Dick Eastman on Prayer

Also by the author

Beyond Imagination
A Celebration of Praise
Seven Keys to a Happy Life

Dick Eastman on Prayer

Three unabridged books
in one volume:
No Easy Road
The Hour That Changes the World
Love on Its Knees

Dick Eastman

Global Christian Publishers
Toronto Carlisle Grand Rapids Sydney Johannesburg

Published 1999 by Global Christian Publishers

Global Christian Publishers is an international alliance of the following:

Baker Book House Co.
P.O. Box 6287
Grand Rapids, MI 49516-6287
U.S.A.

R. G. Mitchell Family Books Inc.
565 Gordon Baker Road
Willowdale, ON M2H 2W2
CANADA

Christian Art Distributors
P.O. Box 1599
Vereeniging 1930
SOUTH AFRICA

STL
P.O. Box 300
Kingstown Broadway
Carlisle, Cumbria CA3 0QS
UNITED KINGDOM

Crossroad Distributors
9 Euston Street
Rydalmere
NSW 2116
AUSTRALIA

Printed in the United States of America

ISBN 1-58558-000-7

PREFACE

To pray in a practical, systematic manner, the prayer warrior needs two things: something to pray about during his or her prayer time, and a quiet place to pray, a place where uninterrupted intercession can be offered for needs of the world. To make your prayer more practical consider these two areas of thought.

How to pray

God gives you 96 fifteen-minute time periods every day. Will you give God at least one or two of these time periods in prayer for your loved ones, friends, and the world? Some, of course, do not respond because they lack a workable method in their prayer life. Some say, "I let the Holy Spirit lead," and when asked how much prayer the Holy Spirit led them into during the last week, they blush with embarrassment. Indeed, why must we wait for a call today when God's Word cries out to all generations: "Pray without ceasing" (I Thess. 5:17)? Thus we have a constant call, and to be obedient to that call, we must answer. That is why we offer the reader several hints on how to pray. . . .

First, divide your fifteeen-minute time period into three periods. The first five-minute time period could be given to praise, adoration, and worship of the Lord. Take time to love God because He is God. Remember, the way to enter the gates of heaven is thanksgiving and praise (Ps. 100). After this you will be ready to pray for other needs.

Second, take five minutes to pray for needs that are close to you. This could mean prayer for family concerns as well as for your local area, including your church and pastor. You will be surprised how much can be included in a five-minute prayer time.

Finally, pray for specific countries of the world. Since there are 210 separate geographical areas we call countries, to name all 210 in five minutes would mean mere mention of each country. Our suggestion is to either extend your prayer time or divide the 210 countries into thirty countries each, each day lifting thirty of the countries before God. Thus, every seven days you will be praying for the whole world.

But what can we pray about concerning these many obscure places? For one thing, most certainly follow the command of Jesus to pray that the Lord of harvest will send forth laborers into the harvest (Matt. 9:38). We should also ask God for the conversion of souls in each country, since His Word declares, "Ask of the heathen for thine inheritance" (Ps. 2:8). Further, pray that God will bless the efforts of all missionary and national-church activities being conducted in that specific area. A sample prayer might be as follows: "Oh, God, I lift before you Indonesia. I claim the precious soils of this country for my inheritance. Please send forth laborers into the harvest of Indonesia, and bless those ministers presently carrying forth the gospel throughout Indonesia. Place a special anointing on the daily efforts of these dedicated workers as they attempt to reach every home with the gospel in many villages today."

The above prayer requires less than twenty seconds and yet calls to God on behalf of that nation. Even if the prayer warrior only mentions the country in but a passing prayer, God will honor such intercession. Of course, in all of this we must covet the precious leading of God's Spirit. He will often prompt us to stop and pray more carefully for a certain country. And remember, when calling on God in behalf of Communist and Moslem nations, be sure to ask God that leaders in the highest levels of these governments will experience changes of attitude so doors will open for an anointed systematic distribution of the gospel to all the people of these countries.

Where to pray

Following several years in which God showed me the impact and value of prayer, I was jolted one night by a startling vision of a prayer center where-college age youth could come from across the country to offer God a gift of time set aside as an offering of intercession. During the year of their commitment these dedicated youth would pray at least two hours a day, praying in specific, assigned time periods so that prayer would never stop day or night at that center. The specific room where these young people would pray was to be called "The Gap," based on God's words to Ezekiel, "I sought for a man among them that should make up the hedge and stand in the gap before me for the land . . ." (Ezek. 22:30). Six months after the evening of this challenging vision, God gave us our prayer center. For years prayer has continued day and night in "The Gap" at this prayer center. Many miracles have resulted from this prayer, not the least of which is the speading of the "gap concept." Today, hundreds of families, churches, and colleges have begun a gap ministry by setting aside a specific place called "The Gap," where people can pray for the needs of the world.

To my knowledge, the first couple to ever begin a gap ministry in the home as the result of hearing about our prayer center were from a Baptist background. Since that time people from many denominations have written us saying," Add us to your 'gap' list! We've begun a family prayer ministry in our home."

My wife Dee and myself have started our own family gap ministry. We had a special family prayer chapel built in our back yard where we could go individually or together for prayer and devotions. It has revolutionized my personal prayer life. Each day I pray for the countries of the world in our gap.

To begin a gap ministry, one must simply set aside a closet or spare room for a place of prayer. Our family saved the necessary money to put down an inexpensive piece of carpet and to panel the walls of our gap so the atmosphere would be conducive to quiet prayer. Of course, the most important thing is a special place reserved just for prayer. Our gap is not a sewing room, den, or office that doubles as a prayer chapel. Every family member knows it is our special "Gethsemane" where we can retreat to be alone with our Lord. I challenge the reader to start a gap ministry soon.

No Easy Road

Inspirational Thoughts on Prayer

CONTENTS

PREFACE

Facing frustrations of an uncertain future I pondered thoughts of never preaching again. My throat became progressively worse and doctors offered no medical solution. I left the pulpit for several months, discouraged. My ministry seriously suffered. Even soft conversation in counseling situations caused severe pain in my throat. At twenty-five years of age I was confused. Why would such a thing occur in my youth?

Nights were long as I sat alone weeping before God. Future plans developed in my thinking. I reasoned, "Africa's the place to go. My experience with the printing press could be the foundation for a life-long literature ministry."

But God's plan differed. It became obvious He had an important lesson to teach me. Prayer was the topic and the closet became the classroom.

After extensive research *NO EASY ROAD* resulted. I believe these important thoughts on prayer are essential to productive living. Prayer, to this writer, is the crux of Christian commitment. We would call it the voice of Christianity or the throat of the Church. It was prayer that ultimately restored this writer's throat and I believe prayer will ultimately restore needed power to the Church.

But the going will be strenuous. Persistence is prerequisite. Expect setbacks but refuse retreat. Prayer is a difficult endeavor. The road to heaven is often obscured by myriad obstacles. Those interested in conquering rugged prayer heights will find challenge and guidance in *NO EASY ROAD*.

Dick Eastman

NO EASY ROAD

The Christian's Journey on the Road of Prayer

Oh, ye who sigh and languish
  And mourn your lack of power,
Hear ye this gentle whisper:
  "Could ye not watch one hour?"
For fruitfulness and blessing
  There is no royal road;
The power for holy service
  Is intercourse with God.

1 NO EASY ROAD

A Communist editor confessed, "The Gospel is a much more powerful weapon for the renovation of society than our Marxist view. Yet it is we who shall conquer you in the end. We Communists do not play with words. We are realists, and because we are determined to reach our end, we also know how to provide necessary means."

Speaking of sacrifice, he said, "Of our salaries and wages we keep only what is absolutely necessary and the rest we give for propaganda purposes. To this same propaganda we also devote leisure time and part of our vacation. You, however, give only a little time and scarcely any money for the spreading of Christ's Gospel."

The angry editor then sneered, "How can anyone believe in the all-surpassing value of this Gospel if you do not practice it, if you do not spread it, if you sacrifice neither your time nor your money for that purpose? Believe me, it is we who shall conquer, because we believe in our Communist gospel and are willing to sacrifice everything, even life itself. But you, you are afraid of soiling your hands."

Perhaps this Communist editor was accurate in his conclusion. Many seek an easy Christianity in this age of affluence. The Christian life, however, is not an easy road.

Rather, it is a challenging journey demanding much of its travelers. Daily we strive in hopeful anticipation for the prize before us. Paul testifies, "I press toward the mark for the prize . . ." (Philippians 3:14).

A most vital but extremely difficult element of the Christian life is prayer. F. J. Huegel writes, "Prayer is work of such a sublime order that it lies beyond the imagination of men." E. M. Bounds emphasizes, "Prayer is not a little habit pinned on to us while we were tied to our mother's apron strings; neither is it a little decent quarter of a minute's grace said over an hour's dinner, but it is a most serious work of our most serious years." This great pray-er adds, "Spiritual work is taxing work, and men are loath to do it. Praying, true praying, costs an outlay of serious attention and of time, which flesh and blood do not relish."

Price of prayer

Relating incidents of the closing days of John Hyde, India's great pray-er, a friend told of the time when his health declined. Deeply concerned, the friend insisted Hyde visit a doctor. Later the physician said: "His heart is in an awful condition. I have never had such a serious case. The heart has shifted from its normal position to the right side. Because of stress and strain it is in such terrible condition that months of strictly quiet life will be required to bring the heart back to anything like its normal state." What caused this rare condition? Praying Hyde's friend says, "We who knew him, knew the cause: his life of incessant prayers day and night, prayers accompanied by exceedingly many tears for his converts, for his fellow-laborers, for his friends, and for the church in India."

Prayer, genuine prayer, has its price. Praying Hyde lost health but gained results few attain in this life. Even after a physician's examination, John Hyde retired to a night of prayer. This turbulent century of social and political problems cries for another man of prayer power like Hyde. One Hyde working at prayer could revolutionize the world. Truly God's pray-ers are societies' best revolutionaries.

Prayer indeed is work. But even more, prayer is an art requiring constant cultivation. Charles Spurgeon declared, "Prayer itself is an art which only the Holy Ghost can teach us. He is the giver of all prayer. Pray for prayer — pray till you can pray."

To learn prayer men must pray. We learn prayer's deepest depths in prayer, not from books. We reach prayer's highest heights in prayer, not from sermons. The only place to learn prayer, is in prayer, bent and broken on our knees. Prayer is skill developed through experience. Learning to pray is like learning a trade. We are apprentices and must serve time at it. Consistent care, thought, practice, and time are needed to become a skillful pray-er.

Great men pray

The Road of Prayer, though tough and rugged, was well-traveled by those who reached spiritual heights. Samuel Rutherford accomplished immeasurable amounts of work for Christ. What was his secret? He rose each morning at three o'clock to converse with God. Scotland's quiet night air was ladened with anguished cries penetrating the darkness as John Welch prayed. Once he remarked his day was ill spent if he could not stay eight or ten hours in secret solitude. It is said of the distinguished and effective Bishop Andrews that he spent more than five hours daily in prayer and Bible study. Charles Simeon rose each day from his bunk to bow on bended knees from four to eight. Martin Luther proclaimed prayer a saintly work of grave necessity. He confessed, "If I fail to spend two hours in prayer each morning, the devil gets the victory through the day. I have so much business I cannot get on without spending three hours daily in prayer."

Although John Wesley's life epitomized work, he gave his best hours to prayer. His motto: "The world is my parish." How did he achieve such saintly goals? He never traveled less than 4,500 miles annually, often as much as 8,000 miles in a single year. From age thirty-six he traveled Methodist circuits, riding over 225,000 miles, preaching over 40,000 sermons. He often spoke to crowds of 20,000 without benefit of modern audio equipment.

Weather never seemed to trouble Wesley. When rain fell in torrents or bitter frost gripped frozen ground, his work continued. His sermons often lasted several hours. But behind every mile and every sermon was a prayer, and backing every word, a tear. Wesley's spiritual strength was gained through someone's faithful prayer.

Most remember the Wesley brothers' triumph and splendor, but overlook the value of a mother's prayers. While John and Charles held crusades she labored on calloused knees. Unfortunately, we have no record of others who fasted and prayed for the Wesleys. Many worked as hard as these evangelists who preached and sang their way to Christian fame. No one cheered the labors of these silent servants. Few, if any, knew they contributed to the Wesleys' spiritual impact. But mark one fact and mark it clearly: behind the saving grace for every soul was someone praying.

Whosoever will may pray

The Road of Prayer may be traveled by all willing to pay the price. Preaching is the exclusive task of preachers. The missionary's task is not for everyone. But anyone can pray! One may lack talent for doing great things, as men count greatness, but one's station in life does not determine greatness in the sight of God. He looks for dedicated hearts carrying prayerful burdens. God longs for those who work at prayer. His Word declares, ". . . the effectual fervent prayer of a righteous man availeth much" (James 5:16). In other words, "He who is in good standing with God and works at prayer will see much done."

In the excellent book, *The Kneeling Christian,* the author says, "Of all the millions in India living in the bondage of Hinduism, none may pray except the Brahmins! A millionaire merchant of any other caste must get a Brahmin — often a mere boy at school — to say his prayers for him. The Muslim cannot pray unless he has learned a few phrases in Arabic, for his god hears only prayers offered in what they believe to be the holy language."

Imagine the bondage Muslims must experience when urgent needs arise. Consider the limitations placed on their prayer lives. Thank God, no limits restrict kneeling Christians. Nothing prevents our kneeling this moment, walking through sparkling gates of heaven, down shining streets of gold, and into the holiest of holies to stand in God's sweet presence. Thank God, whosoever will may pray.

Obstacles on The Road of Prayer

Abundant distractions and seemingly overwhelming obstacles plague Christians who would make progress on the Road of Prayer. At the end of the road lies the prize, the unleashing of God's sustaining power to all who have made the arduous journey. Tragically few ever reach God's place of power. Few will pay the price of work and dedication. It has been said, "The lazy man does not, will not, cannot pray, for prayer demands energy." Because many lack spiritual energy, few conquer these obstacles on the road to prayer.

Beyond the spiraling *Peak of Unbelief,* the first mountain to be conquered, lies *The Mountain of Sin,* hindering many prayers we pray. Next we must pick our way through an *Avalanche of Excuses,* removing them from the road to *The Peak of Habit.* We chose to cross slowly *The Plateau of Intercession,* for difficult lessons must be learned here. Next, we pause for a time in *Holiness Cove.* The road up the towering *Mountain of Self-Will* is especially arduous and our progress is slow. Then, *The Bridge of Balance* beckons. *The Mountain of Persistence* presents a real challenge. Beyond lies the rugged trail to *Burden's Outlook.* Then our goal appears: *Trail's End.* At the summit we stand awed at the power of Christ's promise ". . . ask anything in my name, I will do it." Let us move onward. Before us waits a crucial task. Beyond the obstacles, however, glows God's glory, the glory the psalmist sought: "To see thy power and glory . . ." (Psalm 63:2).

S. D. Gordon comments, "The greatest thing anyone can do for God and man is pray. It is not the only thing; but it is the chief thing. The great people of the earth today are the people who pray. I do not mean those who talk about prayer; nor those who say they believe in prayer; nor yet those who can explain about prayer; but I mean these people who take time to pray."

Glories of answered prayer linger before us this hour. Prayer is work, taxing work, with tireless and endless toil. It is no easy road! A wise poet reminds:

> There's no easy path to glory
> There's no rosy road to fame.
> Prayer, no matter how you view it,
> Is no simple parlor game.
> But its prizes call for fighting,
> For endurance and for grit;
> For a rugged "I can do it"
> And some "don't know when to quit."

2 THE PEAK OF UNBELIEF

"The atomic bomb will never go off, and I speak as an expert in explosives," Admiral Leahy predicted flatly in early 1945. No doubt this famed authority wishes he had never said these words.

"There has been a great deal said about a 3,000-mile high-angle rocket," proclaimed Dr. Vannevar Bush, a few years ago, "but in my opinion such a thing is impossible for many years." Today men walk on the moon.

The aviation pioneer, Octave Chanute, predicted "Airplanes will eventually be fast, they will be used in sport, but they are not to be thought of as commercial carriers." Today we have jumbo jets carrying hundreds daily.

Perhaps most amusing of such negative remarks was voiced by Lt. Joseph Ives in 1861, following exploration of the Grand Canyon. Ives stated abruptly, "The Grand Canyon is, of course, altogether useless. Ours has been the first, and will doubtless be the last, party of whites to visit this profitless locality."

A negative spirit sometimes permeates the minds of praying people. Often we forget that our Master said, ". . . What things soever ye desire, when ye pray, believe that ye receive them, and ye shall have them" (Mark 11:24).

A diary of answered prayer

George Müller stands as one who took Christ's words and prayerfully removed the obstacle of unbelief from his prayers. He testified, "God has never failed me! For nearly seventy years every need in connection with this work [caring for orphans] has been supplied. The orphans from the first until now have numbered nine thousand, five hundred, but they never wanted a meal. In answer to prayer $7,500,000 has been sent to me. We have needed as much as $200,000 in one year, and it has all come when needed. We have no committees, no collectors, no voting, and no endowment. All has come in answer to believing prayer."

Myriad victories fill Müller's diary because he prayed away his unbelief. Those privileged to know Müller saw sparkling faith and received encouragement. Pastor Charles R. Parsons spent a thrilling hour with Müller shortly before death claimed this great orphanage leader. Müller told him an answer to prayer had come just weeks before, when almost all supplies were gone. There were two thousand orphans to care for daily and not enough to feed one hundred.

"I called my beloved helpers together," reported Müller, "and told them, 'Pray, brethren, pray!' Immediately five hundred dollars was sent us, then a thousand, and in a few days seventy-five hundred came in. But always we have to be praying, always believing."

Parsons asked, "Have you saved any money for yourself?"

"He sat erect," declared Parsons, "and for several moments searched my face with an earnestness that seemed to penetrate my very soul. After a brief pause, during which his face was a sermon and the depths of his clear eyes flashed fire, he unbuttoned his coat and drew from his pocket an old-fashioned purse. Placing it in my hands he said quietly, 'All I am possessed of is in that purse — every penny!' "

Müller desired nothing but God. This is all Müller cared to have. He never dwelt on "negatives." Rather, he held constant confidence that God would never fail him. Müller's life became a *diary of answered prayers* because he learned to trust God.

Müller's mustard seed

On one occasion, Müller traveled to Canada for a speaking engagement. Dense fog settled upon the ocean and the uncertain vessel floated motionless on a silent sea. Soon Müller knocked anxiously on the captain's door expressing, "I must be in Toronto by Sunday." The captain quickly replied, "In no way can this vessel move without assuming great danger of colliding with another."

"I understand," said Mr. Müller, "but, in forty years of Christian service I have not failed to keep an appointment. I must be in Toronto Sunday!" He then asked the captain to join in special prayer that the fog lift. Embarrassed, the captain agreed. They knelt and Müller calmly asked God to lift the hindering fog. Somewhat intimidated, the captain said a simple prayer to please his anxious passenger. He no sooner began when Müller stopped him. He gently touched the captain's shoulder saying: "You need not pray. You do not believe."

Startled, the seafarer rose to leave the cabin with this unusual passenger. Walking out on deck, a look of sheer astonishment spread over the captain's face. The fog had completely lifted. George Müller silently stood by with a "just as I expected" look.

Tracing this life of faith to its beginning one finds it started simply. Müller's grain of mustard seed began to grow shortly after college when he quit his job to sacrificially pray, "I now depend on you, God." It was small and simple faith then. But, out of small beginnings grew faith to believe God for almost $200,000 every year. Müller's mustard seed grew to help ten thousand orphans live a healthy life.

Faith . . . as the grain of a mustard seed, Jesus declared, shall remove mountains (Matthew 17:20). Oh, that we would cultivate at least a small amount of faith. Imagine the results waiting for Christians who remove unbelief from their lives. Yet, the age in which we live seems to make this a most difficult feat. If God does not heal, we rely on doctors. If money fails to come for bills, we can always borrow from bank or friend. If mission fields close, we can always erect radio stations to broadcast the Gospel. In a materialistic, "self-oriented" society it is often easy to be caught in a spirit of unbelief.

Charles Allen, in *All Things Are Possible Through Prayer,* writes, "We believe in prayer. Then why don't we pray? The real reason is, we have nothing to pray for. We have everything we want without praying. The supreme tragedy of most people is that they want so little and they are satisfied with almost nothing."

All available power must be amassed to defeat Satan's attempts to fill us with doubts. Nothing defeats him like the prayer of faith. Wise indeed, are those who pray as Christ's disciples — "Lord, Increase our faith" (Luke 17:5).

Billy Bray, a remarkable Christian worker in England's last century, possessed this godly faith. Bray combined prayer with faith and blasted away at Satan. Addressing Satan once, he confidently mused, "What an old fool thee art now; I have been battling thee for twenty-eight years, and I have always beat thee, and I always shall." What a stunning blow to Satan. What a massive portion of unbelief's mountain must have tumbled that day.

This active faith carried Billy through his greatest trials. Once his child was extremely sick. When his wife encouraged him to get the doctor lest the child die, Billy took all the money they possessed, thirty-six cents, and hurried for the doctor. He met a poor man on the way who had lost a cow and was trying to get enough money to purchase another. The poor man's situation so touched Billy's heart that he gave him the entire sum. With no money he saw little use in securing a doctor and rather began praying. Miraculous healing soon came when this father prayed a simple prayer of faith. Satan felt again the sting of defeat.

Raincoats, watches, and fountain pens

Men like Billy Bray are few and far between. The tragedy is seen in lost and dying souls. Unbelievers who look at us often see only wavering, doubt-filled Christians. James proclaimed ". . . ask in faith, nothing wavering . . ." (James 1:6). Moffat translates this, ". . . let him ask in faith with never a doubt. . . ." True prayer, powerful prayer, is doubt-less prayer.

Rees Howells lived doubt-less faith. He became a dedicated twentieth-century intercessor, establishing orphanages and a Bible school during the trying years of World War II. In *Rees Howells: Intercessor,* a masterpiece by Norman Grubb, Howells' stirring story of doubt-less faith in action is related.

Once Mr. Howells made ready his departure for Africa as a missionary. He and his partner were ready to board a train for London to make connections with an ocean-going vessel for the lengthy journey. They had only ten shillings between them, enough to take them twenty miles on the train.

"We felt sure the money would come so we went to the platform to wait for its arrival," relates Howells. "The time for the train to depart came and we decided to go as far as possible."

Leaving the train twenty miles later, they met friends who invited them to breakfast. Surely, thought Howells, God had sent these friends to pay the way, but departure time arrived and no offers of financial aid were given.

Rees Howells testified, "The Spirit spoke to me and said, 'If you had money what would you do?' "

" 'Take my place in the line at the ticket counter,' I said."

" 'Well, are you not preaching that My promises are equal to the need? You had better take your place in the line.' "

Rees Howells stood in line as if he had the money for the ticket. "When there were only two before me," related Howells, "a man stepped out of the crowd and said, 'I'm sorry I can't wait any longer . . . I must open my shop.' He said good-bye and put thirty shillings in my hand."

This indeed was a remarkable victory, as Satan did all he could to place the obstacle of unbelief before Howells. Each time Satan came, however, Howells' faith defeated the devil's arduous attempts. Time and again God blessed Howells with added extras because of unwavering faith.

Upon arriving at the dock, to leave for Africa, these missionaries had everything for their trip except three small items. They each needed a watch, a raincoat and a fountain pen. They had not mentioned these needs to anyone. Before leaving, a friend asked, "What kind of watches have you? My son wants to supply both of you with a watch." Amazingly, his next question, "Have you prepared for the rainy seasons in Africa by getting raincoats?" When Howells replied negatively the friend wrote an address informing them to pick up two fine raincoats at his expense. Finishing writing the address, he asked, "Have you seen this kind of fountain pen?"

"No," Howells replied, and immediately each was given a new fountain pen. How accurate are the words of Paul,

". . . even God . . . calleth those things which be not as though they were" (Romans 4:17).

Can you imagine Rees Howells' joy as each need was provided through believing prayer? Indeed, Howells found the faith William Bathurst sought:

> O for a faith that will not shrink
> Though pressed by every foe,
> That will not tremble on the brink
> Of any earthly woe!

Heroes of faith

Mary Slessor was another godly saint who removed unbelief from her life. Fortified with unfailing faith she performed a lasting labor of love in West Africa. Once asked what prayer meant to her, she quietly replied, "My life is one long, daily, hourly record of answered prayer for physical health, for mental overstrain, for guidance given marvelously, for errors and dangers averted, . . . for food provided at the exact hour needed, for everything that goes to make up life and my poor services. I can testify with a full and often wonder-stricken awe that I believe God answers prayer." Then, with certain confidence she adds, "I know God answers prayer."

Are we really convinced God answers prayer? Why do many travel life's journey uttering prayers but doubting answers? Picture Joshua, an Old Testament hero of faith. He, one of twelve commissioned by Moses to survey the promised land, brought a positive report. Ten came crying, "There are giants in the land . . . we cannot seize it." Joshua, however, is one of two taking the positive approach. His simple faith grew and blossomed, accompanying a man from wilderness wandering to falling walls at Jericho. Jericho is an excellent example of how prayer and faith combined remove an otherwise impenetrable barrier. *In prayer*

Joshua received God's battle plan promising victory over Israel's enemy. *In faith* Joshua led Israel around towering walls, mentally visualizing every stone tumbling to the ground. Here is *praying faith* in action. Prayer — real prayer — sees the answer coming before it actually arrives.

Thank God for those who have left examples of believing prayer. The author of Hebrews' faith chapter lists only a few who occupy faith's hall of fame. They earned this honor not by works, but by unshackled faith in God. God's list includes men such as Enoch, Abraham, David and Samuel. All were men of prayer — *believing men of prayer.* Each earned status by total confidence in His Word. The motto of Moses could simply be stated, "Thus saith the Lord."

The kind of faith these saintly men possessed will always give Christians confidence. Read afresh God's compliment to conquerors of unbelief. . . .

"Through faith they fought whole countries and won. They did what was right and received what God had promised. They shut the mouths of lions, put out fierce fires, escaped being killed by the sword. They were weak but became strong; they were mighty in battle and defeated the armies of foreigners. Through faith women received their dead raised back to life.

"Others died under torture, refusing to accept freedom, in order to be raised to a better life. Some were mocked and whipped, and others were tied up and put in prison. They were stoned, they were sawn in two, they were killed with the sword. They went around clothed in skins of sheep or goats, poor, persecuted, and mistreated" (Hebrews 11:33-37, *Good News for Modern Man*). Then the author adds, "What a record these men have won by their faith" (v. 39).

Tragically, the Word of God also contains accounts of those failing to conquer unbelief. Agrippa weakly admitted, "almost thou persuadest me . . ." (Acts 26:28). He came near to conquering unbelief but failed. Many come close to defeating this doubting spirit and some almost succeed. Faith, however, is never "almost." Real prayer consists of bold, confident petitions and a certainty that the answer will come. Until unbelief is conquered, progress will be halted. We go no further on the Road of Prayer while unbelief obstructs the path. This obstacle must come down, piece by piece. Only then we can sing with assurance:

> Faith in God can move a mighty mountain,
> Faith in God can calm life's troubled sea,
> Faith can make a desert like a fountain,
> Faith will bring life's victory.

3 THE MOUNTAIN OF SIN

One sin allowed in a life wrecks our usefulness, stifles our joy, and robs prayer of its power. With these words fixed in our thinking we journey forward on the Road of Prayer. Nothing makes our journey more difficult than sin.

Tragically, too often many Christians experience unanswered prayer because little things keep them from God. These barriers constantly combine to create another formidable mountain blocking answered prayer.

Sin must be removed from our lives if we wish to be effective warriors of prayer. The psalmist said, "If I regard iniquity in my heart, the Lord will not hear me" (Psalm 66:18).

Consider the dismay we would experience if we suddenly discovered God had turned His back on us. How solemn life would be if God closed His ears to our pleas. If the psalmist is right — and certainly this is the Word of God — sin automatically shuts the ears of God. When sin exists in life the necessary step to answered prayer is confession of that sin.

Satan must be bound

Sin is quickly removed by humble prayer. Luke's account

of the Pharisee and the publican describes how swiftly sin can be removed. The Pharisee entered the temple a proud man — considering himself a supreme example of holiness. He voiced the accomplishments of a saintly life. Included in his list of spiritual genius were fasting twice in a week and strict tithing (Luke 18:12).

Next to him stood a publican, his head was bowed in reverence, his hands clasped to his breast in anguish and remorse. Humbly he cries to God, ". . . Be merciful to me a sinner" (Luke 18:13). In an instant *The Mountain of Sin* is removed and no longer blocks the Road of Prayer.

The Pharisee left God's temple proud and boastful. His sins remained. The publican departed a different person. The sins had been placed in God's sea of forgetfulness, all in a moment's time. Other obstacles standing in this pray-er's way were cast aside. First, unbelief was removed. With unbelief torn away, needed faith came easy. Soon stains of sin were cleansed completely from that sinner's heart.

When sin is removed, we can understand Christ's teachings. F. J. Huegel remarks, "Much of the Savior's ministry and teaching will remain for us an unsolved riddle if we fail to grasp the significance of this great fact of prayer warfare against the powers of darkness. No man can enter into a strong man's house and spoil his goods, except he will first bind the strong man; and then he will spoil his house, our Lord tells us. Only when Satan is bound and defeated are we assured of answered prayer."

Daily we enter a serious battle with the Evil One. If we are to spoil Satan's diabolical efforts we must begin with fervent and persistent prayers. How wise the remark, "Satan trembles when he sees the weakest saint upon his knees."

While still young I learned the value of prayer and what it does to thwart Satan's progress. Once after a time of prayer I thought of the damage one hour in prayer does to Satan. In childlike manner I composed a simple motto, "An hour in prayer gives the devil a scare." While that may be simple, emerging from a child's mind, it remains true. Satan must be frightened when he sees the knees of Christians touch the floor. Satan is bound when people pray.

Real prayer is lethal

C. S. Lewis provides insight to the thought that prayer is lethal to Satan. Comprised of fictitious letters from one demon to another, *The Screwtape Letters* tell of Screwtape, a demon in higher echelons of hellish status, writing to Nephew Wormwood, a novice demon. Many letters flow from Screwtape in attempts to keep Wormwood at his best in driving souls to hell. When Screwtape sees their Enemy (God) reaching one of Wormwood's clients, he quickly writes to correct this matter. In one corrective letter Screwtape writes on need to destroy prayer. He warns: "Interfere at any price in any fashion when people start to pray, for *real prayer is lethal* to our cause."

Some chuckle at discussions of a devil capable of rendering people helpless. Satan is often pictured a shifty little man, arrayed in red attire, with lanky, pointed tail and three-pronged pitchfork. Children are encouraged to think about Satan only in a humorous way. On any average Halloween several little "devils" are certain to appear, asking for treats.

There is, however, a real devil, a fact not to be ignored. Recently a college newspaper had an interesting article on the existence of Satan. Closing the thought-provoking article was this comment, "I see you are one who does not believe in Satan. Next time you attend a party where everyone is laughing, count the people, then count the laughs. There is one more laughing than you think." Could it be Satan spends a wealth of time laughing at man's failure to remove *The Mountain of Sin?*

There are times, however, when Satan's laughing is certainly stifled. These occur as people pray. If we could only fathom how prayers defeat Satan's army of demons! S. D. Gordon, in *Quiet Talks on Prayer,* relates, "Prayer, real prayer, intelligent prayer, it is this that routs Satan's demons, for it routs their chief. David killed the lion and bear in the secret forests before he faced the giant in the open."

Gordon provides illuminating insight into prayer's infinite impact on demonology. "This thing Jesus calls prayer," writes Gordon, "casts out demons. Would that we knew better by experience what Jesus meant by prayer. It exerts a positive influence upon the hosts of evil spirits. They fear it. They fear the man who becomes skilled in its use." Screwtape was more than correct in stating, *"Real prayer is lethal."* Real prayer ruins the pernicious plot of Satan.

The third party in prayer

Often we picture prayer as communication between finite man and his sovereign God. To some extent this is true. However, don't forget a third party involved in prayer — that old deceiver, Satan. The tenth chapter of the Book of Daniel impresses this fact upon our minds and hearts.

Daniel prayed a stirring prayer and waited for an answer. One day passed and no answer came. Five days passed and still no answer. This was most unusual, for prayer was usually answered when Daniel prayed. He might have concluded that his faith was shallow.

Fifteen days passed, and Daniel faced the supreme tests of persistent prayer. Why had the answer been delayed? What hindered his desired request? Once again day dawned — as it had for twenty days — but still no answer. Sunrise met Daniel on his knees, persisting — perhaps discouraged — but never giving up.

Then it happened. On that glorious twenty-first day an

angel of the Lord arrived with prayer's answer. Before Daniel had an opportunity to question, God's representative offered an explanation. The exhausted angel told Daniel how God's answer had been sent the first day prayer was offered. While journeying with God's answer, however, this heavenly courier met a hindering spirit from hell. They became engaged in prolonged battle, lasting more than twenty days. Had Daniel not been persistent in his prayer, the battle would have ended; his prayer unanswered. But prayer continued, day by day, and the hindering spirit was removed.

The lesson from Daniel's life is simple. Satan is a real person, possessing awesome power to fight prayer. Contrary to some modern theologians, Lucifer is not a thought of mind to be discarded as a childish myth. The devil is a real being, doing very real damage.

In truth, the number involved in prayer is three not two. Man seeks God, but in prayer's battle comes another party, one seeking to block the road to God. One author describes it, "The purpose of prayer is not to persuade or influence God, but to join with Him against the enemy. Not towards God, but with God against Satan — that is the main thing to keep in mind in prayer. The real pitch is not Godward but Satanward."

How does prayer destroy *The Mountain of Sin* along with its many temptations? Douglas Steere says, "It is in prayer that you can face temptation and recognize your peculiar weakness at the moment it threatens to overwhelm you. If we stay in prayer we are given the strength needed to refuse the temptation so that we are no longer helplessly vulnerable to it."

It is in prayer's inner chamber that we find a special power against temptation. Philip Henry prescribes, "Pray alone! Let prayer be the key of the morning and the bolt at night. The best way to fight against sin is to fight it on our knees!" Here then is prayer's basic fundamental; sin's greatest battlefield is the inner chamber; its most feared enemy is prayer.

Nothing removes sin but confession of sin. When *The Mountain of Sin* is gone, answers to prayer are sure to come with swiftest speed.

Consider the moving story of Sergeant Johnny Bartek, a close companion of Captain Rickenbacker when both were lost at sea.

"As soon as we were in the rafts at the mercy of God," relates Bartek, "we realized that we were not in any condition to expect help from Him. We spent many hours of each day confessing our sins to one another and to God . . . then we prayed, and God answered.

"It was real. We needed water," reflects Bartek, "And we got water — all we needed. Then we asked for fish and we got fish. And we got meat when we prayed. Sea gulls don't go around sitting on people's heads waiting to be caught. On that eleventh day when those planes flew by, we all cried like babies. It was then I prayed again to God and said: 'If You'll send that one plane back for us I promise I'll believe in You and tell everyone else.' That plane came back and the others flew on. It just happened? It did not. God sent that plane back."

According to Sergeant Bartek's testimony, the answers to prayer came when each confessed his sins, removing *The Mountain of Sin.* This is the crux of prayer — destroy sin and God works. When sin is gone the heavens kiss the earth as people pray. It works. Remove sin and God listens. Defeat the enemy and God responds. It has to work — God says it will.

Sin Number One

Our discussion of sin would profit little if we fail to analyze our nation's number one sin. Indeed, it is probably the number one sin in the world — often rendering prayer ineffective. The sin is criticism, with its roots of bitterness and hate.

Nothing gives Satan a free hand — destroying efforts of bended knees — more than the spirit of criticism. Of all the weapons in Satan's arsenal, this one most assuredly is the greatest. In truth, what prayer means to God, criticism means to Satan.

Travel the globe and you'll find biting criticism rearing its ugly head with alarming frequency. Churches are criticized openly, often rebuked for failing their task. Certainly, improvements are necessary, but claiming the church has failed is nonsense.

Recently my church was invaded by restless, shouting youths, arguing boisteriously that we failed to preach a truthful Gospel. They claimed our preaching lacked tones of judgment needed by our congregation. Ironically, all three sermons that particular Sunday discussed God's judgment. Our pastor's sermon title read, "Has America Forgotten God?" His message vividly described God's ultimate wrath if our nation rejected Christ as Savior. That night, following three dynamic sermons on judgment, these rebel youths claimed we failed to warn people of God's impending wrath. Their screaming, defiant outburst forced cancellation of the last service.

What prompts such outbursts? Why are people so caught up in rebellion today? Indeed, this is the age of the protest sign. No person or institution in America is exempt from criticism's deadly sting. Youth complain college administrations fail to recognize current needs. Ghetto dwellers criticize outsiders for failing to help, while outsiders criticize those inside for lack of effort to excel. Governments of every nation face criticism more than ever in past history. The sad and sickening spirit of criticism abounds.

Removal of a critical spirit is not an easy matter. Saying

"I am sorry," forgiving those who harbor hateful thoughts, is a difficult task. There are times we wish our lovely Lord had never said those searching words, ". . . If thou bring thy gift to the altar, and there rememberest that thy brother hath ought against thee; Leave there thy gift before the altar, and go thy way; first be reconciled to thy brother . . ." (Matthew 5:23-24). One writer said of these words, "It knocks out about one-half of the efficiency and worth of the prayers of Christians. If the church were to really act upon this principle, her prayers could revolutionize the life of nations." Forgiving others is not an easy task. Jesus is asking much of believers here. In fact, He more than asks, He commands. Brotherhood is not optional with Christianity but a steadfast law.

Praying Hyde reports learning an important lesson concerning fault-finding. Seldom in public did critical words of a piercing nature flow from his lips. In his prayer life, however, this was not the case. Once he felt a keen burden on his heart for a native Indian pastor. Upon entering his favorite place of prayer, he developed a bitter spirit toward this pastor's mannerisms. In his mind he criticized that pastor and began praying a bitter prayer: "Oh, Father, thou knowest how cold . . ." but something stopped him in the midst of prayer.

A finger seemed to touch Hyde's lips, sealing them shut. He heard the voice of God softly say, "He that toucheth him, toucheth the apple of mine eye."

Praying Hyde at once cried out, "Forgive me, Father, in that I have been an accuser of the brethren before thee." In the anguish of his prayer, Hyde begged God to show him good things in this pastor's life and as moments passed good points saturated Hyde's mind. As each good quality came to mind Hyde stopped and praised God for this dear pastor.

Soon after Hyde's prayer, revival hit that Indian church. Clearly felt was the impact of a loving spirit. Let it never be forgotten, forgiving hearts are parents to revival. The intercourse of love gives birth to God's outpouring.

The Mountain of Sin, with its plateau of criticism, must be removed. To pray with bitterness toward fellowmen nullifies hours on our knees. The author of *The Kneeling Christian* states, "If we harbor an unforgiving spirit it is almost wasted time to pray. It would be immense gain to our spiritual life if we would resolve not to attempt to pray until we had done all in our power to make peace and harmony between ourselves and any with whom we have quarreled. Until we do this as far as lies in our power, our prayers are just wasted breath. Unkindly feelings towards another hinder God from helping us in the way He desires."

Recently a church in the community in which I live was forced to cancel a weekly service because of criticism. A local television station reported the situation, and quoted the pastor as he spoke of the downward trend in membership. "People no longer desire to come," he said, describing the rebellion of his people. "They seem to resent the message of the church." The number one sin in America had left its effect on another church; criticism had dealt another tragic blow.

Jonathan Edwards offered valuable advice, "If some Christians that have been complaining of their ministers had said and acted less before men and applied themselves with all their might to cry to God for their ministers — had, as it were, risen and stormed heaven with their humble, fervent, and incessant prayers for them — they would have been much more in the way of success."

Empty of love

People harboring critical opinions seldom change attitudes even when the leadership changes. Those signing recall-our-governor petitions will no doubt sign petitions when another is elected. I recently saw a car's bumper sticker, "Happiness is a new Governor." I laughed, thinking of its practicality. "It should be made of metal," I mused, "so they can use it when the next Governor is elected." In reality, critical people are never satisfied. A rebellious spirit hinders satisfaction, leaving men empty of love.

If we would only learn to pray for our leaders! They seem to reach out trembling hands, begging us for prayer. John Welsh begged his congregation, "Pray for your pastor. Pray for his body that he may be kept strong and spared many years. Pray for his soul, that he may be kept humbled and holy, a burning and shining light. Pray for his ministry, that it may be abundantly blessed, that he may be anointed to preach good tidings. Let there be no secret prayer without naming him before your God, no family prayer without carrying your pastor in your hearts to God."

Relatives of the critical spirit also wait for pray-ers seeking to remove *The Mountain of Sin* from their lives. The chasm of hate-filled hearts and the ridge of jealousy loom large. Sin's deceit clouds the peak of pride ahead. The summit is filled with evil places — envy, greed, malice, lust, prejudice, and lies — all used by Satan in his quest to kill the power of prayer.

Before continuing on the Road of Prayer we must destroy these obstacles. Our prayers must drive Satan back, removing his effect from our lives.

One writer observes, "The Master says, 'Faith as big as a mustard seed (you cannot measure the strength of the mustard seed by its size) will say to this mountain — Remove!' Mark keenly — the direction of the faith is towards the obstacle. Its force is against the enemy."

We must learn the greatest hindrance to effective prayer is sin, and Satan's greatest goal is to keep us from our knees. Someone said, "If there were no devil there would be no difficulty in prayer. It is the evil one's chief aim to make prayer impossible."

Though the task is rough — the mountain high — we must move on. *Impossible* must be dropped from prayer's vocabulary. We must face this obstacle on the Road of Prayer with Paul's words of confidence; "I can do all things through Christ who strengtheneth me" (Philippians 4:13).

Have you any rivers you think are uncrossable?
Have you any mountains you can't tunnel through?
God specializes in things thought impossible,
and He will do what no other power can do.

4 AN AVALANCHE OF EXCUSES

"So we come to one of the crying evils of these times," wrote Bounds, "maybe of all times — little or no praying. Of these two evils, perhaps little praying is worse than no praying." Bounds qualifies his statement by saying, "Little praying is a kind of make-believe, a salve for the conscience, a farce and a delusion."

There can be no finer introduction to the excuses for lack of prayer than this quotation of Bounds. Man makes countless excuses covering almost any situation. In truth, there is a sad trend of rationalization present in modern man.

Prisons are packed with inmates giving scores of excuses why they are incarcerated.

"Why did you fail the test?" a mother asks. The child's immediate reply is an excuse — a form of rationalization — "The teacher asked what we hadn't studied."

"Why were you speeding?" asks the officer. The typical reply, "Everyone is going over the limit; why shouldn't I?"

A storehouse of excuses

Satan has a storehouse of tricks that hinder the prayers of hungry Christians. Excuse-making is no exception. The devil rejoices when Christians cultivate fields of excuses.

A fable tells of a man having an unusual dream in which he descends to the council rooms of hell. There a host of demons had gathered, discussing methods of curtailing surges of revival. Satan's army had become alarmed at the number of new Christian converts. This buzz session was organized as a last-ditch effort to stop revival.

"What shall we do?" asked Satan. A daring demon stood, shouting, "I have it . . . I have the answer; I know what we can do."

"Let it out," cried Satan. "We tell people there is no heaven or hell . . . we say men die like animals, having no afterlife."

Satan's face fell as he answered, "It will never work, demon — man is not to be assumed ignorant." Then Satan adds, "Even atheists tell of times they sense a tomorrow after death."

Jubilantly another demon intoned, "Here's the solution. Let's say God is dead, and though He started the universe, He now has left it."

Satan replies in dismay: "Man is too sensible for that. Some may swallow this, but these are fools. Most believe the psalmist's words, 'The fool hath said in his heart there is no God!' No, that will never do."

Other ideas were presented, but none brought hope. Fear of failure gripped those charting plans to stop the rapid rate of revival.

Finally, when ultimate gloom faced them, Satan leaped in glee, "I have it! A sure solution!" Demons listened intently to the master plan.

"Go back and tell them God is real and the Bible is God's Word."

A gasp came from the group as Satan continued his strange command. "Tell them Jesus Christ is God's Son, freeing men from sin." Surely Satan had gone mad!

With a smirking smile Satan added, "Then, brothers, tell them the best time to choose Christ is later. Help them make excuses." Dancing in delight, the demons realized a workable plan was discovered.

Suddenly the sleeping man awoke, completely changed. He had seen the subtle scheme Satan puts in minds of men. In reality, Satan uses every means to destroy the Christian's prayer life. Forces of good and evil contend for the world. If we would, we could add immeasurable power to God's army of prayer warriors. Yet, we hold back from closets of prayer, our lips are sealed, our hands hang limply by our side, and we hinder the very cause we claim to believe in so deeply. Prayer lives suffer severely because of the multitude of excuses which are conjured up. No library could contain the list of irresponsible excuses man makes to keep from prayer. We must become surgeons — cutting out this cancer of excuses hindering prayer.

Prayer is the highest order of business, for it links a powerless human to the creative force of God's sovereign power. When people cease to pray — no matter the reasons — Christians backslide, youth rebel, preachers leave pulpits, mission fields close, and denominations die.

Prayer demands our best

Prayer demands our best. God is not pleased with a few moments at the close of a weary day when strength is at lowest ebb. He longs for us to give our best in traveling the Road of Prayer.

Charles H. Spurgeon preached, "God forbid that our prayer should be a mere leaping out of bed and kneeling down, and saying anything that comes first to mind. On the contrary, may we wait upon the Lord with holy fear and sacred awe."

God's heart must break when listening to a never-ending

tally of excuses as we rationalize away our need for prayer. A saintly man said, "One day we fail to pray because our head aches, the next because it has ached, and three more lest it should ache again."

Pray daily and watch the effect on this Satanic spirit of rationalization. Start today spending time in God's presence before embarking on routine obligations. Henry Drummond advises, "Ten minutes spent in the presence of Christ every day, aye, two minutes, will make the whole day different." Franklin Field says, "The great dividing line between success and failure can be expressed in five words: 'I did not have the time.' "

The "too busy" syndrome

Some ask, "How long need I pray?" Intercessors who have a burden for the lost and realize the worth of souls will never ask this question. To these warriors, prayer is our only hope of reaching a dying world.

"I am too busy," many cry, as souls move endlessly to hell. Our whole society thinks itself too busy to respect God who gave them all they possess. Psychologists call this the "too busy syndrome." Daniel must have had this age in mind: ". . . Many shall run to and fro, and knowledge shall be increased" (Daniel 12:4).

Consider the pace man follows in these closing decades of the twentieth century. In the sixteenth century Ferdinand Magellan took three years to make the first trip around the world. Today, a jet filled with four hundred passengers can accomplish this in less than thirty-six hours. Astronauts fly earth's circumference in less than ninety minutes. Americans have over 100 million cars, some thirty-six for every mile of paved road, another fact indicating man's rapid pace of life.

In religious circles this busyness is alarming. Many Christians are too busy to love, too busy to share, too busy to care, and too busy to pray. Due to vast involvement in secular fields, the willing pray-ers must pray much more. A wise Christian observes, "We say we are too busy to pray. But, the busier our Lord was, the more He prayed." Hildersam cried, "When thou feelest most indisposed to prayer yield not to it, but strive and endeavor to pray even when thou thinkest thou canst not pray." An unknown poet penned these words:

> When prayer delights thee least, then
> learn to say,
> Soul, now is greatest need that thou
> must pray.

The true Christian life is a demanding one, and those who want to live for God must take time to pray. Excuses are not fabricated by those who live close to God. Just as we obey traffic laws or pay a fine when we disobey them, so God's laws are not broken without penalty.

We must pray or pay the price. This is God's law and no excuse diminishes its validity. Godly leaders of past eras feared breaking this law. S. D. Gordon commented, "Those leaders for God have always been men of prayer above everything else. They are men of power in other ways, preachers, men of action, with power to sway others but above all else men of prayer. They give prayer first place."

Consider the disciples. When they made excuses, little was done to build God's kingdom. They had to learn that no excuse should keep them from times of prayer. Christ taught them to preface their actions with prayer. Rev. Thomas Payne, in *Prayer — The Greatest Force on Earth,* relates, "When the apostles prepared for Pentecost they continued in one accord in prayer and supplication. When they would select one to fill the place of Judas, they prayed. When they received three thousand into the church at Jerusalem, they all continued steadfastly in prayer. When Peter and John went into the temple, it was at the hour of prayer. They prayed in the prison, they prayed in the palace, and they prayed in the cottage. They prayed everywhere, lifting up holy hands without wrath and doubting."

Fear of fanaticism

An excuse that often impedes progress on the Road of Prayer involves a fear of fanaticism. Ministers are often accused of being "on a tangent" if they preach much on prayer. College students in our Bible institutes are sometimes dubbed "fanatic" if they have a regular time of prayer. But regular, fervent prayer never lowers a Christian to the level of fanaticism. The emotions of one person may be more apparent than those of another, but prayer is not to blame. True praying may compel men to weep, elevating them to where they feel God's heartbeat. This, however, is never to be construed as fanaticism. Jesus was not a fanatic but a Savior. Luke records His anguished prayer in the Garden of Gethsemane (Luke 22:44). Those who use excuses such as fear of fanaticism seem to develop an immunity toward prayer. None, however, can find the way to God without traveling the Road of Prayer.

Another common excuse involves a false humility. Jesus often spoke of the value of humility, yet He never demands that we whip ourselves for failure. God calls for hallowed and humbled spirits, yet He says, ". . . Come boldly unto the throne of grace . . ." (Hebrews 4:16).

There is yet another excuse that acts as a roadblock. Churches are filled with Christians afraid to pray in public. Many fear praying aloud because they think their ability is not sufficient to pray before a group. One author interjects,

"God does not look at the length or breadth or polish of our prayers. He looks and listens to the Spirit's voice reproduced in and through us."

Bound by excuse

Don't be fooled by the Satanic argument that claims prayer can wait. Don't become a talker about prayer instead of a doer. It has been said, "Truly great people of the earth are people who pray. This does not mean those who talk about prayer, but those who take time to pray." In truth, after all is said and done, more is said than done. Let us cast aside foolish excuses and humbly journey to inner chambers, pleading, "Teach us, Lord, to pray."

Do not think that your fears are impossible to overcome, for God has promised to make us "more than conquerors." The Bible provides numerous examples of overcoming saints. Yet, even these saints failed at times.

In Eden God asked Adam why he took the fruit. An excuse was quick in coming: "Eve did it." Eve was also confronted with her sin, but she placed blame on Satan. Though Adam and Eve made excuses, sin's penalty remained. Adam's excuse may seem partially valid, but in the last analysis a penalty was inevitable and neither excuse was accepted. Both were judged guilty.

Moses did not always stand so tall. Consider his excuses when God called him to free enslaved Israel. Excuse after excuse was presented. After the supply of excuses was exhausted Moses heeded God's call.

Recall Aaron, first high priest of Israel. Moses returned from Mt. Sinai holding God's law. He saw God's people oblivious to the sacredness of the moment, bathing in a river of idolatry, worshiping a golden calf. When confronted with the seriousness of the situation, Aaron retaliated by giving an excuse, "I put gold in the fire and this golden calf came out." This sounds as shabby as some excuses people use in missing times of prayer.

The wait for convenience

The New Testament also contains a long list of excuse-makers. Paul, chief apostle, had a challenging discussion with Governor Felix. Paul, no doubt, used education and logic, coupled with the impact of the Gospel, to drive this intellectual leader to a moment of decision. Felix sat in quiet contemplation very close to Christian commitment. Then, as always, Satan slyly advised, "Think this over, Felix — choose another day." Here it is again: the most common of excuses. Felix said, "Go thy way for this time; when I have a *convenient* season, I will call for thee."

Note the word *convenient* in the reply of Felix. Our nation waits a *convenient* time to change its downward trend toward immorality. Sinners wait for a *convenient* time to make things right with God. Christians wait for a *convenient* time to pray. People everywhere wait for convenience. God, however, calls men everywhere to make today a convenient time for prayer. If we continue ignoring God's call He may force us to take time for prayer. Robert Murray McCheyne had a special word of warning for pastors: "Give yourselves to prayer and the ministry of the Word. If you do not pray, God will probably lay you aside from your ministry, as He did me, to teach you to pray."

Time and again we are admonished to pray, yet we ignore the challenge. Days pass as Satan-sent excuses bind Christians. Convenient times never come. Crime rates rise as blame is placed on lack of law enforcement. Drug abuse soars, affecting little children and youth, while we single out poorly framed laws. Sunday school attendance drops, and blame is focused on inadequate facilities. Marriages approach disaster as counselors point to a lack of communication. Few ever suggest that the absence of prayer may be the root of our problems.

The buck stops here

Prayer could change the world, but do we pray? Communists cry, "We will change the world!" and enforce the pledge with sleepless nights and twelve-hour days. Communists who register in America give an average 38 percent of their annual income to their cause. Many youth become captivated by it, willing to give all for its propagation. One young Communist told his fiancé they could no longer see one another and broke their engagement in this following letter: "There is one thing about which I am in dead earnest and that is the Communist cause. It is my life, my business, my religion, my hobby, my sweetheart, my wife, my mistress, my bread and meat. I work at it in the daytime and dream of it at night. Its hold on me grows, not lessens, as time goes on. Therefore I cannot carry on a friendship, a love affair, or even a conversation without relating to this force which both guides and drives my life. I evaluate people, books, ideas, and actions according to how they affect and by their attitudes toward it. I have already been in jail because of my ideas and if necessary I am ready to go before a firing squad."

This young man was too busy listing areas of dedication to make excuses. Imagine a small army of Christians with such prayer-directed dedication. How many can claim Christianity their life, sweetheart, wife, mistress, bread, and meat? What hinders us from writing in our imaginations, a letter similar to that above, only addressing it to the world? Bundles of manufactured excuses are in effect an avalanche that must be removed before any progress can be made on the Road of Prayer. Excuses kill effectiveness for God and render the prayer lives of Christians helpless.

Think of the many excuses Lucifer sends our way:

Some excuses for not praying are
tenseness, weariness, and pain.
Some excuses for not praying are
tangled lives and broken homes.
Some excuses for not praying are
anxious fears of many sorts.
Some excuses for not praying are
boredom, lack of time, and pride.
Some excuses for not praying are
beautifully articulated.
All excuses for not praying are
good for nothing.

Satan must no longer victimize us with entangling excuses. We must place blame where blame is due, on lack of prayer. We dare not neglect this important duty, hoping other Christians will carry the load.

During President Truman's administration a plaque rested on his desk. When things went wrong this highest official received the blame — the "buck" could not be passed. This is why the plaque simply read, "The Buck Stops Here." A. B. Christiansen penned:

Too busy; O forgive, dear Lord,
that I should ever be
Too much engrossed in worldly tasks
to spend an hour with Thee.

5 THE PEAK OF HABIT

A habit has been defined as an act repeated so often it becomes involuntary. There is no new decision of mind each time the act is performed. Jesus prayed. He loved to pray. Often praying was His way of resting. He prayed so often it became part of His life. It was to Him like breathing — involuntary. With these thoughts in mind we travel the Road of Prayer up *The Mountain of Habit*.

Sadly lacking in lives of countless Christians are good devotional habits. Often I ask how many spend given time in daily prayer, and affirmative responses are always few.

If prayer is indeed the ultimate weapon with which to crush Satan, one must certainly develop proper prayer habits. Without training in use of prayer, God's army of warriors is fearfully inadequate as charges are sounded against the enemy.

God has many soldiers, some excelling in godliness. The generals in God's army are those with holy habits of consistent prayer. One author comments, "Men who know how to use this weapon of prayer are God's best soldiers, His mightiest leaders."

A diet of prayer

Sadly, many Christians never develop good prayer habits.

If people had eating habits similar to their prayer habits, one would be fearful of their physical conditions. Ridiculing the current diet fads, some wag suggested the following low-calorie diet: First day: "One pigeon thigh with three ounces of prune juice (gargle only)." For lunch the next day: "One doughnut hole without sugar with one glass dehydrated water." Another day's diet includes for breakfast: "Boiled out stains of old table cloth." My favorite suggestion: "Prime rib of tadpole and aroma of empty custard pie plate." Also recommended: "A seven-ounce glass of steam to be consumed on alternate days to help in having something to blow off."

This diet is nonsense but, tragically, many spiritual prayer diets have as little substance. Fenelon cried, "In God's name I beseech you let prayer nourish your souls as your meals nourish your body. Let your fixed seasons of prayer keep you in God's presence through the day, and His presence frequently remembered as though it be an everfresh spring of prayer."

Jesus valued prayer highly. As S. D. Gordon reminds us, it was not only Christ's habit, but His resort in every emergency, however slight or serious. When perplexed, He prayed. When hard pressed by work, He prayed. When hungry for fellowship, He found it in prayer. He chose His associates and received His messages upon His knees. If tempted, He prayed. If criticized, He prayed. If fatigued in body or wearied in spirit, He had recourse to His one unfailing habit of prayer. Prayer brought Him unmeasured power at the beginning and kept the flow unbroken and undiminished. There was no emergency, no difficulty, no necessity, no temptation that would not yield to His prayer.

Those who nurture proper habits in prayer testify to amazing supernatural power. Psychologist William James declared, "The man who has daily inured himself to habits of concentrated attention, energetic volition and self-denial will stand like a tower when everything rocks about him and when his softer fellow mortals are winnowed like chaff in the blast. Sow an action and you reap a habit; sow a habit and you reap a character; sow a character and you reap a destiny."

Think of what a meager hour spent in prayer every day would yield. Oscar Schisgall reflects, "If you devote but one hour a day to an engrossing project, you will give it 365 hours a year, or the equivalent of more than forty-five full working days of eight hours each. This is like adding one and one-half months of productive living to every year of life." Our torn world waits to feel the spiritual impact of such pray-ers.

The best time to pray

Those developing the habit of prayer often ask, "What is the proper time of day for prayer?" Some, claiming Christ prayed in the early morning, contend that it is the finest time to pray. In my life, prayer flows more freely in late hours. It should be noted Jesus went to prayer at night as well as early in the morning. In the last analysis, there is never a time we cannot enter God's great throne room. The point is not what time we pray; rather, it is that of developing a constant habit in this matter.

Jesus dramatically declares, ". . . Men ought always to pray, and not to faint" (Luke 18:1). Raymond T. Richey, pioneer evangelical, says, "Men ought to pray when clouds gather and rain descends in torrents; when birds have hushed their songs and flowers no longer bloom; when sorrow lays its crushing weight on the heart and all is wrong with the world. Men ought to pray when it seems God has forgotten to be gracious; when souls seem bleak and barren; when the flour bin is empty; when house rent is past due and there is no money to meet pressing bills; when the job is gone and there is no other in sight."

Richey adds, "Men ought to pray when health and hope are gone and friends are gone and money is gone and everything is gone — for God is not gone. He is ever near. He never changes."

It does not matter when we pray, but that we pray! It was not *when* our Savior prayed that set precedence but *why* and *how* He sought His Father. Some think Jesus prayed only to set a good example. One author reminds, "Our blessed Lord did not pray simply as an example to us: He never did things merely as an example. He prayed because He needed to pray."

New Testament Christians did not pray simply because praying gave pious standing in church or community. They did not develop habits of persistent prayer so throngs of people would read of their exploits centuries later. These people had no idea future Christians would study their acts and analyze their words or preach brilliant sermons on the lives they lived. Early Christians nurtured habits of prayer because no other way existed to win their holy war. They considered prayer a serious business in following Christ.

Spurgeon wrote, "Saints of the early church appear to have thought a great deal more seriously of prayer than many do nowadays. It seems to have been a mighty business with them, a long-practiced exercise, in which some of them attained great eminence and were thereby singularly blest. They reaped great harvests in the field of prayer and found the mercy seat to be a mine of untold treasures."

Perhaps these early warriors of prayer started with a little time each day for prayer, slowly cultivating keen desires for extended times. Someone mused, "We must remember that those men of prayer did not pray by time. They continued so long in prayer because they could not stop praying."

Men of God pray

Men of God are men of prayer!

Bishop Asbury related, "I propose to rise at four o'clock as often as I can and spend two hours in prayer and meditation." They say of Joseph Alleine that when four o'clock arrived he began to pray and continued until eight o'clock.

Dr. Adoniram Judson, a giant for God, spoke clearly on values of creating prayer habits, "Arrange thy affairs, if possible, so that thou canst leisurely devote two or three hours every day not merely to devotional exercises but to the very act of secret prayer and communion with God."

Sir Henry Havelock had a habit of welcoming each day with two hours of prayerful solitude. When he had to leave home at six o'clock he would rise from sleep two hours early for his prayer time. This is living on the valued *Mountain of Habitual Prayer.*

Stonewall Jackson fastened firmly in his mind the habit of prayer. He said, "I have so fixed the habit in my mind that I never raise a glass of water to my lips without asking God's blessing, never seal a letter without putting a word of prayer under the seal, never take a letter from the post without a brief sending of my thoughts heavenward, never change my classes in the lecture room without a minute's petition for the cadets who go out and for those who come in."

In my ministry I meet many fine men of God who have a daily time of meditation. This is certainly essential and yet, too often these same people push aside their need for saintly prayer. Luther taught the need for both study and prayer, "He who has prayed well has studied well."

James Gilmour, pioneer missionary to Mongolia, developed a habit in his writing of never using a blotter. Rather when he completed each page he would wait until the ink dried, spending that time in prayer. He did not elevate time of study above prayer, but made both one.

Putting study time ahead of prayer can endanger our spiritual lives. Preachers do not stand alone in this problem.

In conversation with youth we find Christian teens sorely lacking in daily prayer habits. Some go weeks or months without bending humble knees before God. Yet, where youth pray there seems to be a wave of sweet revival. Let it never be forgotten, youth can be men of God if they first are teens in prayer.

Prayer is the now life

Recently revival came to a Christian college as twelve students gathered for prayer. Soon the number grew to seven hundred at the altars. The end result was a casting aside of many hindering excuses and a fresh resolve to develop new prayer habits. Revival fires flame where hearts are praying. Sinners gloriously find Christ in churches where congregations have faithful habits of prayer.

The greatest habit we can take into our Christian life is living in the presence of Christ. This is more than prayer room experience; it is making Christianity a daily thing. This is how God's pray-ers become God's evangelists. Habits of prayer build habits of evangelism. Habits of evangelism build God's glorious Kingdom. Habits of prayer and evangelism are closely related in God's plan.

We ought to always pray and to always witness. He who effectively communicates with God will effectively communicate with people. We must live prayer and live evangelism. Someone asked George Müller if he had a habit of prayer and if he spent much time at it. His reply: "Hours every day. I live in the spirit of prayer; I pray as I walk, when I lie down and when I rise and the answers are always coming."

Answers always come if we never cease to pray. Satan knows well the power of prayer. No doubt he assigns a massive regiment of demons from the pit of hell to thwart Christians in developing proper prayer habits. There is a place, however — a place Satan does not seem to reach — where the shadow of our Lord hovers over those who pray. The psalmist found this spiritual utopia. "He that dwelleth in the *secret place* of the most High shall abide under the shadow of the Almighty" (Psalm 91:1).

Brother Lawrence knew this place where Satan becomes powerless. He wrote, "There is not in the world a kind of life more sweet and delightful than that of a continual conversation with God. Those only can comprehend it who *practice* and *experience* it." There it is plainly penned by one who found this secret place: *"Practice it and experience it."*

Now is the time for us to dwell in the secret place of the Almighty. Now is the best time to form humble habits of bended knee. Yesterday is gone, tomorrow is not here. All we have is *now*. Prayer is living the "now" life. Everything we intend to do for God must be done *now*. Prayer must be offered *now*. Revival must come *now*.

Churches must grow, Sunday schools increase, reckless youth saved, wounded hearts healed, missionaries sent, preachers trained — all must happen *now*. Habits of prayer set an atmosphere of urgency no other Christian act creates. Those with daily habits of prayer realize we must work hard and fast, accomplishing our task *now!*

Paul reminds us, "Pray without ceasing." In the original Greek, *ceasing* had a special meaning. Scholars say this rendering was used to describe a *hacking cough*. Have you had a constant, hacking cough? We do not set a schedule that indicates we should cough every fifteen minutes. We have no control over the matter. The impulse of a hacking cough is always there and at any moment we may succumb to the overwhelming need to cough.

This is what our prayer life must be. Habit must lodge so firmly in our minds no matter where we are, or with whom we come into contact, we never lose a burden for unceasing prayer. This habit of prayer separates great Christians from mediocre ones.

Wanted: chapped eyes

Songwriter Ira Stanphill talked with me on the subject of prayerful habits. He said he visited a small church where a young pastor labored to establish a work for God. Mr. Stanphill went to the meetings each night, presenting God's message in sermon and song. Less than one hundred were present each night to hear such popular compositions as "Mansion Over The Hilltop" and "Supper Time." Rev. Stanphill said of the young pastor, "One thing impressing me about that man was his unusual habit of prayer. Early each day I would hear him walk down the stairs, and soon sounds of prayer would ring throughout the house."

In this church Mr. Stanphill sang to meager crowds at first, but today thousands attend this church. Success can be accounted for only by the pastor's prayerful motto: "My church will never grow while my eyes are dry." What a splendid way of expressing the flaming burden of a broken heart! Fuel for the flame is habit, and such constant prayer keeps the fire burning.

Years ago this writer selected a motto for life in regards to prayer. I penned it in my Bible and though the ink has long since blurred, one still can read: "Wanted: Chapped Eyes." Oh, that Christians everywhere wept so much each would have chapped eyes.

One great man's prayerful habits became a literal clock to those around him. A neighbor relates: "At the same time every morning, very early, he would rise and go to prayer. When lights came on in his room we knew the time for rising had arrived. It was as positive as coming dawn. Never did he fail. One could use this man for an accurate timepiece."

A constant rule

Habits of prayer affect people close to us. John Fletcher had such beautiful prayer habits friends labeled him, "An angel of the Lord." One describes the outcome of a special prayer time in Fletcher's life, "Now all his bands were broken. His freed soul began to breathe a purer air. Sin was beneath his feet. He could triumph in the Lord. From this time he walked in the ways of God, and thinking he had not enough leisure in the day, he made it a *constant* rule to sit up two whole nights in the week for reading, prayer, and meditation."

Constant is the word to be noted. It was a *constant* rule. In all our groping for a word describing habit, this is best. Even the Webster's Unabridged does no better.

There are certain things we do to stay alive. We must breathe. We must eat foods that nourish. Clothes are donned to shelter from the elements. But another activity must be added, one we must make a *constant rule,* never to be broken. *We must pray today*.

David Livingstone could tell us what godly habits in the art of prayer can do. His habit every birthday was to write a prayer. Next to the last year of life this was his prayer, "O Divine One, I have not loved thee earnestly, deeply, sincerely enough. Grant, I pray thee, that before this year is ended I may have finished my task."

During the following year, Livingstone's faithful servants looked into the hut of Ilala and found their leader on his knees in a position of intercession. He died in prayer; his broken heart soon buried in a savage land. This godly hero, dead and gone, left prayers that live today. He learned well the lesson of developing the habit of prayer. He died on bended knees!

6 THE PLATEAU OF INTERCESSION

"Talking to men for God is a great thing," declared E. M. Bounds, "but talking to God for men is greater still." Intercession is placing emphasis on others, rather than pleading for ourselves. Becoming an intercessor is not easy. Man, by nature, is a selfish creature caring little for others. Strangely, however, this is not the spirit of those crossing *The Plateau of Intercession.* Caring for others is the watchword of those who travel this lonely road.

The climax of prayer

To begin to be an intercessor, we need special preparation. It is necessary to consider certain forms of prayer, giving deeper insight into the reasons for intercession. Understanding why intercession is prayer's highest form is pertinent. S. D. Gordon says, "Prayer is the word commonly used for all intercourse with God. But it should be kept in mind that this word covers and includes three forms of intercourse. All prayer grows up through, and ever continues, in three stages." Gordon went on to list, "(1) The first form of prayer is communion. That is simply being on good terms with God. Not request for some particular thing: not asking, but simply enjoying Him, loving Him . . . talking to Him without words. (2) The second form of prayer is petition. Petition is a definite request of God for something I need. A man's whole life is utterly dependent upon the giving hand of God. (3) The third form of prayer is intercession. True prayer never stops with petition for one's self. It reaches out for others. Intercession is the *Climax of Prayer.* The first two are necessarily for self; this third is for others."

The climax of prayer exists when people discard petty whims and think first of those less fortunate. Intercession battles poverty-gripped ghettos where people starve for lack of love and food. Intercession engages in conflict with a million evils facing our fellowmen. An intercessor must bid farewell to self and welcome the burdens of humanity. In truth, the climax of prayer is intercession.

The scope of intercession

David Wilkerson, founder of Teen Challenge International, is a modern example of one who learned well the lessons of intercession. In extended times of prayer God moved him concerning problem youth. He reflects how, during prayer, he was drawn to a national magazine with sketches of several rebellious youth from New York. They were involved in a brutal criminal act that shocked our nation. Suddenly a burden of intercessory prayer gripped Dave Wilkerson's heart and a love was born for these lost, frustrated youth.

This time of intercession was the impetus which led Rev. Wilkerson to found the greatest private organization in the world for treating hopeless drug addicts. Today his movement aids problem youth in all walks of life.

Teen Challenge, now a multi-million dollar organization, began when one man united with God in humble prayer. Today it reaches most major cities in the United States, and many cities of the world. Dave Wilkerson is indeed an example of an intercessor.

Recently I visited Teen Challenge headquarters in New York City. I shall never forget standing in that inner city center. There a former addict taught me what it means to intercede. He pointed out, "All souls won on the streets are first won in prayer!" Few people realize the power of intercessory prayer. One author notes, "Every convert is the result of the Holy Spirit's pleading in answer to the prayers of some believer."

Word reached me recently of an amazing victory of intercessory prayer in my home church. Our pastor had prayed for years for a wicked man who resisted God. The man's wife, too, became an intercessor. Daily she prayed for her husband, that he might be saved. Finally, the day arrived as her mate accepted Christ. Another victory for intercessory prayer. Intercession is basically love praying. In the very truest sense, intercession is love on its knees. When we love someone we seek his very best. Douglas V. Steere wrote, "If I really engage in prayer, 'The business of business' as Bernard of Clairvaux called it, I really awaken to the love with which I am encompassed." Later he elaborated, "When we begin to pray for another, we begin to know and to understand and to cherish him as never before. There is vivid confirmation of Phillips Brooks' well-known word that 'If you want to know the worth of a human soul, try to save one.' "

Imagine occupying God's throne and seeing one lost, lonely soul. Could we give our only son! Would we love others enough to pay this price? Sacrificial prayer is true intercession. In truth, *prayer for other men is the scope of intercession.*

"No one seemed to care"

We live in a fast-paced society with few caring for those

around them. In a large West Coast city a policeman was almost kicked to death by a pack of rebellious youths. Hundreds filed past, glancing quickly as blood flowed freely. None stopped to question. No one offered help! Rebels kept on beating, finally leaving him for dead. Blood on the pavement seemed to form five frightful words — *no one seemed to care.* Even more tragic is how Satan pushes helpless souls around while Christians lack concern. Intercession is our only means to hinder Satan's drive, yet few cultivate this kind of prayer. Oh, that God would place a burning drive within us to pray this type of prayer.

Troubled Job learned a priceless lesson about intercessory prayer. Early in his prayer experience he thought only of his horrible condition. Daily he petitioned God to remove those dreadful sores. Relief, however, didn't come when he prayed for himself, but while he prayed for friends who caused him such grief. It was when he learned the lesson of intercession that his body was restored to perfect health. Job tasted victory only after prayer for others.

Moses knew well the role of the intercessor. On one occasion his prayer reached intensified proportions while he interceded for God's children. Israel was warned to cease its constant bickering. Time and again warnings came as Jehovah cried, "I shall destroy them." But, mark one fact: Moses cared! Using every ounce of strength, he prayed, "Please, O God, forgive them." You can see hot tears flow freely down Moses' face, as he begs, "Blot my name from Your great book — kill me if You wish — but please forgive Your people."

Anyone praying this intensely has learned the meaning of intercession. How much this reminds us of that great praying Christian, Billy Bray. They say he was small in stature but a giant in things of God. Daily he went to work inside a filthy English coal mine with the prayer: "Lord, if anyone of us must be killed, or die today, let it be me; let not one of these men die, for they are not happy and I am, and if I die today I shall go to heaven."

Bray possessed an "I care" attitude throughout life. For example, once, not having received wages for some time, he had no money. He approached the Lord in prayer. He had potatoes and bacon but no bread. He went to the manager of the mine and borrowed a small sum. Walking home he met two families more destitute than himself. He gave each half his money and went home penniless. His wife felt discouraged but Billy assured her the Lord had not forgotten them. Soon twice the amount was given them. Most agree the world is lacking men such as this — men of intercessory prayer. We ought to pray for modern Billy Brays — men who think of others in their prayer, men who care.

Every Finney needs a Father Nash

Through past centuries, revivals of consequence have come through intercessory prayer. Finney's revival rocked America's Eastern states in the first half of the nineteenth century. One man, known as Father Nash, would precede Finney to cities scheduled for crusades. Three or four weeks in advance of meetings Father Nash humbly journeyed to town. No great crowds waited to welcome him and no bands played fanfares of greeting. Father Nash would quietly find a place of prayer. During the revivals countless souls were won and lives changed. Finney's name soon gained acclaim, and his sermons pierced the hearts of multitudes.

Somewhere alone, however, knelt humble Father Nash. After revival came, he quietly left town for another crusade, there to labor on bended knees. He, too, knew the meaning of intercession. Father Nash concerned himself with others, often sacrificing the finer things of life. He had no home, no church support, and often missed the taste of home-cooked meals. Nights were spent without a bed, and clothes became frayed.

What did Nash receive for this? Little in this life, perhaps, but much in the life to come. He owns stock in two and one-half million Finney converts. Few realize how many souls found Christ because of Father Nash. Time, no doubt, will show that behind every soul won for Christ was intercessory prayer. Indeed, Finney had remarkable talent to preach. Certainly he had a special touch from God. But mark this fact — *Every Finney* needs a Father Nash! Every preacher needs an intercessor.

Consider for a moment the challenge of becoming an intercessor. The needs for intercessory prayer are staggering. Frank C. Laubach says, "All the following people need to be floodlighted with prayers: the President of the United States and Congress (especially the Senate), the Prime Minister and Parliament of England, Russia's Premier and leaders, China's leaders, delegates at every peace conference, Japanese, Germans, church members and the clergy of Christians and Jews, the missionaries, motion picture leaders, radio broadcasters, all kinds of slaves and oppressed peoples, Negroes, Americans of Japanese ancestry. We must pray for illiterates, for all teachers, mothers and fathers, for understanding between capital and labor, for human brotherhood, for cooperatives, for the enlargement of people's minds to world vision, for children and youth, for wholesome literature, for victims of liquor, drugs and vices of all kinds, for educators and better education. We must pray for hatred to vanish and love to rule the world; we must pray for more prayer, for it is the world's mightiest healing force." Laubach's list seems long, but even this is incomplete. Intercessors never lack needs to occupy prayer lists. Always flowing from the intercessor's heart is prayer for someone, prayer that says, "I love you."

Aspects of intercession

All ages, nationalities, and races may kneel at *Intercession's* summit. Physician Luke from apostolic days declares, "And there was one Anna, a prophetess . . . and she was a widow of about fourscore and four years, which departed not from the temple, but served God with fastings and prayers night and day" (Luke 2:36, 37). Here was an elderly lady possessing more purpose in life's twilight hours than in her younger years. These words of Luke are of special worth, indicating that all are welcome at God's throne.

Someone has said, "We may have a wonderful gift of speech pouring itself out in a torrent of thanksgiving, petition, and praise like Paul; or we may have the quiet, deep, lover-like communion of a John. Brilliant scholars like John Wesley and humble cobblers like William Carey are alike welcome at the throne of grace. Influence at the court of heaven depends not upon birth, or brilliancy, or achievement, but upon humble and utter dependence upon the Son of the King."

True intercessors, unfortunately, seldom come along prayer's trail. Rees Howells was such a man. He learned the power of intercessory prayer while building Bible schools, orphanages, and mission churches throughout Africa. Howells' associates say he was a man of prayer. Early in his Christian life God challenged him concerning intercessory prayer. Once, when emerging from his prayer chamber, Howells gave a three-fold explanation of intercession.

"These three aspects," taught Howells, "are never found in ordinary prayer." Included, first of all, is *identification;* law number one for every intercessor. Christ remains the supreme example of this crucial law. He was numbered with transgressors. He became the great High Priest interceding on our behalf. Christ came to earth from ivory palaces, born in a humble manger. God's Son pitched His tent within our camp, making Himself a brother to all men. Temptation became a snare to Him and death the taste upon His lips. He suffered with the suffering and walked the rocky roads we mortals walk. Jesus epitomized lasting love. His lovely life defines the intercessor: *one who identifies with others.*

Secondly, Mr. Howells listed *agony* as the next law of the intercessor. "If we are to be an intercessor," felt Mr. Howells, "we must be fully like the Master."

The author of Hebrews (5:7) says our Master prayed with ". . . strong crying and tears. The apostle Paul says, ". . . the Spirit itself maketh intercession for us with groanings which cannot be uttered" (Romans 8:26).

Jesus reached deepest depths in the sea of agony; Gethsemane, no doubt, was the very ocean floor. Here is defined the agony of agonies. Here our Master's heart was broken as none have known. His life teaches intercession's key: *learn to agonize for souls.*

Howells' third law concerns *authority*. He states, "If the intercessor is to know identification and agony, he also knows authority. He moves God, this intercessor. He even causes Him to change His mind." Rees Howells claimed that when he gained a place of intercession for a need, and believed it God's will, he always had a victory.

"Who cares about North Africa"

Amazing victory for Mr. Howells followed a week of intercessory prayer during World War II. Prayer meetings were not usually held on Saturday afternoons, but on one particular Saturday the college was called to spend an afternoon in prayer, to ask God to turn the tide of the war in North Africa. This was a heavy burden.

That evening Mr. Howells and the college came through to victory. "I thought Hitler might be allowed to take Egypt," he said, "but I know now he will never take Egypt — neither Alexandria nor Cairo will fall." At the end of the meeting he declared, "I have been stirred to my depths today. I have been like a man ploughing his way through sand. But now I am on top of it, now I am gripping it; I am handling it. I can shake it."

One week later, while scanning a newspaper, Mr. Howells read how grave the condition was that Saturday when they called the extra prayer meeting. That very weekend, according to the article, Alexandria was saved. Involved in the battle was a Major Rainer, the man responsible to supply the Eighth Army with water. Later he described the incident in a book, *Pipe Line to Battle*. Rommel, the Desert Fox, was moving his men toward Alexandria with hopes of capturing the city. Between him and the city was a remnant of the British Army with only fifty tanks, a small number of field guns, and five thousand soldiers. The Germans had approximately the same number of men but held decisive advantage with their superior 88 mm guns. One thing in common with both armies was sheer exhaustion from intensifying heat, and urgent need for water.

Major Rainer relates, "The sun was almost overhead, and our men were fast reaching the end of their endurance, when the Nazis broke. Ten minutes more and it might have been us. Suddenly the Mark IV tanks lumbered back from the battle smoke. And then an incredible thing happened: eleven hundred men of the 90th Light Panzer Division, the elite of the German Africa Korps, came stumbling across the barren sand with their hands in the air. Cracked and black with coagulated blood, their swollen tongues were protruding from their mouths. Crazily they tore water bottles from the necks of our men and poured life-giving swallows between their parched lips."

Later in his account Mr. Rainer gives the reasons for this totally unexpected surrender. The Germans had gone an entire day and night without water. While the battle raged they over-ran British defenses and to their joy discovered a six-inch water line. Craving water they shot holes in the pipe and carelessly began to gulp the contents. Because of extreme thirst they consumed tremendous amounts without realizing it was sea water.

Major Rainer, the man in charge of the pipe line construction, had decided to give it one last test. Fresh water was far too valuable for testing and therefore sea water was used. "The day before, it would have been empty," wrote the Major. "Two days later," he added, "it would have been fresh water." The Nazis didn't detect the salt at once since their sense of taste had been anesthetized by the brackish water they had been used to, and by extreme thirst."

The startling point to note concerning this entire event is that intercessory prayer was responsible. Had Rees Howells not called a special time of prayer this account could well have been different.

"Who cares what happens in North Africa?" may have been the attitude of some, but others cared. Thank God for those intercessory giants. An intercessor's concern for others often shapes the destiny of nations, changing things no other power can change.

Sowing seeds of love

This is an age when people cry incessantly for social action. Popular songs contain lyrics as, "Come on, people now . . . everybody get together, try to love one another, right now." Society seeks a force to heal man's ill — to bring about a special change. From philosopher to musician the cry is, "What the world needs now is love."

Indeed, no force transmits human love more than intercessory prayer. No greater gift could man give society than bended knee. In the last analysis, when all history is written and we stand before God, we will know what really shaped this age. When we talk with God in eternity we will quickly learn everything of worth that was accomplished was connected to an intercessor's prayer.

7 THE COVE OF HOLINESS

Billy Bray was once asked how the world was getting on. His answer, "I don't know; I haven't been there for twelve years." This hero of faith lived in *Holiness Cove,* a place of spiritual beauty reached only by prayer. Few aspire to reach this abode. Those who do sacrifice all to reach the top.

The Road of Prayer must ascend to this cove if answers are expected. Those who bid farewell to earth's thrills learn what real holiness affords in making prayer more effective.

Dress up in Christ

Never has there been a greater need for holiness. Dr. Joseph Parker said, "When the church forgets to put on her beautiful garments of holiness, though it be made up of a thousand Samsons, it cannot strike one blow at the enemy. Count the church by the volume of its prayers; register the strength of the church by the purity and completeness of its consecration."

Dr. Parker adds this striking observation: "Genius is nothing, learning is nothing, organization is a sarcasm and an irony, apart from that which gives every one of them value and force — the praying heart and the trustful spirit."

Paul told the Roman church, "Put . . . on the Lord Jesus Christ . . ." (Romans 13:14). This could be paraphrased "Dress up in Christ."

When climbing to *Holiness Cove* one plainly sees a wide road in the valley below. This road is filled with frivolous throngs gayly going their willful way. Follow this road to its tragic ending. There you see the horror at its terminal point — hell.

More leave every day to join the throngs on that lower road. The great tragedy is the scarcity of sermons calling men to holiness. Burning sermons on holiness come only from praying hearts — and few preachers have a "closet" time each day. Bounds relates, "Dead men give out dead sermons, and dead sermons kill. Everything depends on the spiritual character of the preacher." Praying Jewish priests in Old Testament times had inscribed in jeweled letters on their golden frontlet, "Holiness to the Lord."

Personal integrity and character are sure foundations for a life of prayer. As a man is, so he prays. He cannot be shallow and frivolous by nature and yet pray with depth and intensity. Our prayers are worth what we are worth!

Holiness is seeing God

Results achieved by godly men have always been backed by holy living. Holiness is doing all within one's power to become like Jesus. Holiness is seeing Christ in His completeness; doing all we can to pattern our life after His example. One preacher proclaimed, "Romanism trembled when Martin Luther saw God. The great awakening sprang into being when Jonathan Edwards saw God. The world became the parish of one man when John Wesley saw God. Multitudes were saved when Whitefield saw God. Thousands of orphans were fed when George Müller saw God."

Holiness brings us close to God, whom the Bible calls a

consuming fire. In His presence we become flaming torches spreading this great fire of God. William Bramwells illustrates this thought. Of him a biographer says, "He is famous in Methodist annals for personal holiness, for his wonderful success in preaching and for the marvelous answers to his prayers. For hours at a time he would pray. He almost lived on his knees. He went over his circuits like a flame of fire. The fire was kindled by the time he spent in prayer."

Holiness is lived, not just talked about. Praying Hyde talked little about his holy living and life of prayer. There was no need for him to stand before a crowd and say, "I have spent a night in prayer." Those hearing him knew he prayed earnestly. Francis A. McGraw in writing of John Hyde relates, "I have carefully and prayerfully gone over the facts and incidents and experiences in the life of my dear friend and I am impressed that the one great characteristic of John Hyde was holiness." Hyde once challenged, "Self must not only be dead but buried out of sight, for the stench of the unburied self-life will frighten souls away from Jesus."

John Hyde accomplished much for God because of prayer, but at the root of prayer is holiness. Holiness is the soil nourishing roots of prayer. Holiness testifies emphatically that sin has been cast from our lives. Without real holiness genuine prayer cannot be uttered. One pray-er observes "All hindrance to prayer arises from ignorance of the teaching of God's Holy Word on the life of holiness He has planned for all His children, or from an unwillingness to consecrate ourselves fully to Him."

Happiness is holiness

It is true that holiness is difficult to attain. Worldly weights often hold us back. God's Word succinctly says, ". . . Let us lay aside every weight . . ." (Hebrews 12:1).

Worldly weights hinder more prayers than one realizes. We must rid ourselves of the "sin that doth so easily beset us" as Scripture states, and "run with patience the race that is set before us."

Achieving holiness is not impossible, as some suggest. Holy living is joyful and exciting. Brother Lawrence, though dead four centuries, remains a great example. His position in life was humble — washing pots and pans in a monastery. Yet an acquaintance said, "His very countenance was edifying, such a sweet calm devotion appearing in it as could not but affect the beholders. And it was observed that in the greatest hurry of business in the kitchen he still preserved his recollection and heavenly mindedness."

Holiness to Brother Lawrence was not the result of painful endeavor. He loved living close to Jesus, "I renounce, for the love of Him, everything that was not He, and I began to live as if there was none but He and I in the world."

Those striving for holiness soon learn to live within God's holy presence. It is said of Horace Bushnell, "When he buried his face in his hands and prayed, I was afraid to stretch out my hand in the darkness, lest I should touch God."

Holiness is not a lengthy list of negatives. Holiness is never whipping our spiritual selves in attempts to become humble. It is not bidding farewell to everything in life that resembles honest fun. Holiness does not mean we abolish humor and ignore all pleasure. Rather, it is simply living near the heart of God. Holiness creates an inner craving for more of God. David Brainerd blazed a trail across North America while preaching about his lovely Lord. He penned, "I long for God, and a conformity to His will, in inward holiness, ten thousand times more than for anything here below." Brainerd did not live a miserable life. He learned the holy life is a happy life and holiness begets happiness.

Society today is on a happiness "kick." Americans will consume three and one half gallons of hard liquor per person this year. Multiply this times two hundred million and we envision a vast ocean of liquor. All this is craved to provide a moment's happiness in a trying age. Recently a teen-ager came to me from a life of hopeless drug addiction. His habit drove him to jail on many occasions. He found Jesus as Savior and began his climb up to *Holiness Cove.* He described his experience, "I have a permanent high . . . a forever fix." To him holiness is not drudgery, but real living. Holiness is happiness.

Holiness is shared

Holiness is something shared. Those walking close to God affect others. Norman Grubb says of Rees Howells, "But if at the beginning the world was affecting him, by the end it was he who was affecting the world, for people sensed the presence of God with him, and said so." Some with no religious faith doffed hats when Howells passed them in the streets. One man used to say, "You mark my words: there goes a modern John the Baptist." Evidence of Howells' effect was seen when a man, not knowing Howells' name, simply asked the train ticket collector where "the man with the Holy Ghost lived." He immediately was directed to Howells.

Charles Finney led two and one-half million persons to profession of Christ as Savior. Services were marked with the unusual because Finney wore spotless garments of holiness. He testified, "I once preached for the first time in a manufacturing village. The next morning I went into a manufacturing establishment to view its operations. As I passed into the weaving department I beheld a great company of young women, some of whom, I observed, were looking at me, then at each other, in a manner that indicated a trifling spirit, and that they knew me. I, however, knew none of them. As I approached nearer to those who had recognized me, they seemed to increase in their manifestations of lightness of mind. Their levity made a peculiar impression upon me: I felt it to my very heart."

Finney further relates, "I stopped short and looked at them, I know not how, as my whole mind was absorbed with the sense of their guilt and danger. As I settled my countenance upon them I observed that one of them became very much agitated. A thread broke. She attempted to mend it; but her hands trembled in such a manner that she could not do it. I immediately observed that the sensation was spreading, and had become universal among that class of triflers."

Finney concludes, "I looked steadily at them until one after another gave up and paid no more attention to their looms. They fell on their knees, and the influence spread throughout the whole room. I had not spoken a word; and the noise of the looms would have prevented my being heard if I had. In a few minutes all work was abandoned and tears and lamentations filled the room."

The effect of a life of holiness was felt. Hundreds of factory workers were changed, their lives revolutionized. Finney had prepared himself in prayer, but prayer alone cannot bring revolution. A praying man must be a holy man. Finney was a man of prayer — and more. He was a holy man of prayer. Indeed, holiness is linked with prayer as sterling is with silver. "Prayer and holy living," wrote a godly man, "are one. They mutually act and react. Neither can survive alone." We cannot talk of praying hands unless we talk of holy hearts. The two become one in traveling prayer's trail.

Not all are comfortable when they come into contact with holy lives. Holiness often brings conviction of the highest order. Whitefield's holiness left an impact long remembered. His first sermon was delivered to a large audience in his old home church at Gloucester. Following this sermon the bishop received severe criticism and complaints. He heard reports of fifteen people going mad as Whitefield preached. Respecting Whitefield's holy life the bishop said, "I truly hope the madness will not be forgotten before next Sunday."

Holiness and the Holy Spirit

God's Holy Spirit holds a vital place in teaching holy living. Presently we witness growing hunger by all faiths to understand more fully this Third Person of the Trinity. Never have people needed the Holy Spirit as today. He is One who comes beside us, always helping attain holiness. We must make a constant effort — ever praying, always seeking — to gain the Comforter's help.

John Fletcher, of Swiss fame, became synonymous with holiness. A Methodist leader said of him, "I conceive Fletcher to be the most holy man who has been upon earth since the apostolic age." Fletcher displayed a gnawing need to have God's Spirit. Once he cried, "O for that pure baptismal flame! Pray, pray, pray for this! This shall make us all of one heart, and of one soul. Pray for gifts — for the gift of utterance; and confess your royal Master. A man without gifts is like a king in disguise; he appears as a subject only. You are kings and priests unto God! Put on, therefore, your robes, and wear on your garter, 'Holiness to the Lord.' "

To attain holiness we must be honest with ourselves. Frankly, there are times we seem to lose footing and even times we fall. It is then we praise our Lord for being near us with His Spirit. He alone can lift us from the fall. We thank Him for the words, ". . . If any man sin [slip], we have an advocate with the Father . . . (I John 2:1). An advocate is a helper; a friend who picks us up when down. Some forget that even saintly men needed an advocate with the Father.

Fletcher told Wesley how Satan often tempted him to end his life. According to Wesley his friend was so passionate by nature he often prayed whole nights to gain victory. Sometimes he stretched prostrate in agony of grief to gain victory over self. Yet, we remember Fletcher for his holiness and gentle spirit. We, too, face moments when we feel the coldness of this sinful age. Often we catch a death of a spiritual "cold" for lack of wearing garments of holiness. There are countless times Satan tries to blow us from this sheltered spot with his forceful breath of wrong desires. Then, we must move closer to our ever-present Lord.

Take time to be holy

One visit to *Holiness Cove* leaves people changed for years. Moses came from the top of Mt. Sinai where he bathed in God's great glory. His person was like a burning star — his face shining and aglow. Moses' life was changed forever. He learned real holiness is not to be associated with mountain-top experiences alone. Holy living is a daily thing, and Moses lived it everyday. His godly living gave him dynamic power when he prayed. Moses took time to be holy; he walked with God as did Enoch. His life of holiness prepared him for his times of prayer. In truth, *holy living is essential preparation for prayer.*

Oh, that each would spend time in this sheltered spot before we lose our bravery, strength, and dare desire. We must attain holiness to be effective pray-ers. With "Holiness unto the Lord" inscribed on our hearts we journey forward on the trail of prayer. W. D. Longstaff encourages:

Take time to be holy;
    The world rushes on;
Spend much time in secret
    With Jesus alone;
By looking to Jesus
    Like Him thou shalt be;
Thy friends in thy conduct
    His likeness shall see.

8 THE MOUNTAIN OF SELF-WILL

Dr. Roy C. DeLamotte, chaplain at Paine College, Augusta, Georgia, preached the shortest sermon with the longest title in the college's history. "What Does Christ Answer When We Ask, 'Lord, What's in Religion for Me?' " His complete sermon was, "Nothing!"

Dr. DeLamotte later explained his sermon was a corrective for people "brought up on the gimme-gimme gospel." When asked how long it had taken to prepare his message he replied, "Twenty years."

Unfortunately, it takes some Christians a lifetime to realize the importance of God's will in prayer. Too often prayers fail because we possess a "gimme-gimme" attitude. This is why praying Christians must learn to scale this towering *Mountain of Self-Will.*

A silent surrendering

In some churches of today there is the danger of taking on a form of prayer with one intention in mind — using God. Recently I noticed a book on prayer called, "How to Use God." I never read it, for the title frightened me away. F. J. Huegel said, "Prayer is not the cunning art of using God, subjecting Him to one's selfish ends in an effort to get out of Him what you want."

George MacDonald provides depth to our consideration: "It is not what God can give us, but God we want." One peasant described his prayer, "God just looks down at me and I look up at Him."

Essential to our understanding of God's will is this basic fact: God desires, above all else, devoted worship. Sören Kierkegaard labels prayer "a silent surrendering of everything to God."

No one has learned better the value of such surrender than the monk Brother Lawrence. A simple book on Lawrence's life has affected many millions. The book *The Practice of the Presence of God* contains a friend's analysis of Lawrence: "His prayer was nothing but a sense of the presence of God, his soul being at that time insensible to everything but Divine love; and that when the appointed times of prayer were past, he found no difference, because he still continued with God, praising and blessing Him with all his might, so that he passed his life in continual joy." This is a *silent surrendering* to God. Dare we hope our friends would write the same of us when we are gone?

Brother Lawrence found the will of God because His perfect will calls men everywhere to praise, worship, and adoration. Brother Lawrence wrote, "The end we ought to propose to ourselves is to become, in this life, the most perfect worshipers of God we can possibly be, as we hope to be through all eternity."

Shadow of God's presence

The more we stand in a friend's presence the more we understand his personality. In growing to know this friend we grow to know his will. Thus it is with children of God. Often we bring petitions to God voicing them with boldness at His throne. Seldom do we talk of simply waiting in His presence.

Jehovah says, "Be still, and know that I am God . . ."

(Psalm 46:10). This is the listening part of prayer.

The fondest moments of my married life are spent quietly in the presence of my wife. Earlier a dialogue existed as we pondered events of the day. Love was shared in dialogue as we voiced personal interest in one another. Later, however, love reaches a higher plane although speech ceases. There is no great dialogue, no fancy words, just a wonderful feeling of being near one you love. Love finds completeness at this stage. Nothing more is needed for romance. We are near the one we love, which after all, is fundamental love. This, then, is how we find the perfect will of God. It is learning to live within *the shadow of God's presence.*

Remember Enoch, a prime example. "And Enoch walked with God . . ." the Bible says (Genesis 5:22). What a thought-provoking epitaph! How could Enoch fail to know the will of God? He "walked with God"! When walking with God, man understands unanswered prayer. He knows why problems often plague our way. How else could Paul accept his "thorn in the flesh" (II Corinthians 12:7)? Satan buffeted him daily, but God's grace was sufficient (II Corinthians 12:9). Perhaps Paul knows today, while resting in Paradise, why God permitted his thorn. Paul, no doubt, sees value in it all, sensing the beauty of God's will.

Only when he denies himself and lives close to God does man learn His beautiful will. When one really understands God's perfect will, the effectiveness of prayer is staggering. S. D. Gordon adds this insight: "The first thing in prayer is to find God's purpose, the trend, the swing of it; the second thing, to make that purpose our prayer." Gordon continues: "Now prayer is this: finding God's purpose for our lives, and for the earth, and insisting that it shall be done here. The great thing then is to find out and insist upon God's will. And the 'how' of method in prayer is concerned with that."

The force of prayer cannot be fathomed without understanding what submission to God's will involves. God answers every sincere prayer; not a single real prayer can fail of its effect in heaven. Answers will always come, although they may not be exactly what we seek. When asked if her prayers were answered, a little girl replied, "Yes, God said No."

"You choose, God"

Recently in prayer I heard God say, "What would you like if I should give you one particular gift today?"

This question passed from my mind, but seconds later it came another way: "If I should hand you a silver platter with one item, what would you like?" In contemplation my mind wandered from desire to desire. First, vast sums of money came to mind; money to begin a special mission work overseas. Then, I thought of perfect happiness, certainly an item valued highly. Next, the fullness of God's Spirit crossed my mind — indeed a perfect gift from God, for nothing aids our ministry like a double portion of His Spirit.

Time passed as myriad thoughts paraded through my mind. Suddenly a staggering thought occurred. If I could have one gift from God — absolutely anything — I would want above all else, His will. "Give me your will for my life, O God; with this, there is nothing more."

S. D. Gordon relates a similar experience, "I sometimes thought this: what if God were to say to me: 'I want to give you something as a special love-gift; an extra because I love you: what would you like to have?' Do you know that I thought I would say, 'Dear God, you choose. I choose what you choose.' " What a beautiful way of describing God's will. Oh, that God would choose what He thinks best, no matter what the situation. Horatius Bonar prayed poetically:

Choose thou for me my friends,
My sickness or my health;
Choose thou my cares for me,
My poverty or wealth.

Not mine, not mine the choice
In things of great or small.
Be thou my guide, my strength,
My wisdom and my all.

Our lovely Lord time and again spoke of His Father's will — the "works of Him that sent me" (John 9:4). Christ was always cognizant of His Father's will, keeping in mind the Master's plan. Once His disciples uttered their request, "Lord, teach us to pray." Jesus answered with the prayer of prayers. It would do well to note that a key portion of our Master's prayer included the petition, "Thy will be done" (Luke 11:2). Our own prayers will not be effectual if we do not first pray our Master's prayer and say, "Thy will be done."

Once I visited a lady in the hospital whose new baby lay near death. One can only imagine the agony of this broken heart as tears flowed endlessly — the pain more intense than a dread disease. Finally, in sensing the sovereign will of God this grieving mother cried, "God, choose what you think best." Heaven called this little baby home that day, as a mother wept those scalding tears of love. (It calls to remembrance those wise words, "It is worth noting that the greatest pain in prayer comes from the tightness of our grip on that which holds us back.") In speaking with this lady twelve months later I saw God's purpose. Tragedy struck a close friend and she seemed the only one who understood. She stood with the family, giving comfort none other could give. Experience had taught the beauty of God's will — the real reason for these tests and trials. Her battle, waged a year before, prepared for her a balm to soothe wounded hearts. She learned the value of allowing God to choose.

Tragedy at Christmas

God always desires our greatest good. In sorrow, however, we often miss God's "why" of certain things, observing only that painful moment rather than God's total plan.

Evangelist Kathryn Kuhlman tells of God's will. Recently I came across her excellent book *God Can Do It Again.* It told of a young couple who found Christ through tragedy.

It was winter time, a matter of days before Christmas, as Joe and Dora made preparations for the holiday. Joe was a successful television repairman, father of two young boys, Mike and Steve. One morning Joe embarked on another day's work as Dora let Mike and Steve out to play on the front driveway. She knew the boys would soon return for a taste of warm cookies she was baking. Only twenty minutes passed when a terrified neighbor pounded frantically on their door. News of tragedy was soon to set a gloom upon that house for months. Her neighbor ominously cried, "Two boys fell in the pond. I think they're yours."

Joe and Dora soon found themselves standing sadly in a funeral home, the boys lying in twin caskets. Following a solemn service, burial was held in freezing wind and rain. Imagine, standing in this mother's place asking God "why?" Follow Dora as she returns home. She tries every human way to forget. Entering the kitchen she notices two little gifts Mike and Steve made at school; gifts they placed on the countertop the day they died. She silently reads, "To the best mom and dad in the world," penned in childlike manner. Follow this broken mother just one day and sense the difficulty of submitting to God's will.

Dora serves dinner now, but two empty chairs rest beside the dining room table, constant reminders of two little boys. Try to measure a mother's love — it cannot be done. The object of love is gone. The love itself remains with no release, eating at this mother's heart like a cancer. Stay with her as she enters the boys' room, only to find a rumpled pile of little boys' clothes. She pulls out drawers of a nearby chest noticing things boys collect — bottle caps, empty shotgun shells, and children's books. Consider the anxiety this father felt. He could not eat, sleep, or even dress himself for weeks. His hair began to fall, his eyes constantly bloodshot, and his body soon was covered with huge boils. Trace his steps for a day, noticing the striking parallel with Job of old. Imagine his thoughts as a school bus of joyful children passed. Kneel beside Joe as he repairs a broken television set, moving the cabinet only to discover a child's toy. Tears flow freely as he looks in retrospect. Vividly he recalls times Mike and Steve snuggled close to him showing childlike love.

"How on earth could this possibly be God's will?" It reminds me of a tragic train wreck in which a father saw his only son killed. The father, tense and terrified, ran along the wreckage yelling, "Where was God when my son was killed?" One after another he seized people, shouting again and again, "Where was God when my son was killed?" Finally he approached an elderly bearded man, upon whose aging face appeared a look of calm. "Where was God when my son was killed?" the father begged. In love and understanding came the reply, "I suppose where He was when His own Son died."

Just as cheap and easy to rejoice

It is imperative that we realize there is a reason behind all God allows. In the lives of the parents who lost two fine boys we note the husband brought thirteen relatives to Christ in the months following this tragedy. Now we see more clearly God's will — the "why" of it. Only with this understanding can we make progress on the Road of Prayer. We must recognize the value of accepting all that happens, knowing well the need to have God's plan. Here we learn the "why" of every failure, the purpose for each trial.

My mind goes back to a classic psalm, "Yea, though I walk *through* the valley of the shadow of death . . ." (Psalm 23:4). We must not miss the impact of the simple word *through.* The psalmist does not with frightened eyes scan the valley. He does not center fearful thoughts on death's shadow. In actuality, David sees *through* the valley, *past* the shadow, looking in confidence toward the other side.

Here we understand James Whitcomb Riley's thought:

> It is no use to grumble and complain;
> It's *just as cheap and easy to rejoice;*
> When God sorts out the weather and
> sends rain —
> Why, rain's my choice.

Oh, that man could look *through* moments of tragedy and see the blessedness of submitting to God's will. Here, alone, we find full comprehension of Paul's thought, ". . . All things work together for good . . . to them who are called according to His purpose" (Romans 8:28).

After conquering our own self-will and submitting to God's will, we bask in the glow of God's sweet presence. Here, in tragedy, we hear God's voice silently say, "All is well." Robert Louis Stevenson describes a raging storm at sea. Passengers below were greatly alarmed as waves dashed over the vessel. Many thought the end had come. Finally one, against orders, crept to the deck where the captain steered the bothered vessel. There he stood, strapped to the wheel, doing his job without flinching. The pilot caught sight of the terror-stricken man and quickly gave a reassuring smile. The passenger immediately went below to comfort all by saying, "I have seen the face of the pilot, and he smiled. All is well." Here is essence of true prayer: looking into our Captain's face, realizing all is well. Robert Browning mused:

> God's in His heaven,
> All's right with the world.

Prayer, then, must be a reaching out to God, rather than a constant groping after our own trivial desires. Real prayer craves God; selfish prayer so often craves things. We recall that communication in friendship is not always begging for things. Real communication occurs when we stand by a friend, merely enjoying his company. The author of *The Kneeling Christian* said, "All that true prayer seeks is God Himself, for with Him we get all we need."

Having conquered *The Mountain of Self-Will* and submitted ourselves to God's will, we sense a special clarity of God's master plan. We know now that Christ will not allow us to be tempted above that which we are able (I Corinthians 10:13). Here we realize trials on the Road of Prayer build, teach, and strengthen Christian lives. Within God's will everything holds a special beauty, a calm serenity.

James Mudge penned this verse:

> Unfaltering trust, complete content,
> The days ensphere;
> Each meal becomes a sacrament,
> And heaven is here.

Only the pray-er who has subdued his own self-will senses the impact of John's words: "And this is the confidence that we have in him, that, if we ask any thing according to his will, he heareth us" (I John 5:14). Without stamina to stand firm in God's will we will never conquer other spiraling peaks along the Road of Prayer. We must know God's highest will, His perfect master plan.

Müller and God's will

What does God will? For one thing, He wills that all be saved. The Bible clearly states, "The Lord is not . . . willing that any should perish . . ." (II Peter 3:9). Secondly, God wills that men seek His will. We recall a time God scanned His world, observed the wickedness of men, and purposed to destroy the earth He created. "But Noah" — mark these words — "found grace in the eyes of the Lord" (Genesis 6:8), and the course of history was changed. Noah sought God's perfect will. He sought the Creator in a rebel age. Because he sought God's will, he was given the master plan to save the race of man. How true it is that God longs most for men to long for Him. Audrey Mieir sings:

> All He wants is you;
> Nothing else will do.
> Not just a part,
> But all of your heart,
> All He wants is you.

God's will, in truth, becomes the key to all true prayer. Man must seek, above all else, God's perfect will. He must do all within his power to ascertain God's blueprint for his life.

As extra help along the Road of Prayer, we share Müller's six-point plan to understanding God's will.

1. I seek at the beginning to get my heart into such a state that it has no will of its own in regard to a given matter.

2. Having done this, I do not leave the result to feeling

or simple impression. If I do so, I make myself liable to great delusions.

3. I seek the will of the Spirit through, or in connection with, the Word of God.

4. Next I take into account providential circumstances. These often plainly indicate God's will in connection with His Word and Spirit.

5. I ask God in prayer to reveal His will to me aright.

6. Thus, through prayer to God, the study of the Word, and reflection, I come to a deliberate judgment according to the best of my ability and knowledge.

Few men over the centuries have relied not on themselves but on God, as did George Müller. In God's will he reached highest heights in Christian service, and remains for modern missionaries a model in the art of trusting God. All because he took this simple plan and made it work.

So, here we are, "pressing for the mark" along the Road of Prayer. One more mountain is conquered as we crush our own desires and reside in God's will.

What a prize God's will is for those who submit to it daily. It must be prayer's partner, always kneeling at our side. It's sure to guide us to prayer's answer.

I cannot say,
Beneath the pressure of life's cares to-
day,
I joy in these;
But I can say
That I had rather walk this rugged way,
If Him it please.

I may not try
to keep the hot tears back — but hush
that sigh,

"It might have been";
And try to still
Each rising murmur, and to God's sweet
will
Respond "Amen."

Ophelia G. Browning

9 THE BRIDGE OF BALANCE

"We should plow carefully and pray carefully," Charles Spurgeon noted in challenging his congregation to a life of balance. Jesus remains the perfect example of the balanced life. Physician Luke relates how Christ increased in all essentials of life. His mind developed keenly and His body, too, was not neglected. Socially, Christ became the example of examples. He spent hours with crowds, and yet, there were many times He prayed alone. Indeed, He led the balanced life by combining the mental, physical, and social, with the spiritual.

As Jesus walked the sandy beaches and rugged, stony roads of Galilee, His life became the perfect example of the disciplined, balanced life He wished others to emulate. Later John penned these words: "He that saith he abideth in him [Christ] ought himself also so to walk, even as he [Christ] walked" (I John 2:6). Certainly our keenest desire is to follow Christ's example. The words of the following camp meeting chorus echo this thought:

> To be like Jesus, to be like Jesus,
> All I ask: to be like Him.
> All through life's journey,
> From earth to glory;
> All I ask — to be like Him.

"Ten percent Christians"

Needed today are more conquerors who set out to be balanced pray-ers. Spurgeon preached, "To be anxious in the shop and thoughtless in the closet is little less than blasphemy, for it is an insinuation that anything will do for God, but the world must have our best."

Within the framework of our worship, dangerous habits often exist, many hindering proper balance. Tithing is one example. Although it is God's law, some take advantage of the law. Since tithe of material things is 10 percent, some assume God seeks only 10 percent of man's time. This thought becomes an evil dart the enemy has thrown. Pity the army going to battle with soldiers committing only 10 percent of their energy. How tragic would the church be with only "10 percent Christians."

There is little doubt that Satan spends much time destroying balance in our giving and praying. Of these two aspects of the Christian life, prayer has received the hardest of blows. A prayerful writer reflects, "As poor as our giving is, our contributions of money exceed our offerings of prayer. Perhaps in the average congregation fifty aid in paying, where one saintly ardent soul shuts himself up with God and wrestles for deliverance of the heathen world."

Christians cannot afford to live their lives without proper spiritual development. If lives must be overbalanced, may the fault lie in too much prayer rather than works. Church historians indicate truly successful men of God not only persisted physically, but had ample prayer time. Praying hands, indeed, become God's select tools in building a mighty work for God. Someone wisely said, "We are shut up to this: only praying hands can build for God. They are God's mighty ones on earth, His master-builders." With brilliant insight S. D. Gordon penned:

"The whole circle of endeavor in winning men includes

such an infinite variety. There is speaking the truth to a number of persons, and to one at a time; the doing of needed kindly acts of helpfulness, supplying food, and the like; there is teaching; and the almost omnipotent ministry of money; the constant contact with a pure unselfish life; better writing; printers' ink in endless variety. All these are in God's plan for winning men."

Gordon fervently adds this prescription for victory, "The intensely fascinating fact to mark is this: that real victory in all service is won in secret, beforehand, by prayer, and these other indispensable things are the moving upon the works of the enemy, and claiming the victory already won."

Constant communion with God

The Bridge of Balance symbolizes exactly what it says — a place in Christianity where we value all Christ taught. God plainly teaches that prayer and work become one. Brother Lawrence bridged the gap, "The time of business does not with me differ from the time of prayer, and in the noise and clatter of my kitchen, while several persons are at the same time calling for different things, I possess God in as great tranquillity as if I were upon my knees at the blessed sacrament." Thus the key to becoming a balanced pray-er is fusing work and prayer as one. It is living in *constant communion with God*. Rev. Calixto Sanidad of the Philippine Islands reflects, "I used to farm with my hand on the plow, my eyes on the furrow, but my mind on God." He found a secret to the balanced life, that of keeping thoughts fixed firmly on our Lord. No matter where we go, how hard the task, or great the labor, we must always think of Jesus.

A crucial lesson we must learn in prayer is proper use of time in this age of wasted minutes. We live in a busy time, where a strange paradox occurs. We work hard, accomplishing little. Perhaps we pour too much time into meaningless endeavors. One writer has said, "In this restless and busy age most of us live too much in public. We spend our spiritual strength and forget to renew it. We multiply engagements and curtail our prayers. By an error of judgment, or perhaps by the subtle force of inclination, which we mistake for necessity, we work when we ought to pray, because to an active mind work is far easier than prayer." Shamefully, some Christians fail to see need for proper balance. We are compelled to remember, however, those who pray most, work best. Martin Luther, when asked his plans for tomorrow answered: "Work, work, and more work from early until late. In fact, I have so much to do that I shall spend the first three hours in prayer."

Luther knew that prayer paves the highway of accomplishment. To this end he prayed — often and hard. Through prayer and Bible study Luther learned Satan's goal in fighting warriors of prayer. Satan tries to make them think they pray too much and work too little. Martin Luther, examining his church, noted a frightful emphasis on works, but little value given faith. From this burning conviction sprang the reformation — a movement shifting balance from physical to spiritual; from works to faith. Someone aptly said, "God requires soul worship and men give Him body worship: He asks for the heart and they present Him with their lips: He demands their thoughts and minds, and they give Him banners and vestments and candles."

What God seeks most in the lives of Christians is balance; time for prayer, time for work. Often, however, God receives nothing but moldy crumbs and leftovers of tired lives, tired because energies have been drained. Christianity, however, is not a fifty-fifty, "this is mine, that's the Lord's," proposition. Christianity is a daily commitment . . . *a constant communion with God.*

Doing grows from praying

If more ministers and laymen would attempt to maintain balance between prayer, and work, the results would be staggering. E. M. Bounds vividly declared, "If the twentieth century preachers will get their texts, their thoughts, their words, their sermons in their closets, the next century will find a new heaven and new earth." No statement is more accurate. We live in an age in which some think academic genius essential to evangelism. In secular association some Christians feel status in life is the key to winning souls. They spend endless time raising themselves to lofty heights of influence, hoping to win high-class friends to Christ. When arriving at this desired place they find their goal most difficult. They quickly realize God's Spirit draws men rather than man's accomplishments. How much more could be achieved if men sought God instead of newer, more novel methods. Cure for this troubled world is not in how we sway neighbors by notches carved in shotguns of success. The cure is Christ, and men must be convinced of personal need to have this cure. Real prayer summons God's convicting Spirit, putting in man's heart a want for cure.

We must recognize that, more than any other force true and concentrated prayer challenges men to service. A praying preacher declared, "The truth is that when one understands about prayer, and puts prayer in its right place in his life, he finds a new motive power burning in his bones to be doing; and further he finds that *it is the doing that grows out of praying* that is mightiest in touching human hearts."

Wilbur Chapman stressed connection between prayer and evangelism. He emphasized, "Revivals are born in prayer. When Wesley prayed England was revived; when Knox prayed Scotland was refreshed; when the Sunday school teachers of Tannybrook prayed, eleven thousand young people were added to the church in a year. Whole nights of prayer have always been succeeded by whole days of soul winning." Here then is prescription for revival: Persistent pray-ers become worthy workers, winning multitudes of men to Christ.

A "bottled-up" society

We would neglect proper analysis of the balanced life if we failed to consider the emotions. Emotions are a vital part of prayer.

Satan observes the manner in which humans are affected by emotion. Our world operates on emotion. Billy Graham relates, "The movie stars emit emotion on our giant screens as ladies in the audience sob and restrained gentlemen unashamedly wipe a tear from their eyes. Television stars use all of their histrionic powers to move the viewers, employing highly emotional sights and sounds to evoke feelings of sympathy, contempt and passion in the hearts and minds of the audience."

Why should we assume serving God — especially in the act of prayer — does not involve our emotions? The word *emotion* is derived from the Latin word *movere,* which means "to move." Its deeper meaning reflects a strong, keen feeling for an object, truth, or person.

Dr. Leslie Weatherhead, preaching at City Temple in London, asked, "What is wrong with emotion? If Christianity is falling in love with Christ, has anyone ever fallen in love without emotion? Can we imagine somebody advising a young lover saying: 'I would not marry her if I were you, you evidently feel too deeply about it.' How could anyone come into contact with the living Christ and feel both His forgiving love and His relentless challenge without the very deepest emotion?"

Jesus certainly left an example of our need to use emotions in building balanced lives. He wept with "strong crying and tears" over the city of Jerusalem. Certainly Gethsemane is a living example of emotional outflow. The late Dean Farrar has said, "The disciples saw Him, sometimes on His knees, sometimes outstretched in prostrate supplication upon the damp earth; they heard snatches of the sound of murmured anguish in which He humanly pleaded with the divine will of His Father. They saw Him before whom the demons had fled in terror, lying on His face upon the ground. They heard that voice wailing in murmurs of broken agony which had commanded the wind and the sea, and they obeyed Him."

From college days I recall a professor's words, "The trouble with men over thirty years old is their inability to cry." Because of pent up problems we find ourselves a *bottled-up society.* Wise is he who frees his burden in scalding tears, releasing "bottled-up" anxieties. He learns that the inner chamber is the place to drive away anxious fears.

Upon retiring to our inner chambers a vision of a hell-bound world should constrain our thoughts. Only then do we join the psalmist, "Rivers of waters run down mine eyes, because they keep not thy law" (Psalm 119:136).

Try tears

Several young Salvation Army officers asked General Booth, "How can we win the lost?" Booth's return letter said only — "Try tears."

David of old made a worthy statement concerning emotions: "The sacrifices of God are a broken spirit: a broken and a contrite heart, O God, thou wilt not despise" (Psalm 51:17).

Spurgeon's pleading cry was, "Oh, for five hundred Elijahs, each one upon his Carmel, crying unto God, and we should soon have the clouds bursting into showers. Oh, for more prayer, more constant, incessant mention of the mission cause in prayer, then the blessing will be sure to come."

Today we do not have enough broken hearts in pulpits. Not only church pulpits suffer but personal pulpits too. The back fence of a housewife is a pulpit for the Gospel. Grocery counters, gas pumps, and restaurant tables all become preaching points and pulpits. The person who weeps in prayer before standing in his pulpit is indeed wise. When people weep in prayer before confronting neighbors, chances of conversions increase. All Christians — not preachers alone — must heed God's exhortation, ". . . Weep between the porch and the altar . . ." (Joel 2:17). Bounds emphasizes, "A preacher may preach in an official, entertaining, or learned way without prayer, but between this kind of preaching and sowing God's precious seed with holy hands and prayerful, weeping hearts there is an immeasurable distance." God says, "He that goeth forth and weepeth, bearing precious seed, shall doubtless come again with rejoicing, bringing his sheaves with him" (Psalm 126:6). Here is the key to effective evangelism. It is possession of a broken and weeping heart. Indeed, the greatest blow sent Satanward is made by weeping warriors of prayer.

Consider the weeping heart of Charles Finney. Once he decided to pour out his heart in prayer in the woods north of his village. So great was his pride, he kept hidden for fear someone should see him on the way to the woods and should think he was going to pray. Says Finney, "An overwhelming sense of my wickedness in being ashamed to have a human being see me on my knees before God, took such powerful possession of me, that I cried at the top of my voice, and exclaimed that I would not leave that place if all the men on earth and all the devils in hell surrounded me."

"I prayed," reports Finney, "until my mind became so full that, before I was aware of it, I was on my feet and tripping up the ascent toward the road." On reaching town he found it was noon, although he had gone into the woods at dawn. He had been so lost in prayer, time had become unimportant. Later Finney went to dinner, but found he had no appetite. He went to his office to play hymns on his bass viol but was so moved of God he could not sing without weeping. Finney said of that night, "All my feelings seemed to rise and flow out. The utterance of my heart was, 'I want to pour my whole soul out to God.' The rising of my soul was so great that I rushed into the room back of the front office, to pray. I wept aloud like a child, and made such confession as I could with my choked utterance. It seemed to me that I bathed His feet with my tears."

This weeping man sowed precious seed and two and one-half million souls found Christ. Surveys indicate 75 percent of these remained true till death.

A time to weep — a time to laugh

How can we possibly travel the Road of Prayer and never mark the value of a balanced life? How often have people said, "Prayer is fine, but I will work. Somebody has to get the job done!" Look closely at the average twentieth-century church roster. Count those at the annual church picnic, then count those at the annual day of prayer.

Psalmist David was so burdened he declared, "I am weary with my groaning; all the night make I my bed to swim; I water my couch with my tears" (Psalm 6:6). Prayer's "wanted list" seeks warriors who pray as David — those who pray with scalding tears.

Real "joy unspeakable," is found only when Christians learn the need for work and prayer. We must understand Solomon's reflection — "To every thing there is a season, and a time to every purpose under the heaven. . . . A time to weep, and a time to laugh . . ." (Ecclesiastes 3:1, 4).

Here we sense the value of a hearty laugh and recognize the priceless worth of tears. Here we pray as Dr. Bob Pierce, "Let my heart be broken with the things that break the heart of God."

> Prayer is the burden of a sigh,
> The falling of a tear,
> The upward glancing of an eye
> When none but God is near.
>
> James Montgomery

10 THE MOUNTAIN OF PERSISTENCE

"In spite of monsoon or summer heat, the Ganges never stops; so why should I?" Words of a humble praying Indian lead us to the towering *Mountain of Persistence.*

History indicates much is achieved for God by those who pray persistently. In our secular world those who persevere become leaders. Men who work with total commitment are those earning highest salaries — ones who receive better jobs. In a major magazine recently, an authority wrote on, *The Four Pricetags Of Success.* Prescribing success, the writer states, "First of all, there is painstaking preparation. Secondly, aim high." Next, he adds, "Help others to grow. Last, expect long days and sleepless nights."

John Wesley challenged people to harness the power of persevering prayer. "Bear up the hands that hang down by faith and prayer," says Wesley, "support the tottering knees. Have you any days of fasting and prayer? Storm the throne of grace and persevere therein and mercy will come down."

Age of quitters

Much of society has forgotten to persevere. We live in an age of quitters. Society constantly seeks new methods to solve "drop-out" problems of schools. America's armed forces utilize hundreds of psychiatrists in hopes of curtailing desertions. Executives of corporations flee busy cities to hippy communes where "drop-outs" congregate. Spreading of this "quitter's spirit" is felt in every corner of the globe. Few have a striving spirit like the artist Raphael. Once he was questioned, "What is your greatest painting?" He smiled, saying, "My next one." One finds Raphael always striving to do better. This is what we need in prayer, an attitude of persistence.

Satan fears this persevering power in prayer. He hates to see persistent pray-ers. As one aptly said, "The intense fact is this: Satan has the power to hold the answer back — to delay the result for a time. He has not the power to hold it back finally, if someone understands and prays with quiet, steady persistence." Indeed, Satan has power to stifle ordinary prayer, but loses this power when people persevere.

Testimony of one dear lady adds insight to our study. "For thirty-two years I have prayed that God would save my husband." Then a diamond-like tear glittered as she added, "And this week he bowed, accepting Christ as Savior." Think of it . . . thirty-two years persisting in prayer. Thirty-two years with 365 nights of intercession.

Ask this dear one if she would live those years again. Truly she would. Every time she prayed aeons of eternal flames spread before her eyes. This is why she persisted. She saw the intense horror of a single soul, lost for eternity.

George Müller wrote, "The great point is never to give up until the answer comes. I have been praying for sixty-three years and eight months for one man's conversion. He is not saved yet but he will be. How can it be otherwise . . . I am praying." The day came when Müller's friend received Christ. It did not come until Müller's casket was lowered in the ground. There, near an open grave, this friend gave his heart to God. Prayers of perseverence had won another battle. Müller's success may be summarized in four powerful words: "He did not quit."

First cousins: waiting and persistence

Charles Finney takes us back nineteen hundred years to learn about persistent prayer. "Observe," preached Finney, "those who gathered in the upper room and the work they had before them. They had a promise of power to perform it. They were admonished to wait until the promise was fulfilled. How did they wait? Not in listlessness and inactivity; . . . not by going about their business, and offering an occasional prayer that the promise might be fulfilled; but they continued in prayer, and persisted in their suit till the answer came." These pioneer Christians remembered well Isaiah's words, ". . . They that wait upon the Lord shall renew their strength . . ." (Isaiah 40:31). They learned *waiting* and *persistence* are first cousins in prayer.

Painstaking, persistent prayer has always been a special mark on every man of God. We are told Mr. Payson prayed grooves into the floor where he knelt long and often. They say, "Payson's continuing instant in prayer, be his circumstances what they might, is the most noticeable fact in his history, and points out the duty of all who would rival his eminency." Adoniram Judson spent his life in persistent prayer. He said, "I never prayed sincerely and earnestly for anything but it came at some time; no matter at how distant a day, somehow, in some shape, probably the last I would have devised, it came."

We can change the world

History is replete with testimonies showing the value of persistent prayer. Persevering prayer has changed the course of nations. Armies have stood frozen in their tracks because of prayer. Raging elements have subsided when persistent prayers were prayed. Mountains are conquered, cliffs scaled, rivers crossed and deserts cultivated when people persevere in prayer. No one — no matter what his status or academic brilliance — could make this preacher think obstacles of life crumble without prayer. We must press on, conquering *Persistence Mountain.* We cannot cancel our quest.

A story is told of an atheist who made his home in London. His wife possessed a Bible she consistently read. One day in raging anger he hurled this Book of books into a flaming fire and stormed out the door. Later he returned to watch this Bible burn. Gazing into the fire he noted one small portion unburned. Fastening trembling fingers to the page he read, "Heaven and earth shall pass away, but my word shall not pass away." Soon the infidel fell before the fire seeking God's forgiveness. The story seems to end with happiest of endings, yet, we note an interesting sequel. A sister of this wicked man had prayed for years for his conversion. In fact, the very night of his conversion she had engaged in persistent prayer. Here it is again, the power of a persevering prayer.

There is a special place of prayer on *Persistence's* summit. This type of prayer is fasting, a form of prayer used little today. Those totally lost in prayer often lose want for food. Before long they find the epitome of persevering prayer, that place of fasting.

Elder Knapp labored daily until strength left his body. This did not hinder Knapp's prayer time. Once he said, "It is really surprising what a small amount of sleep and food we can get along with, and how much we can endure, when we are filled with the Spirit. Well-oiled machinery can be run day and night for years together with but little friction." Christians well oiled by God's spirit do amazing things to make His kingdom richer. We would do well to learn God's oil flows freely in persistent prayer.

Prayer must be intense

Some think persistent praying means waiting weeks and years for answers. Although at times this is true, it is not the total picture. A person's prayer may be persistent in a quarter hour's time. Lengthy prayers may not qualify as persistent prayers. Most important is how intensely we pray. *Prayer must be intense.* When one prays with intense feelings of humility — fused with utter dependence on God — he learns the definition of persistent prayer. Persistent prayer is frantic prayer. It is prayer with depth and intensity.

A captain of a whaling vessel illustrates this thought. He tells how years ago he was hunting whales in desolate seas off Cape Horn. They were bearing directly south in face of a high velocity wind as the ship made little headway. About eleven o'clock the idea suddenly came into this captain's mind, "Why batter the ship against these waves? There are probably as many whales north as south. Suppose we run with the wind instead of against it?" In response to this sudden idea the captain quickly changed course and began sailing north. An hour later the lookout at the masthead shouted, "Boats ahead!" Soon four lifeboats, in which fourteen sailors lay, tossed about them. Days before, their ship had burned to water's edge and they had been adrift ever since, praying frantically for rescue. The lives of fourteen men were saved. They could not have survived another day.

Duration was not the key to success for these praying men. It was how they prayed. Their prayer was intense. The answer came in ten short days, but to these alone at sea days seemed months.

Here we see the basis of prevailing prayer. It is not how long we pray, or how choice our words, but our level of urgency that counts. We must not only pray, but we must pray fervently, with great urgency and intenseness. We must not only pray, but we must storm heaven's gates with unfaltering persistence. It is this type of prayer that has changed whole societies and destroyed Satanic influence over the years.

"The Miracle of Salerno"

Rees Howells talks about a miracle at Salerno. Salerno was a city of decisive value on the Italian front in World War II. In the battle for Italy, Salerno was the real danger spot. Allied troops landed here in September 1943 to seize this strategic location thus preparing for the invading forces to reach Rome. This is an eye-witness account of Howell's activities that night: "We had the first evening prayer meeting as usual in the conference hall, and gathered again at 9:45 P.M. The meeting had a solemn tone from the outset. The Director, Mr. Howells, voice trembling with the burden of his message and scarcely audible, said, 'The Lord has burdened me between the meetings with the invasion at Salerno. I believe our men are in great danger of losing their hold.' "

Howells then called the congregation of Bible students to prayer. It was not an ordinary prayer time. Prayer was intense and urgent, and in the greatest sense, true prevailing prayer. Howells relates, "The Spirit took hold of us and suddenly broke right through in the prayers, and we found ourselves praising and rejoicing, believing that God had heard and answered. We could not go on praying any longer, so we rose . . . the Spirit witnessing in all our hearts that God had wrought some miraculous intervention in Italy. The victory was so outstanding that I looked at the clock as we rose to sing. It was the stroke of 11:00 P.M."

The story continues with amazing tribute to the value of persistent prayer. Several days later one of the local newspapers displayed the headline in large print, "The Miracle of Salerno." A front line reporter gave his personal account of the battle. He was with the advanced troops in the Salerno invasion on Monday. The enemy was advancing rapidly, and increasing devastation was evident. It was obvious that unless a miracle happened the city would be lost. British troops had insufficient strength to stop the advance until the beachhead was established. Suddenly, with no reason, firing ceased and deathlike stillness settled. The reporter describes the next few moments, "We waited in breathless anticipation, but nothing happened. I looked at my watch — it was *eleven o'clock at night*. Still we waited, but still nothing happened; and nothing happened all night, but those hours made all the difference to the invasion. By morning the beachhead was established."

One easily observes the value of persistent prayer when reading of Salerno. We see God's intention when telling Jeremiah, "Then shall ye call upon me, and ye shall go and pray unto me, and I will hearken unto you. And ye shall seek me, and find me, when ye shall search for me with all your heart" (Jeremiah 29:12).

My mother prayed

Someone has said, "God's best men and women have been reared by a mother's prayers and views, and a father's solemn consecration. Blessed indeed, is the life of a man or woman, boy or girl, who has been heralded into the world not only by pain but also by prayer — their advent prefaced by the hand of a father or mother laying hold upon God."

Nine lovely children of the Scudder family in India served Christ as missionaries because a mother prayed. Mr. Scudder reflects, "Our children were literally prayed into the Kingdom by their mother." Mrs. Scudder had a custom of spending each child's birthday in prayer.

Impact of a praying mother is certainly seen in John Newton's life. Friends say he learned to pray beside his mother's knee, where prayer's influence became staggering. His mother died when John was only eight years old, but the impact of her testimony never departed. Once when lost at sea he simply prayed, "My mother's God, thou God of mercy, have mercy upon me."

From youth I recall the manner in which I awoke for school. No alarm was set to wake me. Daily at 6:00 A.M. the cry of prayer would rouse me from sleep. It was mother praying again. Looking back at my youthful years, I do not remember all the schools I attended, nor the names of my teachers. The names of most of my early friends have vanished from my memory. Many things are vague in my remembrance save one fact which is vividly clear. Mother prayed! And she prayed persistently. Her prayers were never voiced in swift and careless fashion. Many hours drifted away in tear-filled rivers while mother prayed. The result is a family of ministers. Every child grew to serve God. Each has his special ministry. A clear result of persistent prayer.

Climb this mountain at all cost. Bridge its chasms, crevices and cracks. Conquer every inch of this great pinnacle. Tap the valuable reservoir of persevering prayer. Learn to cry as Jacob in his battle with an angel. "I will not let thee go, except thou bless me." Sing along with Charles Gabriel:

> I want to scale the utmost heights
> And catch a gleam of glory bright;
> But still I'll pray till heaven I've found,
> Lord, lead me on to higher ground.

11 BURDEN'S OUTLOOK

It has been reported that at present rates of Scripture distribution it will take thirteen years to reach all the people of North America with the Gospel. Consider further that it will require sixteen years to reach Latin America, thirty years to reach Australia, seventy-five years to reach Africa, ninety years to reach Europe, ninety years to reach East Asia and three hundred seventy years to reach West Asia. How can we reach people with the Gospel when statistics indicate seven out of eight Christians in the world do not possess a Bible?

Can we read these reports and fail to have a burden for the lost? Can we keep ourselves from falling prostrate — overcome by the agonizing burden — crying out as John Knox did, "O God, give me Scotland or I die"? Can we help but pray as Whitefield, "O Lord, give me souls or take my soul"?

World population increases even as more than one hundred thousand die each day. Man's only way to save this world is by prayer — prayer which carries this agonizing burden to the Lord. One wise writer said, "I question if any believer can have the burden of souls upon him — a passion for souls — and not agonize in prayer." Never has there been a greater need for burdened hearts. If we cease our prayers for miracles to reach this world for Christ it will not happen. Mere machinery cannot do the task. Great computers of this age are of little help. We have printing presses, television, and radio to aid in spreading the Gospel, yet we seem to fail. What, then, is the crying need? We must catch a fresh and desperate burden for lost men — a burden expressed only in prayer.

When prayer becomes desperate

We must advance to desperation in prayer to meet the desperate challenge of this age. Huegel writes, "There are times when the Christian's praying is something so desperate, so awful, so tremendous that one trembles before the very record of it." How true this is! Often we walk into prayer rooms where people tremble in God's presence. They tremble because a burden aches deep inside their breasts. They seem to bow at the foot of Calvary watching their Savior's blood drip upon Golgotha's ground. We gain a special sense of where the writer was who wrote, "Were you there when they crucified my Lord? Were you there when they crucified my Lord? Sometimes it causes me to tremble, tremble, tremble. Were you there when they crucified my Lord?"

We must climb to *Burden's Outlook* if we are to make progress on the Road of Prayer. This lofty height must be explored thoroughly and better understood. We can not cast it aside or go around.

Learn from Sir Thomas Broune, a great English physician, who developed a curious prayer burden. Once he vowed, "To pray in all places where quietness inviteth; in any house, highway or street; and to know no street in this city that may not witness that I have not forgotten God and my Savior in it; and that no town or parish where I have been may not say the like. To take occasion of praying upon the sight of any church which I see as I ride about."

Broune further pledges, "To pray daily, and particularly, for my sick patients, and for all sick people, under whose care so ever. And at the entrance into the house of the sick to say, 'May peace and the mercy of God be upon this house.' After a sermon to make a prayer and desire a blessing and to pray for the minister."

Keep the fire

A burden for souls must not be kept for bended knee alone. We must not save it just for quiet times amid prayer's inner chamber. The intercessor's burning heart must keep its flame, notwithstanding those around or the time of day. A renowned evangelist provides good example. He recently returned from several crusades overseas. While in Brazil he and a missionary attended a soccer game. They viewed the contest in one of the world's largest stadiums. Crowds surpassing two hundred thousand often gather there for contests. These men were caught amidst the thrill of this vast multitude. "This is time for pleasure" — some would say — "forget your calling momentarily. Blot from your mind the burden of your heart." When you have a flaming burden, however, forgetting souls is not easy. Soon this evangelist's eager eyes wandered through the crowd. He noticed, too, the missionary had lost interest in the game. Looking at him he asked, "Are you thinking what I'm thinking?" and heard a quick reply, "I'm sure I am." Their thoughts were centered on the mammoth soccer stadium. Could it be filled with hungry hearts in search of Christ?

Recent reports indicate this colossal stadium is available for future crusades. Preliminary rallies are drawing over fifty thousand. Soon, crowds four times as large will attend. All because a moment's joy was forgotten, and the flame of burden kindled.

John Wilkerson composed a simple chorus with this line, "Lord, give me a vision — a sanctified vision — keep the fire on the altar of my heart." Three words of this chorus ought to be life's motto. *Keep the fire!* What a glorious theme to take along prayer's journey. "Let me burn out for God," said Henry Martin. "After all, whatever God may appoint, prayer is the great thing. Oh, that I may be a man of prayer."

Hyde and his burden

Some think burdens are to be reserved for special times. For Brother Lawrence, however, the burden of his praying heart never died — the flame never quenched. He wrote, "I made this my business as much all the day long as at the appointed time of prayer; for at all times, every hour, every minute, even in the height of my business, I drove away from my mind everything that was capable of interrupting my thoughts of God."

Think of Praying Hyde who often went into the hills to visit friends and pray. A friend relates, "It was evident to all he was bowed down with sore travail of soul. He missed many meals and when I went to his room I would find him lying as in great agony, or walking up and down as if an inward fire were burning in his bones." It was from intense burden that Hyde asked God to give him a soul a day that year. Praying Hyde departed from his friends no ordinary man. He became a burden-bearer for mankind. At year's end four hundred souls had been won to Christ. As the new year came John Hyde approached God's throne with greater burden. Now Hyde begged for two souls daily. Twelve months later more had been won than Hyde anticipated. In fact, some eight hundred souls were claimed that year. This, however, did not satisfy Praying Hyde. Soon we hear him pleading, "Give me four souls every day."

Hyde's intent was not to win these with tent crusades or massive rallies. He went for every soul, one at a time. It is said Hyde approached sinners on the street of any village at any time. Conversation ensued and before long both would kneel in prayer. Hyde would lead this new convert to water and perform baptismal rites. This event repeated itself four times daily because Hyde's burden reached out to lost men. Multitudes of souls found Christ when this humble man assumed a burden for the lost.

A trip to Gethsemane

St. Francis of Assisi had a personal retreat, Mount Averno, where he spent hours in anguish of a burdened heart. Those close to Francis say he prayed for hours, never voicing any word but "God." We often look at mortals like this and quickly label them saints. Artists often place halos above their heads in paintings. Consider the One who led the way along the path of prayer as it climaxed in Gethsemane. Luke paints a picture of Gethsemane as it ought to be — not one of Christ calmly kneeling, halo fixed above his head. Luke reflects in retrospect, "And being in an agony he prayed more earnestly: and his sweat was as it were great drops of blood falling down to the ground" (Luke 22:44). A Bible commentator remarks, "Doubtless, the battle of the cross was first fought and won in Gethsemane. It is considered that the soul anguish which he suffered on that occasion was equal to that which he suffered on the cross of calvary." In reality, Christ died in Gethsemane before He ever died on the cross. He, no doubt, was nailed to Gethsemane's ground by burden before nails of Roman soldiers hanged Him to the cross. Have you been to Gethsemane? Consider the words of William Gaither:

Have you had a Gethsemane?
 Have you prayed in despair?
In the dark of the dreary hour,
 Did the Lord meet you there?

Burden's brother

God's word states, "Where there is no vision people perish" (Proverbs 29:18). Vision is brother to the force we call burden. We could almost paraphrase the words of Proverbs: "Where there is no burden people perish." What is vision? Jonathan Swift relates, "Vision is the art of seeing things invisible." *Vision is seeing a need* in our mind before it arises in the physical. *Burden is feeling a need* in our heart before it happens. Vision, or burden, prompts us to pray for those suffering across rolling oceans of despair. We may not suffer trials they experience, yet, we sense how they feel. We may not stand beside them physically, yet vision takes us there. We pray as they pray. We feel as they feel. Vision is ability to see remote villages waiting for the Gospel. Human limitation builds a wall of separation but prayerful vision removes all barriers. We pray for converts overseas and with vision see results. Indeed, "Vision is the art of seeing things invisible." As Charles Allen stresses, "The only limit to your prayer, says Christ, is the limit of your own belief. What is belief? It is *mental visualization.* It is seeing in your mind what you want accomplished in your life."

Out of this vision for a dying world grows the greatest vision, the vision of visions. It is a yearning for prayer warriors. This was Christ's vision. He states, ". . . The harvest is truly plenteous, but the labourers are few; Pray ye therefore the Lord of the harvest, that he will send forth labourers into his harvest" (Matthew 9:37, 38). Jesus wants all to hear His glorious Gospel but realizes workers are few. Christ does not say here, "Build new Sunday schools, train new workers." He does not say, "Enlarge Bible schools." No, indeed, Christ first points men to prayer. Not that we should cease other labors, but, with them, pray.

Picture Dr. Bacchus of Hamilton College as he lay near death. His doctor entered the room and quietly gave him a quick examination. With a solemn look he departed. Passing through the door he softly spoke to friends standing by.

"What did the doctor say?" asked Mr. Bacchus.

"He said, Sir, you cannot live more than half an hour."

"Then take me out of bed," cried Bacchus, "and place me on my knees. Let me spend the time in prayer for this sinful world." Moments later Dr. Bacchus passed from bended knees to Paradise.

What a beautiful vision Dr. Bacchus possessed! Few will ever realize how much his final prayer accomplished. No one knows how much is achieved by the powerful combination of a visionary's vision and a pray-er's burden. As one so aptly stated, "Who can tell how many towns and cities have been saved in answer to prevailing prayers of God's people since the time that Abraham interceded in behalf of Sodom."

Go back over history's records and observe the many times destinies of nations were changed because of prayerful vision. "Nobody but God knows," cried a wise preacher, "how often prayers have changed the course of history." God and Satan know well the value of a visionary's prayers. No wonder Satan condemns this saintly act God encourages.

Prayer is limitless

Consider John Wesley's burden. Burning in his heart was

vision for a worldwide visitation. He sought revival to shake the world. Long before revival fires flamed he had a vision of the flames. In his journal he describes the start of this revival, "Monday, January 1, 1739, Mr. Hall, Kinchin, Ingham, Whitefield, Hutchins, and my brother Charles were present in Fetterslane, with about sixty of our brethren. About three in the morning, as we were continuing instant in prayer, the power of God came mightily upon us, insomuch that many cried out for exceeding joy, and many fell to the ground."

Wesley received a powerful outpouring of God's Spirit at this meeting. Soon his preaching changed whole cities. His unction and power were far greater than before. Methodist societies witnessed amazing upsurges in attendance as vision from months of prayer had become reality. Soon the world became Wesley's parish. Cities burned with revival, just as Wesley had anticipated in prayer. Richard Watson Gilder said of Wesley:

> In those clear, piercing, piteous eyes
> behold
> The very soul that over England
> flamed!
> Deep, pure, intense; consuming shame
> and ill;
> Convicting men of sin; making faith live;
> and, this the mightiest miracle of all,
> Creating God again in human hearts.

Intense prayer took Wesley's vision around the world. Indeed, *prayer is limitless.* No limitations hinder those who pray. "Ask of me," cries God, "and I shall give thee the heathen for thine inheritance, and the uttermost parts of the earth for thy possession" (Psalm 2:8). Imagine the all-comprehending possibilities prayer provides under such promises of God! The only real limitation of our prayers is our inability to ask.

God seeks men of burden

How broken God must be when looking daily for students in His school of prayer and seeing countless absentees. How it must have pierced His heart to say, "And I sought for a man among them, that should make up the hedge, and stand in the gap before me . . . but I found none" (Ezekiel 22:30). Can this possibly be? The God of the universe unable to find a candidate to hedge the gap? We wonder if the time will come when God will cry again, "I sought for a man but found none!" Praise God He sent Christ to hedge the greatest gap, the gulf of sin. Thank God, too, for those burdened prayer warriors whose petitions bridge the gap between God and man. We rejoice for men like Elder Knapp who testified, "I often repaired to the barn in the silent hours of the night, and poured out my soul in prayer to God." Every time an Elder Knapp performs an act like this, he fills the gap, making up prayer's hedge.

I recall one dear lady who stood in a prayer room on a quiet Sunday afternoon. There was no scheduled time of prayer, as she stood alone before God's throne. Our whole congregation should have been there to observe. Opening the prayer room door I could see this dear saint, her back to me, weeping before a large missionary list. Here was a praying saint, well past eighty years, standing in the gap.

Days later another incident reminded me of those who fill such a need. I returned for something I had left in our youth chapel days before. Entering the darkened room, I saw the shadow of a lonely figure on the wall. There a burdened girl knelt, crying to God. It was afternoon when most youth involve themselves in school activities. There she was . . . making up prayer's hedge, pleading that God would send revival.

How earnestly God seeks young lives to stand in the gap — to travel the Road of Prayer. Frankly, the trail is rough, the task rugged. It offers challenge not found elsewhere.

12 TRAIL'S END: THE MOUNTAIN OF GOD'S POWER

Dr. Courtland, twentieth century scientific genius, says, "Prayer is the mightiest force in the universe." Here is a scientist's explanation of the power awaiting praying Christians. Charles Spurgeon adds, "The power of prayer can never be overrated. They who cannot serve God by preaching need not regret. If a man can but pray, he can do anything. He who knows how to overcome with God in prayer has Heaven and earth at his disposal."

The Road of Prayer has been a challenging journey. Many obstacles have been overcome on this rugged road. In prayer we have removed *Sin's Mountain,* leveled *The Peak of Unbelief* and cast aside an *Avalanche of Excuses.* Together we scaled *The Peak of Habit,* crossed *The Plateau of Intercession,* and spent some time in *Holiness Cove.* There have been other barriers on the Road of Prayer. We will long remember *The Bridge of Balance, The Mountains of Self-Will* and *Persistence,* along with the rugged trail to *Burden's Outlook.* Now before us, at the edge of prayer's horizon, towers a mountain above the others. Here rises life's mountain of mountains for pray-ers. It is *The Mountain of God's Power* with a towering peak that reaches out to God. Here we learn as Bounds suggests, "prayer can do anything God can do."

While preaching on the mighty power of prayer, Spurgeon cried, "The very act of prayer is a blessing. To pray is, as it were, to bathe oneself in a cool stream, and so to escape from the heat of earth's summer sun. To pray is to mount on eagle's wings above the clouds and soar to heaven where God dwells. To pray is to enter the treasure house of God and to enrich oneself out of an inexhaustible storehouse. To pray is to grasp heaven in one's arms; to embrace the deity within one's soul and to feel one's body made a temple of the Holy Ghost."

A sovereign remedy

Prayer is the only cure for spiritual sickness. "Enough people praying," someone penned, "will release into the human blood stream the mightiest medicine in the universe, for we shall be the channels through whom God can exert His infinite power."

Imagine a world with sickness abolished. Think how much greener rolling hills would be — how lovelier the rose would seem — if sin were driven from the earth. Dr. Payne declared, "Prayer hath brought health to the sick, hearing to the deaf, speech to the dumb, and eyes to the blind; life to the dead, salvation to the lost. And hath even driven Satan from the hearts of many, and brought the God of Heaven to dwell in his room."

The power of prayer is not merely good medicine but the only medicine for a troubled age. Prayer is the only cure. Robert Hall declared, "The prayer of faith is the only power in the universe to which the great Jehovah yields. Prayer is *the sovereign remedy*." Faith-filled prayer, indeed, is mankind's key to unlock God's eternal power.

Nothing should restrain us from drawing on this great

source of power. We must ask, as Hudson Taylor did, "Should we not do well to suspend our present operations and give ourselves to humiliation and prayers for nothing less than to be filled with the Spirit, and made channels through which He shall work with resistless power? Souls are perishing now for lack of this power. . . . God is blessing now some who are seeking this blessing from Him in faith." How accurate are Taylor's timely words! Billions of lost souls seek a redeemer, while Christians seek new means to reach these dying men.

Shall we build better machines? Can computerized programming provide necessary power? Frankly, what we need is a God-given power to reach this rebel world. What is this power? James Cowden Wallace answers:

> That power is prayer, which soars on high
> Through Jesus to the throne,
> And moves the hand which moves the world
> To bring salvation down.

Quest for power

Man seeks power in many ways. His quest reaches out into God's universe as he travels to the moon and dreams of planetary exploration. Real power, however, is found only in prayer. Isaac Newton, the brilliant scientist, relates, "I can take my telescope and look millions of miles into space but I can lay my telescope aside, get down on my knees in earnest prayer and I see more of heaven and get closer to God than I can when assisted by all the telescopes and material agencies on earth."

The power of prayer reaches every human need. Prayer provides the power for saving souls, for the cure of diseases, for victory in battles, for sleepless nights and trials. Prayer grants power for conflicts of old age, for calmness in the tempest, for comfort during sorrow, and guidance in life's storms. Our list grows as we consider the possibilities of prayer. Man in quest of real power finds it in faith-filled prayer. Jesus says, ". . . ask any thing in my name, I will do it" (John 14:14). One word sums up what prayer can do. Anything!

Church achievements are directly related to its prayer life. Churches ignoring prayer refuse the only real world-changing power. Rev. Mark Guy Pearce declares, "The prayer meeting is the thermometer of the church. It tests what degree of warmth there is. The prayer meeting is the barometer of the church and points to showers of blessing or seasons of drought. The church's warming apparatus is the prayer meeting room." Unfortunately, many churches no longer place enough value on prayer. Congregations often fail to recognize prayer as man's best weapon. Bounds, challenging preachers, cried, "The preaching man is to be the praying man. Prayer is the preacher's mightiest weapon." Prayer is everyone's best weapon, not the preacher's alone. We are reminded of America's powerful howitzer cannons of World War II. Without ammunition, however, these guns could not be considered weapons of war. This is why our enemies sought first to destroy our munition dumps. Likewise, Christians are rendered useless without prayer. Satan's goal becomes clear. He desires to destroy the Christian's ammunition storehouse, the secret place of prayer.

Prayers are deathless

"Prayer is not given us as a burden to be borne," wrote a man of God, ". . . but to be a joy and a power to which there is no limit." The greatness and power of prayer provide Christians the greatest challenge. It is not a gruesome task or irksome duty. The art of the bended knee is a royal honor of the highest order. Prayer is man's highest privilege, his greatest responsibility. It places in our human hand God's sovereign power. Prayer, genuine prayer, is the most powerful act a creature of God can perform.

The power gained on bended knee has accomplished more for God than all combined forces of Christianity in two millenia. Works are fine, but works die with men. A remnant of man's works may live but to a great extent they die. Prayer, however, lives. Prayer is power uncontained by death or grave. A praying man relates, "God changes the world by prayer, *prayers are deathless,* the lips that uttered them may be closed in death, the heart that felt them may have ceased to beat, but prayers . . . outlive the lives of those who uttered them; outlive a generation, outlive an age, outlive a world." The power of prayer is not reserved for any certain class of people. Historians tell us Whitefield took a little crippled man with him to crusades. His job was not crusade director nor chief musician. He prayed! That was the extent of his duty. As Whitefield preached, this handicapped Christian prayed. Now we see more clearly why Whitefield's sermons rocked the hearts of men.

The vividness with which he preached seemed supernatural. Once, while preaching to sailors, he described a vessel lost at sea. He portrayed her as on her side, ready to sink, and then cried aloud, "What next?" So anointed was Whitefield's preaching that sailors sprang to their feet, crying, "The life boat! Grab the life boat!" On another occasion he pictured a blind man walking near the edge of a precipice. Without knowing where he was going he came to the edge. Whitefield's portrayal was so vivid at this point that the famous Lord Chesterfield sprang to his feet crying, "My God! He's gone!" Famous actors Garrick, Foote, and Shuter loved to hear Whitefield preach. Garrick was so impressed he declared Whitefield could make people weep by the mere enunciation of the word, "Mesopotamia." So run the accounts of Whitefield's anointed preaching. Yet, remember a little crippled man's prayers. Early morning and late night we see those twisted legs bending in supplicating prayer.

Potency of prayer

Writers attempt to adequately describe the essence of prayer. Authors amass words, expressions, and clichés to explain it. Volumes have been penned to stress it. Yet, a simple word describes it — *power!* "Prayer brings power," writes Gordon. "Prayer is power, the time of prayer is the time of power. The place of prayer is the place of power. Prayer is tightening the connections with the divine dynamo so power may flow freely without loss or interruption." This defines true prayer. It is power to defeat Satan's hellish demons any place, any time, no matter what odds. "More things are wrought by prayer than this world dreams of," cries Tennyson. In fact, more dread blows are driven Satanward by prayer than hell would care to mention.

Before his death, Dale Carnegie was kind enough to share this secret of his life. "Every day I pray. I yield myself to God, and tensions and anxieties go out of me and peace and power come in." True prayer — coming from those in the right standing with Christ — brings untold blessings and power. By means mortals cannot comprehend, prayer releases inward tension and anxieties. A noted psychiatrist reports, "After a long life observing human behavior, I have no doubt, whatever, that entirely apart from its religious significance, prayer is one of the most effective methods of tapping the wisdom and power that exists in the great reservoir of the unconscious." People reflect inward peace following prayer. Recently scores of Christian teenagers gathered for a weekend devoted only to prayer. Being present, I decided to watch closely the results. Most noticeable was a special happiness each teen possessed following the prayer camp. Anxious, troubled teens departed free from cares — a fact demonstrating the power of prayer over life's attitudes. Prayer, indeed, touches every aspect of human experience. Prayer is power, for it links man to God's sovereign power source, His Holy Spirit. ". . . Ye shall receive power, after that the Holy Ghost is come upon you . . ." (Acts 1:8). Luke said it, Pentecost proves it, and God still chooses to extend this power to praying men. Chrysostom said it dramatically:

"The potency of prayer hath subdued the strength of fire; it hath bridled the rage of lions, hushed anarchy to rest, extinguished wars, appeased the elements, expelled demons, burst the chains of death, expanded the gates of heaven, assuaged diseases, repelled frauds, rescued cities from destruction, stayed the sun in its course and arrested the progress of the thunderbolt. Prayer is an all-efficient panoply, a treasure undiminished, a mine which is never exhausted, a sky unobscured by clouds, a heaven unruffled by the storm. It is the root, the fountain, the mother of a thousand blessings."

Heroes of the closet

We cannot leave this discussion of the power of prayer without recalling heroes of the faith from former years. Perhaps we should label them *heroes of the closet,* for here they gained needed faith for service. Truly, heroes of the closet are heroes of the faith. Look again at Praying Hyde. Hyde's prayer power stimulated thousands for Christ. Dr. J. Wilbur Chapman recalls the time he spent praying with Hyde:

"He came to my room, turned the key in the door, dropped on his knees, and waited five minutes without a single syllable coming from his lips. I knew I was with God. Then with upturned face, down which the tears were streaming he said, 'O God.' "

Recalling this joyous time Chapman adds, "Then for five

minutes at least, Hyde was still again, and then when he knew he was talking with God his arms went around my shoulder and there came up from the depth of his heart such petitions for men as I had never heard before. I rose from my knees to know what real prayer was." Such results are gained only when people touch God through unwavering prayer.

Elder Jacob Knapp was another hero of the closet. Knapp was so endued with prayer's power his very name became synonymous with spiritual power. Reports indicate over one hundred thousand found Christ under his ministry.

Edward Payson provides another excellent example of the power of prayer. He was the most illustrious of Congregational preachers of New England. "His pulpit utterances," wrote McClintock and Strong, "were of the most startling and uncompromising character. It may be truly said of Edward Payson he labored not to please men, but God; and his pulpit thundered like another Sinai. . . ." Payson's fire was kindled by traveling the Road of Prayer.

Peter Cartwright, too, was a hero of the closet. When he preached, God's power fell in torrents like driving rain. Following a campaign, he relates, "The encampment was lighted up, the trumpet blown, I rose in the stand, and required every soul to leave the tents and come into the congregation. There was a general rush to the stand. I requested the brethren, if ever they prayed in all their lives, to pray now."

In certain confidence Cartwright continues, "My voice was strong and clear, and my preaching was more of exhortation and encouragement than anything else. My text was, 'The gates of hell shall not prevail.' In about thirty minutes the power of God fell on the congregation in such a manner as is seldom seen: The people fell in every direction, right and left, and front and rear. It was supposed that not less than three hundred fell like dead men in mighty battle."

Charles Finney, too, must have felt similar impact as a result of time spent in prayer. In Finney's meetings God's power was so intense that entire audiences fell prostrate on hardwood floors. At times God's power would come on Finney as a literal cloud. Historians say a holy calm, noticed even by sinners, settled on cities where this modern John the Baptist preached. Amazing results always accompanied Finney's preaching. Two and one-half million Finney converts stand as living testimony to prayer's power. Oh, that God would teach us to pray. Only then will we sense the positive power of prayer.

Prayer's sustaining power

Prayer's power is not given only for man's urgent and serious needs; this power must be secured for even daily trivialities. Dr. Alexis Carrel, Nobel Prize winner, says, "As a physician, I have seen men, after all other therapy failed, lifted out of disease and melancholy by the serene effort of prayer. It is the power in the world that seems to overcome the so-called 'laws of nature.' The occasions on which prayer has dramatically done this have been termed 'miracles.' But a constant, quieter miracle takes place hourly in hearts of men and women who have discovered that prayer supplies them with a steady flow of sustaining power in their daily lives" (*Voyage to Lourdes,* Harper: 1950).

Christ drew daily from the sustaining power of prayer. At dawn we find Him praying. As evening shadows lengthen Jesus prayed. Often during daylight hours Jesus stopped for heavenly conversation. Before facing Calvary He spent a painful night in prayer. Decades of His human life were given much to prayer. Jesus walked on water, healed the sick, calmed the raging tempest and raised the dead. But most of all He prayed. His private prayers produced His public miracles. Everything in Jesus' life was seasoned with prayer. In the truest sense, Christ is the greatest Example of prayer in the greatest Book on prayer. His very name is the crux of all prayer. Weekly His name stops wheels of commerce, silences our halls of justice, empties our universities, and locks industry's mighty doors. When Sunday arrives millions enter temples of worship, cathedrals of Christianity, mud huts of praise, and brush arbors of prayer, all because of Jesus.

Much has been said of the power of prayer. Volumes have discussed the force of prayer. Sermons have stressed the need for prayer. People have proven the value of prayer. But were it not for Jesus' name, prayerful lips would be sealed in deathlike silence. When one really prays in His name, intelligently and scripturally, it is as though Christ Himself prayed. To the sinner, Jesus' name means forgiveness. To the sick, His name means healing. To the lonely, His name means comfort. To the pray-er, His name means power.

Prayer's trail at last has led to the Source of all power. Upon the lofty peak at the end of the Road of Prayer we see the cross of Jesus. Were it not for this cross, prayer would be altogether useless. Had it not been for John's four powerful words, "and bearing his cross," prayer would hold no impact. Yet, because of Jesus' name there is no force, might, or authority on earth that can prevent prayer's answer. Those who learn to kneel in humility and weakness will soon feel God's supernatural power. The man of prayer is the man of power.

> We kneel — and all about us seems to lower;
> We rise — and all, the distant and the near,
> Stands forth in sunny outline, brave and clear.
> We kneel, how weak! We rise, how full of power!
>
> — Richard Chenevix Trench

BIBLIOGRAPHY

Allen, Charles L., *All Things Are Possible Through Prayer.* Old Tappan, N.J.: Fleming H. Revell, 1958

Bounds, Edward M., *Purpose in Prayer.* Chicago: Moody Press, n.d.

________, *Power through Prayer.* Grand Rapids: Zondervan, n.d.

Gordon, Samuel D., *Quiet Talks on Prayer.* New York: Grosset and Dunlap, 1904

Grubb, Norman P., *Rees Howells: Intercessor.* Fort Washington, Pa.: Christian Literature Crusade, 1962

Huegel, F. J., *Prayer's Deeper Secrets.* Grand Rapids: Zondervan, 1959

Laubach, Frank C., *Prayer, the Mightiest Force in the World.* Old Tappan, N.J.: Fleming H. Revell, 1959

Lawrence, Brother, *Practice of the Presence of God.* Old Tappan, N.J.: Fleming H. Revell, 1956

Lawson, J. Gilchrist, *Deeper Experiences of Famous Christians.* Anderson, Ind.: Warner Press, 1911

McGraw, Francis A., *Praying Hyde.* Chicago: Moody Press, n.d.

Payne, Thomas, *Prayer — the Greatest Force on Earth.* Chicago: Moody Press, n.d.

Sims, A., ed., *George Müller: Man of Faith.* Chicago: Moody Press, n.d.

Spurgeon, Charles H., *Effective Prayer.* London: The Evangelical Press, n.d.

Steere, Douglas V., *Dimensions of Prayer.* New York: Harper & Row, 1963

Unknown, *The Kneeling Christian.* Grand Rapids, Zondervan, 1945

The Hour That Changes the World

A Practical Plan for Personal Prayer

CONTENTS

THE CHALLENGE

Have you ever considered giving God a daily gift of time? Not just a few spare minutes here or there, but a substantial gift of at least sixty minutes every day? It would be time spent alone with God in prayer and the study of His Word.

Before you cry "Impossible!" and toss this book aside, please turn to page 10 and look briefly at the diagram. It shows a basic, workable plan for daily prayer.

This plan is designed to place special emphasis on affecting the world we live in through prayer. When properly focused, prayer does more than just change one's life. Prayer reaches out in love to a dying world and says, "I care!"

"*But why set one hour daily as my goal*?"

The most reasonable answer is that Jesus requested an hour. It was in a lonely, quiet garden under a heavy Judean sky that Jesus pleaded with His disciples, "Could ye not watch with me one hour?" (Matt. 26:40). Our Lord knew that prayer is the only answer to our daily confrontations with the enemy. This is why, when we read the Gospels, we constantly find Jesus praying. He prayed among the hypocrites in the temple, in crowds, on hillsides cluttered with disciples, in a crowded upper room, and alone on mountains outside Jerusalem. Prayer was more than a part of Christ's life, it *was* His life.

Sometimes Jesus spent whole nights praying. In His moment of greatest need, He asked His disciples to watch with Him for just one hour; but it was night and the temptation for sleep was too great. The sheep were sleeping and the Shepherd had to wage His war alone!

"*But how can anyone possibly pray an entire hour?*" is another recurring question. It was a question I, too, had to answer from the moment I determined to personally accept Christ's call to "watch" with Him daily for one hour.

Seeking an answer, I brought the matter before God in prayer. After all, if prayer really works in the first place, then to pray a prayer concerning "how to pray" ought to be the first order of business.

God answered my petition with a simple plan. He showed me how to structure my devotional hour into twelve scripturally-based aspects. Since I started using the plan it has seemed impossible to miss keeping this daily prayer appointment. Suddenly my devotional exercise became the delight of my day. Often the time allotted to each aspect of prayer has expanded quite by accident, transforming an hour into a whole day. It is difficult to explain fully, but the delight steadily increases.

To begin using this simple plan you can divide your hour into twelve five-minute "points of focus." This allows a specific amount of time for each aspect of prayer. At times some areas may require only a few moments, while others—like interceding for lost souls—may require far more than five minutes.

Regardless of how you apply these prayer elements, you will most certainly find them fresh and exciting. And think of the impact this daily gift of sixty minutes will have on a troubled world. One hour each day for an entire year equals 365 hours, or forty-five continuous "eight-hour" days. Imagine asking your employer for six weeks off work next year so you can spend the time with Jesus praying for the world. That's the power of giving God just sixty minutes a day (when projected for a full year).

So, let us go forth in joyful anticipation to discover new secrets of "world-changing" prayer. Soon we shall sing with fresh excitement:

> Oh, the pure delight of a single hour
> That before Thy throne I spend,
> When I kneel in prayer
> and with Thee, Oh, God,
> I commune as friend with Friend.

"Oh! One hour with God infinitely exceeds all the pleasures and delights of this lower world.

—David Brainerd

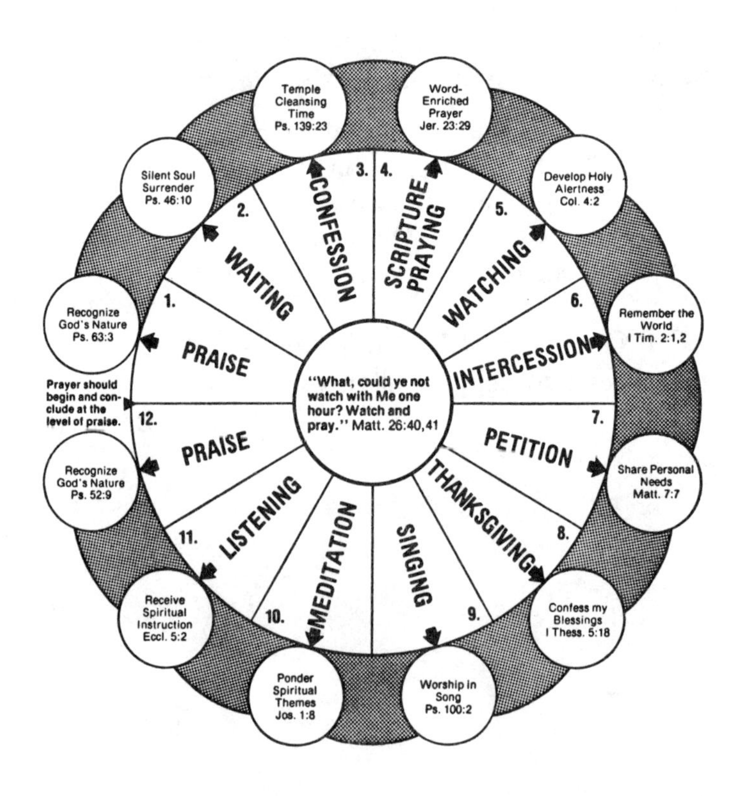
Temple Cleansing Time Ps. 139:23
Word-Enriched Prayer Jer. 23:29
Silent Soul Surrender Ps. 46:10
Develop Holy Alertness Col. 4:2
Recognize God's Nature Ps. 63:3
Remember the World I Tim. 2:1,2
Prayer should begin and conclude at the level of praise.
Recognize God's Nature Ps. 52:9
Share Personal Needs Matt. 7:7
Receive Spiritual Instruction Eccl. 5:2
Confess my Blessings I Thess. 5:18
Ponder Spiritual Themes Jos. 1:8
Worship in Song Ps. 100:2
1.
PRAISE
2.
WAITING
3.
CONFESSION
4.
SCRIPTURE PRAYING
5.
WATCHING
6.
INTERCESSION
7.
PETITION
8.
THANKSGIVING
9.
SINGING
10.
MEDITATION
11.
LISTENING
12.
PRAISE
"What, could ye not watch with Me one hour? Watch and pray." Matt. 26:40,41

INTRODUCTION

PRAYER

THE SLENDER NERVE OF POWER

Prayer is the divine enigma—that marvelous mystery hidden behind the cloud of God's omnipotence. Nothing is beyond the reach of prayer because God Himself is the focus of prayer. E. M. Bounds agreed when he wrote, "Prayer is the contact of a living soul with God. In prayer, God stoops to kiss man, to bless man, and to aid in everything that God can devise or man can need."[1] Charles Spurgeon adds, "Prayer is the slender nerve that moveth the muscles of omnipotence."[2]

Prayer! What exactly is it? Basically, prayer is the simplest act a creature of God can perform. It is divine communion with our heavenly Father. Prayer does not require advanced education. Knowledge is not a prerequisite to engage in it. Only an act of the will is required to pray.

But prayer is more. Prayer is the vision of the believer. It gives eyes to our faith. In prayer we see beyond ourselves and focus spiritual eyes on God's infinite power.

Prayer is also man's ultimate indication of trust in his heavenly Father. Only in prayer do we surrender our problems completely to God and ask for divine intervention.

But, sadly, few make prayer a part of their daily experience. They pray only if extra time is available or if their emotions draw them to prayer. Oh, that Christians would see prayer in its proper perspective!

Prayer is not optional. On the contrary, it is quite obligatory. Where there is an absence of prayer there will be an absence of power. Where there is frequency of prayer there will be continuing display of God's power. God said, "If my people, which are called by my name, shall humble themselves, and pray, and seek my face, and turn from their wicked ways; then will I hear from heaven, and will forgive their sin, and will heal their land" (II Chron. 7:14).

THE SEARCHING INSTINCT

But where do we begin in our quest for spiritual power? We need only follow the instinct of the heart to pray. This searching instinct fills the human spirit. The moment we turn to Christ it comes alive. We suddenly yearn to fellowship with the Father. As Charles Spurgeon said, "To seek aid in time of distress from a supernatural Being is an instinct of human nature. I believe in the truthfulness of this instinct, and that man prays because there is something in prayer. As when the Creator gives His creature the power of thirst, it is because water exists to meet its thirst; and as when He creates hunger there is food to correspond to the appetite; so when He inclines men to pray it is because prayer has a corresponding blessing connected with it."[3]

This prayer instinct is somewhat difficult to understand and explain. Somehow, the simple act of prayer links a sovereign God to a finite man. When man prays, God responds. Difficult situations change. Unexplained miracles occur.

But when we neglect the closet of prayer we remove ourselves from the focus of God's power. Dr. E. Stanley Jones explains, "In prayer you align yourselves to the purpose and power of God and He is able to do things through you that He couldn't do otherwise. For this is an open universe, where some things are left open, contingent upon our doing them. If we do not do them, they will never be done. For God has left certain things open to prayer—things which will never be done except as we pray."[4]

MEN OF PRAYER

Look again at the lives of God's warriors from past generations. What qualified men like Wesley, Luther, Finney, or Brainerd for their high calling in Christ? J. C. Ryle, the nineteenth-century Bishop of Liverpool, provides a worthy answer: "I have read the lives of many eminent Christians who have been on earth since the Bible days. Some of them, I see, were rich, and some poor. Some were learned, some unlearned. Some of them were Episcopalians, and some Christians of other denominations. Some were Calvinists, and some were Arminians. Some have loved to use a liturgy, and some chose to use none. But one thing, I see, they all had in common. They all have been men of prayer."[5]

No matter our position in life or natural abilities, to be mightily used of God we must first understand a fundamental principle of spiritual power. What we do for the Lord is entirely dependent upon what we are in the Lord. Further, what we are in the Lord wholly depends upon what we receive from the Lord. And what we receive from the Lord is directly proportional to the time we spend alone with the Lord in prayer.

To spend little time with Jesus is to accomplish little in Jesus. Simply stated, there is no *true* spiritual growth apart from the devotional habit. Consistency in prayer is the evidence of true commitment. As David Hubbard shares, "Our prayer expresses our commitment to Christ. By talking to God we affirm our basic decision to depend on Him."[6]

If I seldom talk with God, it indicates He plays a secondary role in my life. Soon the world commands more of my attention than does God. Adam Clarke warns, "Apostasy begins in the closet. No man ever backslid from the life and power of Christianity who continued constant and fervent in private prayer. He who prays without ceasing is likely to rejoice evermore."[7]

THE GIFT OF TIME

Once we determine that prayer is important, our

spiritual battles begin. Professor Hallesby explains in his classic book *Prayer*, "The first and decisive battle in conjunction with prayer is the conflict which arises when we are to make arrangements to be alone with God every day."[8]

The moment we determine to pray daily, Satan fills our path with distracting hindrances. Job responsibilities increase. The children demand more time. It seems we are more weary than usual.

As Dr. Hallesby further suggests, "The carnal mind will always instinctively and automatically mobilize every possible reason it can possibly conceive for not praying at a particular time. For example, you are too busy; your mind is too preoccupied; your heart is not inclined toward prayer; later on you will have more time, your mind will be more calm and collected, and you will be able to pray in a more devotional frame of mind. Before we know it, the entire day is gone, and we have not had a single quiet hour alone with Christ."[9]

Carefully mark this in your mind: *It is possible to make time for prayer*! Consider Susanna Wesley. With nineteen active children, including John and Charles, Susanna Wesley still found time to pray daily. This godly saint seldom gave the Lord less than a full hour each day for prayer.

"But I have no place to get away for prayer!" some might object. Susanna Wesley, likewise, had no specific place for prayer. So, at her chosen time for spiritual exercise she would take her apron and pull it over her face. Her children were instructed never to disturb "mother" when she was praying in her apron.

Like Susanna Wesley we must *make* time for prayer every day. Until we do, prayer will never become the force God intends it to be in our daily walk. Only as we apply our knowledge of prayer to the actual practice of prayer will we discover the practical power of prayer.

Fletcher of Madeley, a fellow worker with John Wesley, illustrates the importance of making prayer practical. This dedicated warrior had a most unusual conclusion to many of his lectures. Often, after discussing themes on prayer and spiritual growth, Fletcher would say to his students, "That is the theory; now will those who want the practice come along up to my room!"

Often all of Fletcher's students would quietly follow this godly saint to his room for one or two hours of actual practice in the art of prayer. They knew the secret was in "doing," not merely in "knowing."

Prayer is much more than mere theoretical power—it is practical power. But to tap this practical power we must willingly sacrifice much time. Samuel Chadwick cautions, "In these days there is no time to pray; but without time, and a lot of it, we shall never learn to pray. It ought to be possible to give God one hour out of twenty-four all to Himself."[10]

A PATTERN FOR PRAYING

To be effective our sixty minutes with God should be carefully arranged. Systematic prayer adds health to the devotional habit. Most tasks in life are accomplished systematically. In fact, without a systematic approach to life, many goals would remain unreached.

The same is true with prayer. The devotional exercise needs careful planning and preparation to function properly. Harold Lindsell cautions, "Prayer does not come naturally to men. It must be learned. Learning to pray . . . includes knowledge of the laws governing prayer as well as experience gained in the practice of prayer. Prayer must be nourished and cultivated if it is to grow."[11]

Scripture is filled with numerous concepts related to prayer that should form the basis of the devotional habit. *The Hour That Changes the World* is an attempt to present these major elements so each may be applied systematically, on a daily basis.

Although each element is clearly based on Scripture, the particular order in which they are employed may vary. To spend five minutes on each of the twelve aspects of prayer will take exactly one hour. However, some prayer warriors may desire to spend more time on certain elements than others. On occasion only eight or nine of the twelve elements may be included during your devotional hour.

Be careful not to become a slave to any "prayer system." Indeed, prayer is not a system at all but the development of a relationship between man and God. The highest goal of the devotional habit is to strengthen this relationship.

PRAYER WORKS

When the question surfaces, "Why pray?" a twofold answer must be our response. First, because *Jesus calls us to prayer*. Secondly, because *prayer works*.

How well the author recalls the impact of a personal experience concerning the first reason for engaging in daily prayer. I had always believed God answers prayer, but my prayer life was never consistent. During a devotional transformation, I was gripped with the realization that Jesus asked His disciples only one question specifically related to the subject of prayer. During His intense experience in Gethsemane, Christ approached His sleeping disciples. Speaking first to Peter, Jesus asked, "What, could ye not watch with me one hour?" (Matt. 26:40).

Suddenly I realized Jesus was speaking to *me*. I, too, was a follower of Jesus. I was being challenged to make a daily sacrifice of at least one hour of my time specifically for prayer. It was my choice. No one would force me. I could either sleep or pray. I chose the latter—a decision I shall never regret. Although the battles have sometimes been difficult, the victories have always been sweet.

But there is a second reason why daily prayer is profitable. *Prayer works*! Dr. Walter Judd, missionary to China, frequently enjoyed sharing his prayer experiences from missionary days. Of these experiences the doctor related, "There would come into my spirit something that supported and helped steady me, gave me confidence and assurance during the day. I can't explain it. I can't explain how some of the food I ate tonight for supper becomes brain, some blood, some bone, but I haven't stopped eating just because I can't explain it! In the same way, I can't explain this. It is not in the realm of explanation yet, or of logical proof. It *is* in the realm of demonstration; prayer works."[12]

From the first pages of Genesis to the last words of Revelation we see scriptural evidence that God answers prayer. Bishop J. C. Ryle adds these insights: "Prayer has obtained things that seemed impossible and out of reach. It has won victories over fire, air, earth and water. Prayer opened the Red Sea. Prayer brought water from the rock and bread from Heaven. Prayer made the sun stand still. Prayer brought fire from the sky on Elijah's sacrifice. Prayer overthrew the army of Sennacherib. Prayer has healed the sick. Prayer has raised the dead. Prayer has procured the conversion of countless souls."[13]

Indeed, God has said nothing lies beyond the potential of prayer. Beloved, let us ask with new confidence . . .

Lord, teach me to pray!

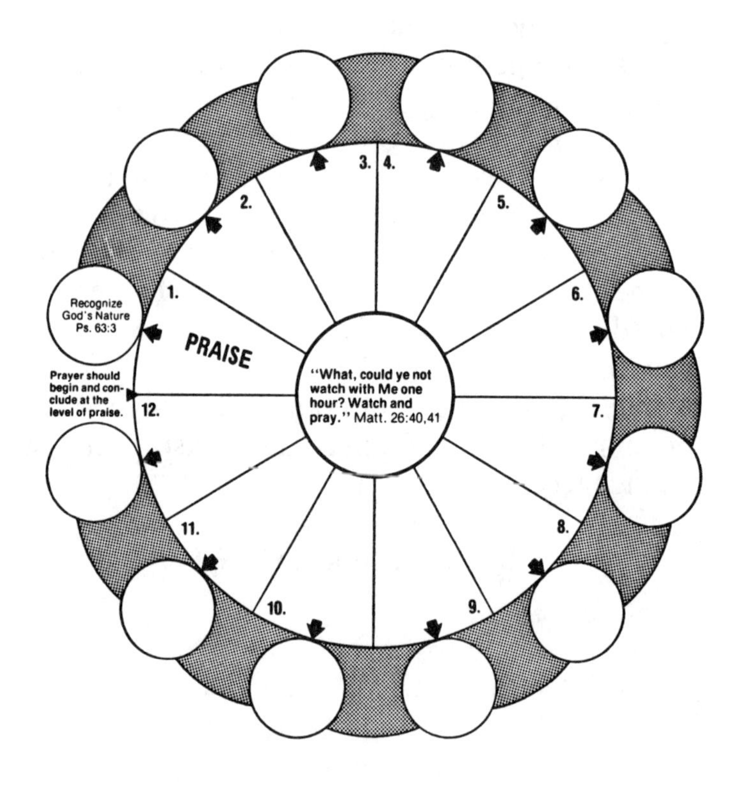
Recognize
God's Nature
Ps. 63:3
PRAISE
"What, could ye not
watch with Me one
hour? Watch and
pray." Matt. 26:40,41
Prayer should
begin and con-
clude at the
level of praise.
1.
2.
3.
4.
5.
6.
7.
8.
9.
10.
11.
12.

PRAISE 1

THE ACT OF DIVINE ADORATION

Jesus left His disciples but a single prayer as an example upon which to base their praying. Although several of Christ's prayers are recorded in Scripture, only once did He say, "After this manner therefore pray ye." The prayer is recorded in its entirety in Matthew 6:9-13 and appears somewhat abbreviated in Luke 11:2-4. It is commonly called The Lord's Prayer, although The Disciples' Prayer would be a more accurate label. The first ten words of this important prayer provide the believer with a biblical foundation for commencing all prayer with a season of praise. The prayer begins, "Our Father which art in heaven, Hallowed be thy name" (Matt. 6:9).

The goal of all praying is summed up in the expression "Hallowed be thy name." *Hallowed* is a New Testament expression used only in reference to the name of God. The Greek word for our word *hallow* is *hagiazo*, meaning "to revere or to sanctify." Since *sanctify* means "to set apart," our prayer time should include several moments, at the very outset, when God's name is set apart strictly as the object of our divine worship. During these moments of praise our sole purpose is to bring glory to God with our words. God declared through the psalmist, "Whoso offereth praise glorifieth me" (Ps. 50:23).

THE CHIEF END

Praise is more than a single aspect of prayer. Praise is a way of life. An old Presbyterian catechism explains, "The chief end of man is to glorify God and to enjoy Him for ever." Praise helps the believer achieve this "chief end." In fact, praise might well *be* the "chief end."

Brother Lawrence, a sixteenth-century monk, accurately summarized this thought when he wrote, "The end we ought to propose to ourselves is to become, in this life, the most perfect worshipers of God we can possibly be, as we hope to be through all eternity."[1]

What is praise? First, praise is the vocal adoration of God. Adoration is the act of rendering divine honor, esteem, and love. The word *adoration* is derived from an ancient expression that meant "to apply the hand to the mouth," or "to kiss the hand." In certain countries a kiss of the hand is still a symbol of deep respect and submission.

The act of vocal adoration is important because it implies we acknowledge God as God. Harold Lindsell explains, "Since adoration brings man into immediate and direct contact with God, in the role of servant to Master, or the created to the Creator, it is foundational to all other kinds of prayer."[2]

WHY PRAISE FIRST?

Aside from the fact that Jesus listed praise first in His prayer, there are numerous reasons for placing it first when we pray. Only praise puts God in His rightful position at the very outset of our praying. In praising God we declare His sovereignty and recognize His nature and power.

Some have taught that confession should be first in prayer because sin makes effective praying impossible. True, sin does rob prayer of power. And confession is important. But were it not for a loving, merciful God, confession of sins would mean very little, regardless of when it was included during prayer. So, we must first draw our attention to God in prayer before we draw our attention to self.

Another major reason for offering praise early in prayer is the fact that, in its very nature, praise is unselfish. Paul Billheimer relates, "Here is one of the greatest values of praise: it decentralizes self. The worship and praise of God demands a shift of center from self to God. One cannot praise God without relinquishing occupation with self. Praise produces forgetfulness of self—and forgetfulness of self is health."[3]

We soon discover spiritual health has its roots in divine adoration. Thus, praise is quite practical. It is practical because it changes our focus. As the believer recognizes God for all He is, he soon realizes it is this all-powerful God to whom he will be presenting all of his later petitions.

THE VOICE OF PRAISE

Offering praise at the outset of prayer is also wise because of the biblical precedent given to praise. Praise sparks victory. Note the scriptural account of God's glory flooding His earthly temple: "It came even to pass, as the trumpeters and singers were as one, to make one sound to be heard in praising and thanking the Lord . . . that then the house was filled with a cloud, even the house of the Lord; So that the priests could not stand to minister by reason of the cloud: for the glory of the Lord had filled the house of God" (II Chron. 5:13, 14).

Preaching on this passage, Dwight L. Moody said, "Solomon prevailed much with God in prayer at the dedication of the temple, but it was the voice of praise which brought down the glory that filled the house."[4]

Not only does praise open our devotional hour to an outpouring of God's glory, but it promptly sends Satan running. He cannot tolerate the presence of God.

Where do we find God's presence? In Psalm 22:3 we are reminded that God inhabits "the praises" of His people. God manifests His living presence in the praise-saturated chamber of prayer. Adoration is the antidote to the poison of satanic oppression. To develop the "praise-life" is to develop a certain immunity to the enemy's attacks. Paul Billheimer further suggests, "Satan is allergic to praise, so where there is massive triumphant praise, Satan is paralyzed, bound, and banished."[5]

OUR PRIZE POSSESSION

"Praise the Lord" is an expression gaining increased popularity in the vocabulary of many believers. But what exactly do we mean when we say, "Praise the Lord"? Basically, praise is the act of expressing one's esteem of a person for his virtues or accomplishments. It is to pronounce that person "worthy of honor."

But rendering praise to God is even more. The full meaning of praise can be captured only in its Old French origin, *preiser*, which means "to prize"! To *praise* God is to *prize* God. The word *prize* means "to value, esteem, and cherish something." During our time of praise we cherish and esteem God with our words of adoration.

Prize also means "to estimate the worth of." In "praise" we mentally gather together all the facts we know about God and we put these facts into words. Praise literally becomes "the fruit of our lips" unto God (Heb. 13:15).

Because praise is to verbalize our esteem for God, it seems unlikely we will exhaust any potential list of possibilities for praise. The following are but a few scriptural suggestions for your moments of ministering unto the Lord through praise.

First, we should *praise God for His name*. The psalmist said, "Not unto us, O Lord, not unto us, but unto thy name give glory" (Ps. 115:1). Although various titles describing God are shared throughout the Old Testament, the actual "name of the Lord" is not specifically revealed until the pages of the New Testament. His "name" is *the Lord Jesus Christ*.

It greatly honors God when we take time during prayer to "prize" the name of Jesus Christ with words of praise. An elderly Bible teacher once declared, "If you want to get in good with God, just brag on His Son."

When praising the name of Jesus in prayer we may use expressions from Scripture, such as those used by Isaiah: "And his name shall be called Wonderful, Counsellor, The mighty God, The everlasting Father, The Prince of Peace" (Isa 9:6).

Secondly, we should *praise God for His righteousness*. All that God is deserves our praise. The psalmist intoned, "And my tongue shall speak of thy righteousness and of thy praise all the day long" (Ps. 35:28).

Righteous means "meeting the standards of what is right and just." God does more than meet certain standards; *God is the standard*. All that a prayer warrior can imagine concerning God's faithfulness, justice, and mercy may become a theme for these moments of praise.

Thirdly, we should *praise God for His infinite creation*. The psalmist said succinctly, "Praise him for his mighty acts" (Ps. 150:2).

Because we are challenged to praise God for His "mighty acts," there is no limit to praise. God created countless species of plant and animal life, each serving as an individual basis for praise. The scope of praise ranges from the microscopic particles of the atom to the spiraling galaxies of the universe. All of creation is a treasure house of praise.

Finally, we should *praise God for His Word*. During moments of deepest depression King David wrote, "In God will I praise his word" (Ps. 56:10).

How do we praise the Word of God? The answer is revealed in Psalm 19. Note this excellent outline for praising God's Word. We may offer praise because . . .

1. "The law of the Lord is perfect, converting the soul."
2. "The testimony of the Lord is sure, making wise the simple."
3. "The statutes of the Lord are right, rejoicing the heart."
4. "The commandment of the Lord is pure, enlightening the eyes."
5. "The fear of the Lord is clean, enduring forever."
6. "The judgments of the Lord are true and righteous altogether."

Truly, the possibilities for praise stretch beyond the limits of our imagination. Because God has no limit, our praise is limitless.

Early in prayer take time to recognize all that God is. Express these thoughts vocally. And don't be in a hurry to go beyond praise until you have taken adequate time to adore God with your words of worship . . .

Lord, teach me to adore you!

PRAISE
THE FIRST STEP IN WORLD-CHANGING PRAYER

1. Sanctify, or set aside, a period of time specifically to praise God at the beginning of your prayer.
2. Select a specific theme for praise, such as God's righteousness, His Word, or His creative acts.
3. Drawing on your selected theme, declare vocally all that God is.
4. Expand your theme as much as possible. Allow God to reveal new themes for worship as your time of praise develops.

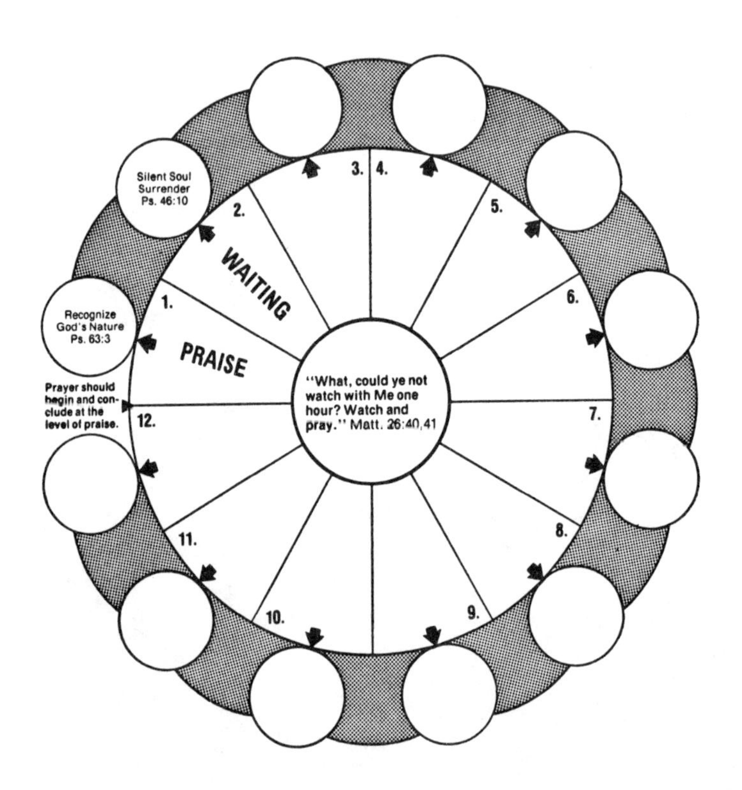
Silent Soul
Surrender
Ps. 46:10
Recognize
God's Nature
Ps. 63:3
Prayer should
begin and con-
clude at the
level of praise.
WAITING
PRAISE
"What, could ye not
watch with Me one
hour? Watch and
pray." Matt. 26:40,41
1.
2.
3.
4.
5.
6.
7.
8.
9.
10.
11.
12.

WAITING 2

THE ACT OF SOUL SURRENDER

Few saints have longed after God with such sincerity as did Madame Guyon. Early in life, seeking spiritual encouragement, she approached a devout Franciscan friar. The young woman explained that her desire for God had grown shamefully weak.

After hearing her story the friar engaged in silent contemplation for a considerable time. Slowly the old Franciscan gazed up at Madame Guyon and declared, "Your efforts have been unsuccessful, because you have *sought without* only what you can *find within*. Accustom yourself to seek God in your heart, and you will not fail to find Him."[1]

Madame Guyon had received her introduction to a most vital element of prayer, that of silently waiting in the presence of God. All who would be used of God must learn this secret of silence. In her classic study, *Creative Prayer*, Bridgid E. Herman explained, "If we read the biographies of the great and wise, we shall find they were people of long silences and deep ponderings. Whatever of vision, of power, of genius there was in their work was wrought in silence. And when we turn to the inner circle of the spiritual masters—the men and women, not necessarily gifted or distinguished, to whom God was a living, bright reality which supernaturalized their everyday life and transmuted their homeliest actions into sublime worship—we find that their roots struck deep into the soil of spiritual silence."[2]

A DOSE OF SILENCE

To be complete, prayer needs an early, significant dose of spiritual silence. Such silence is necessary if the believer hopes to minister effectively for Jesus. Just as virtue went out of our Lord when He ministered, a certain amount of spiritual virtue seems to depart the believer during his daily ministry (see Luke 8:46). A student of prayer said, "We cannot be made a blessing to others without perceiving that virtue has gone out of us, and unless this is constantly renewed with loving communion with Heaven, our service becomes little more than dead works, and our message loses the ring which bespeaks its divine origin."[3]

J. Gregory Mantle says, "Work is not food for the spirit any more than for the body. Amidst a multitude of works the worker's soul may wither, and his activities will prove this in due time."[4]

What does it mean to "wait" upon God? And how does waiting differ from praise? Scripture includes numerous insights into the ministry of waiting: "I will wait on thy name" (Ps. 52:9). "My soul waiteth upon God" (Ps. 62:1). "My soul waiteth for the Lord more than they that watch for the morning" (Ps. 130:6). "They that wait upon the Lord shall renew their strength" (Isa. 40:31).

Waiting on the Lord is basically the silent surrendering of the soul to God. John Bisagno observed, "Waiting upon God requires our entire being. It is not drifting into daydreaming, but is rather an exercise that demands our keenest attention, our most alert frame of mind and all of our soul's attention to the Heavenly Voice."[5]

Waiting is not praise, though it is closely related to praise and flows directly from it. Praise is verbalizing our esteem of God. Waiting is a time of silent love. Praise cries boldly, "God, I see these excellent qualities in your nature." Waiting says softly, "God, I love you."

A SPIRITUAL LOVE AFFAIR

The act of waiting is well illustrated by the experience of an elderly saint. One day an acquaintance asked her how she usually spent her days.

The lady quickly replied, "Well, I always begin my day with a good season of prayer. In fact, I pray until I can't pray any more. Then I take my Bible and read until I can't read any more. After that, I take my hymnbook from the shelf and I sing until I can't sing any more. Then I just sit quietly and let God love me."

To a great degree our time of waiting might be termed "wordless worship." It is a spiritual love affair with intimate supernatural.union. Professor Hallesby spoke of this intimacy as the "soul's fellowship with God in prayer." The saintly Bible teacher added, "There is something in our lives, also in our fellowship, which can never be formulated in words, which can be the common experience, nevertheless, of two who share with each other everything that can be expressed in words."[6]

The professor illustrated this intimacy with an experience from his early ministry. One day his son bumped his head in the entryway of the professor's study. The lad knew his father was not to be disturbed during these important hours of study. His conscience troubling him, the youngster quietly approached his father. Gazing tenderly with loving eyes, the lad pleaded, "Papa, dear, I will sit still all the time if you will only let me be here with you."[7]

Being alone with God is the central issue of waiting. Genuine prayer is not merely asking for things; it is a relationship. Asking is only a part of prayer, and asking must come later. Strong relationships are best cultivated in silence. My wife and I were much in love long before words could adequately express that love. Being with each other was enough.

It is also important to understand that our time of waiting is not necessarily a time of listening. Listening is crucial to prayer, but as with the aspect of asking, listening will come later. For now we simply surrender our hearts to the Lord in quiet love. In these silent moments we respond as Job: "What shall I answer thee? I will lay mine hand upon my mouth" (Job 40:4).

THE FOCUS OF WAITING

John of Damascus, the ancient Greek theologian, defined waiting as "the elevation of the mind to God."[8]

Here we find the true focus of waiting. All attention must center in our heavenly Father. We come to know the Lord only at this most intimate level. The knowledge of God is best revealed in silent waiting. Scripture declares, "Be still, and know that I am God" (Ps. 46:10).

As one author expressed, "The highest worship of almighty God consists in being wholly taken up with Him. It is the most intimate form of communion in which the creature adores his Creator, the finite before the Infinite, the powerless before the Powerful, the nothing before the All."[9]

Of course, for very practical reasons God must be the central focus of our praying. There is no power for prayer apart from God. Scripture does not say, "Have faith in prayer," but, "Have faith in God" (Mark 11:22).

Far more important than the answer to our prayer is the focus of our prayer. Donald E. Demaray accurately wrote, "The point of prayer is to get God. Answers are most meaningful when they are thought of least. Prayer is most meaningful when God is thought of most."[10]

Waiting on God is especially essential to prayer

because it strengthens our knowledge and concept of God. To focus attention entirely upon God places God on the throne of our praying. Ralph Herring shares the following insight in his *The Cycle of Prayer*: "Only a sovereign God can inspire prayer, and only a sovereign God can answer it. A man's concept of God, therefore, determines the depth of his prayer life. Real prayer begins and ends with God enthroned."[11]

Remember, we were not only challenged by the psalmist to "Be still," but to "know God" as well. Knowing someone intimately is impossible with limited attention. Intimacy takes time and concentration. This is why these early moments of prayer need a careful silencing of the mind, with all thoughts directed toward the person of God alone.

THE VALUE OF WAITING

Tragically, many believers become deceived by a spirit of selfishness that often follows them directly into the closet of prayer. Waiting helps deal with this spirit. It is an important step that prepares us for our time of confession, which is next on our list of prayer elements. Bridgid Herman wrote, "The most formidable enemy of the spiritual life, and the last to be conquered, is self-deception; and if there is a better cure for self-deception than silence, it has yet to be discovered."[12]

Not only does waiting prepare the prayer warrior for *confession* in prayer, but it actually serves to snatch us away from the things of the world. To wait in silence is to bid farewell to earthly conversation and attention. It is that vital bridge that takes us from a carnal world to a spiritual world. This silent surrendering of the soul to God opens the door to the "higher plane" of His divine love.

Thoughts from Dr. Andrew Bonar illustrate this concept. Bonar, a man greatly used of God, carefully kept a diary never intended for publication. Fortunately, one of his daughters knew his code system and was able in later years to translate the diary. An especially meaningful entry reads, "Some people have got the beauty of the rose of Sharon, and there are others who have the fragrance, too. Spent two hours today in prayer, seeking that I might have the fragrance."[13]

THE DIVINE LINK

Like any worthy spiritual vocation, waiting in prayer takes time. "A great part of my time," said Robert Murray McCheyne, "is spent in getting my heart in tune for prayer. It is the divine link that connects earth with heaven."[14]

We must not rush these moments of spiritual silence. If any quality seems typically "Christian," it is our impatience with God's timing. An unknown saint confessed, "Many a man asks in April a gift of divine fruit that will be ripe only in June."

We must wait for the best of God's blessings, even in prayer. Consider the case of Paul. When he surrendered his life to Christ, he immediately sought a mission: "Lord, what wilt thou have me to do?" (Acts 9:6). And what was God's answer? He immediately sent Paul into the solitude of a quiet Arabian desert.

A spare ten or fifteen minutes here and there, listening to the latest cassette of a noted minister, or reading a best-seller on Christian growth, will never provide the food needed for true spiritual development. Building a friendship takes much time. The Bible says, "And the Lord spake unto Moses *face to face*, as a man speaketh unto his friend" (Exod. 33:11; italics added).

Little wonder Moses came from the mountain with his face shining. He met God "face to face." Here was a man who waited decades in a barren wilderness before catching a glimpse of the true glory of God. But, oh, the results of his lonely desert sojourn. Moses touched God, and God, in turn, touched Moses in those years of waiting.

TAKE TIME TO WAIT

Concerning the importance of spiritual waiting, Andrew Murray wrote, "Here is the secret of a life of prayer. *Take time* in the inner chamber to bow down and worship; and *wait on Him* until He unveils Himself, and takes possession of you, and goes out with you to show how a man can live and walk in abiding fellowship with an unseen Lord."[15]

Especially strive to conquer the spirit of misspent conversation that permeates the very fiber of human life. Practice the art of silence throughout your day. A wise writer reminds, "The one fact we forget is that the saints of old were capable of spiritual silence simply because they had not contracted our modern habit of ceaseless talk in their ordinary life. Their days were days of silence, relieved by periods of conversation, while ours are a wilderness of talk with a rare oasis of silence.''[16]

Oh, that more believers would earnestly seek the power of sacred silence. Scripture declares, ''Be silent, O all flesh, before the Lord: for he is raised up out of his holy habitation'' (Zech. 2:13).

Strive to devote the early moments of your devotional hour to a time of silent sharing with the Lord. Wait patiently for a greater glimpse of His infinite glory. May our hearts cry out with the unknown poet,

> Oh, to see our Saviour's face!
> From sin and sorrow to be freed!
> To dwell in His divine embrace—
> This will be sweeter far indeed!
> The fairest form of earthly bliss
> Is less than nought compared with this . . .

Lord, teach me to wait!

WAITING
THE SECOND STEP IN WORLD-CHANGING PRAYER

1. After your moments of praise, bring your mind and spirit into a time of complete silence to the world.
2. Think no thoughts but thoughts of God the Father, His Son Jesus, or the Holy Spirit.
3. If words are to be voiced, let them be quiet whispering like, ''I love you, Lord,'' or, ''I long for your presence, O God.''
4. Concentrate full attention on the ''love'' aspect of God's nature in these minutes of silence.

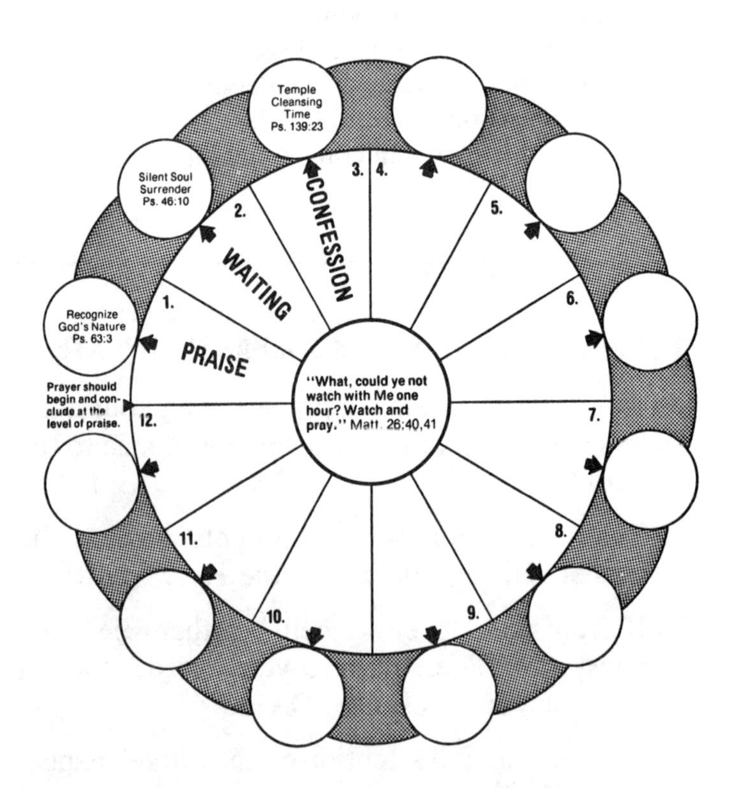
Temple
Cleansing
Time
Ps. 139:23
Silent Soul
Surrender
Ps. 46:10
Recognize
God's Nature
Ps. 63:3
Prayer should
begin and con-
clude at the
level of praise.
1.
2.
3.
4.
5.
6.
7.
8.
9.
10.
11.
12.
PRAISE
WAITING
CONFESSION
"What, could ye not
watch with Me one
hour? Watch and
pray." Matt. 26:40,41

CONFESSION 3

THE ACT OF DECLARED ADMISSION

Having honored God with vocal praise and silent love, we find the door now opens for truly effective praying. Immediately we must deal fully with the matter of personal sin. Andrew Murray reminds us, "God cannot hear the prayers on our lips often because the desires of our heart after the world cry out to Him much more strongly and loudly than our desires for Him."[1]

An awareness of our past failures especially tends to buffet the mind as we pray. Suddenly we feel hopelessly unworthy of offering our petitions. The devil has gained a victory and soon we stop praying altogether.

To combat these spiritual attacks we must take at face value all the promises of God concerning confession. "If we confess our sins," declared the apostle John, "He [God] is faithful and just to forgive us our sins, and to cleanse us from all unrighteousness" (I John 1:9). If unrighteousness renders our praying ineffective, then confession is the solution to the problem of sin-guilt in prayer.

What is confession? The New Testament Greek word for *confess* means "to agree with God" concerning His opinion of a matter. It also means "to admit my guilt." When we confess our sins we are agreeing with God concerning the sin in our lives, as revealed through His Word by the Holy Spirit.

Confession is to verbalize our spiritual shortcomings and admit we have sinned. Simply stated, confession is the act of declared admission.

At no other time in prayer does the believer look so carefully at his own spiritual growth as during *confession*. Both King David and Solomon spoke of this as communing with their own hearts. Dwight L. Moody called it a "personal debate betwixt ourselves and our hearts." Defining this aspect of prayer, Moody added, "Commune—or hold a serious communication and clear intelligence and acquaintance—with your own hearts."[2]

HEARTFELT RECOGNITION

Confession is a heartfelt recognition of what we are. It is important to God because it indicates that we take seriously our mistakes and failures. Of course, God does not ask us to confess our sins because He needs to know we have sinned, but because He knows that *we* need to know we have sinned.

William R. Parker and Elaine St. Johns, psychologists who carefully studied the psychological impact of prayer, also discussed the importance of confession. According to these authors, "People should think less about what they ought to do and more about what they ought to be. If only their being were good, their works would shine forth brightly."[3]

This brings to our attention an essential law of prayer: *My prayer life will never rise above my personal life in Jesus Christ*. If my personal life touches too much of the world, my prayer life suffers. The psalmist put it succinctly, "If I regard iniquity in my heart, the Lord will not hear me" (Ps. 66:18).

According to Scripture there can be no effective prayer life where sin maintains its grip in the life of the believer. This is why confession is critical to our praying and should be implemented early in prayer. It clears the conscience of faith-killing guilt and opens the heart to truly believe God will hear our petitions.

Why is confession so difficult for some? Perhaps because confession is really the most painful part of personal prayer. The moment we admit that a particular act displeases God, we recognize the responsibility to change it. Immediately an inner battle of the will begins to take place.

Speaking of confession, E. M. Blaiklock explains, "This period of our devotions must contain a moment of pain. It is not God's intention that we should writhe under it, or linger in it. But specific and sincere confession of our own sin is no joyous exercise; and self-contempt, however salutary, is not pleasant. But let evil in conduct, thought or motive be brought into the open, fully, without excuse, and under proper names. It is of no use, after all, to pose before God."[4]

SPIRITUAL SURGERY

This act of declared admission gives God access into the heart of a believer, removing all hindrances to effective prayer. It could well be described as a spiritual work of surgery. "It [confession] works healing to the wound incurred in the heart," Harold Lindsell writes. "Just as the surgeon lances a boil to permit the infection to drain and to heal from the inside, so confession opens the sore, drains the poison, and heals from within."[5]

There can be no healing *within* until there is first confession *without*. Confession is conditional to cleansing. Until known sin is fully dealt with, we are not ready to pray. Meister Johannes Eckhart said, "God is bound to act, to pour Himself into thee as soon as He shall find thee ready."[6]

The great question confronting us at this stage of prayer is, "Am I truly ready to pray for a lost and unevangelized world?" And what about the personal needs of my family and friends? Their well-being depends upon my prayers. But my prayers depend upon *my* spiritual well-being. John Allan Lavender accurately suggests, "Before you pray for a change in circumstances, you should pray for a change in character."[7]

As Christians our ultimate goal in prayer must

be to glorify God by changing the world. God desires to pour Himself through us into our world, thus bringing about this change.

Herein lies the problem. How can a holy God pour Himself through a believer whose life is clogged with the debris of this world? Sin causes indifference, and it is impossible for indifferent people to change the world. Daily we must pray as the psalmist, "Search me, O God, and know my heart: try me, and know my thoughts: And see if there be any wicked way in me, and lead me in the way everlasting" (Ps. 139:23, 24).

A careful study of Scripture reveals how important confession truly is. Those most mightily used of God were also those most willing to confess their weaknesses. Only after Isaiah cried, "I am undone," did the Lord invite him to serve. When Job confessed his sins and prayed for his friends God changed his circumstances and gave him more blessings than during his greatest days of prosperity.

Daniel is another example. His life was so godly that the evil princes could find no fault in him (see Dan. 6:4). But note Daniel's awareness of personal sin. He wrote, "And while I was speaking, and praying, and *confessing* my sin and the sin of my people Israel, and presenting my supplication before the Lord my God for the holy mountain of my God . . . even the man Gabriel . . . touched me about the time of the evening oblation" (Dan. 9:20, 21; italics added).

These godly servants of ancient days had

learned an important secret of power. The Holy Spirit works best through a clean vessel, and confession begins the process of cleansing.

THE NECESSITY OF CONFESSION

Confession is not optional to spiritual growth. Through Isaiah God told His people, "Your iniquities have separated between you and your God, and your sins have hid his face from you, that he will not hear" (Isa. 59:2).

Confession is crucial for all spiritual growth, not merely for effective prayer. It is that necessary "first step" to repentance. Before we will ever willingly turn *from* sin, we must first admit that what we are doing *is* sin.

Preaching on Pharaoh's earnest plea to Moses, "Entreat the Lord, that he may take away the frogs from me" (Exod. 8:8), Charles Spurgeon said, "A fatal flaw is manifest in Pharaoh's prayer. It contains no confession of sin. He says not, 'I have rebelled against the Lord: entreat that I may find forgiveness.' Nothing of the kind; he loves sin as much as ever."

Spurgeon concludes, "A prayer without penitence is a prayer without acceptance. If no tear has fallen upon it, it is withered. There must be confession of sin before God, or our prayer is faulty."[8]

During your times of confession especially be on guard for little things—those unseen sins that grow to cause such severe damage. Every major spiritual failure begins as a tiny seed of misconduct.

Virginia Whitman, in her excellent book *The Excitement of Answered Prayer*, tells of an incident that occurred in New York City. "Someone tossed an empty beverage can in front of a subway train just as it was entering a tunnel. It was only a tin can but somehow that can landed on the 'live' electrical rail, causing a major power failure. The result was an hour and a half delay that affected an amazing 55 trains and 75,000 passengers."[9]

THE HOW OF CONFESSING

The author has found a particular psalm to be of special help in establishing a pattern for daily confession. Each day during this phase of prayer I center my attention on David's confession found in Psalm 51. David prayed, "Create in me a clean heart, O God; and renew a right spirit within me. Cast me not away from thy presence; and take not thy holy spirit from me" (Ps. 51:10, 11). Here David provides a practical fourfold pattern for daily confession.

First, David cries out for *divine holiness*. "Create in me a clean heart," he pleads. I cannot be cleansed or forgiven by my own actions. Forgiveness is a work only God can do. So during confession I amplify David's request, elaborating on areas that I believe need improvement in my life. I quietly ask God to show me what needs cleansing.

Often a quick mental trip through the previous twenty-four hours reveals the need for confession. Ask yourself, "Did I fail God in any areas of personal conduct?" "Was I honest in my dealings with others?" "Were my thoughts pleasant to God?" As God reveals various spiritual shortcomings, confess them and claim total victory.

Next, David cries out for a *divine attitude*. He continues, "And renew a right spirit within me."

Whereas David's first petition concerns a right relationship with God (a clean heart), this petition concerns a right relationship with others (a renewed spirit). Helen Shoemaker observes, "Unless our attitude toward others is forgiving and redemptive, God will not hear us."[10]

Mrs. Shoemaker illustrates her thought with a legend concerning the noted artist Leonardo da Vinci. According to the account, during the painting of "The Last Supper," da Vinci chose as his subject for Judas a much-hated enemy. Later, prior to the day the face of Jesus was to be painted, da Vinci was deeply troubled. All night long he tossed and turned in his sleep. Morning finally arrived and the time came to paint the figure of Christ. But, as the legend relates, when da Vinci tried to paint the picture, the Lord's face became strangely blurred.

That night the artist tossed and turned again. Suddenly he jumped from his bed and rushed to the studio. In moments he erased the likeness of the enemy from the face of Judas. Then, in a flash, Leonardo da Vinci saw the picture of Christ clearly.

One's attitude is crucial to dynamic praying. Bitterness toward others drains prayer of power. David Hubbard reminds us, "The great danger in having enemies is not what they may do to us—it is what we do to ourselves as we allow harsh, bitter, angry reactions to develop."[11]

A third quality ought to be sought during this aspect of prayer. David confessed his need for *divine guidance*. The king entreated, "Cast me not away from thy presence." Here we confess our need for God's presence throughout the day, especially to defeat temptation. In the prayer Jesus gave His disciples, He taught us to pray, "Lead us not into temptation" (Matt. 6:13). To confess my confidence that God will be with me when temptation comes helps prepare me for these attacks.

Finally, David cries out for *divine unction*. Almost desperately the king confesses his need for the Holy Spirit: "Take not thy holy spirit from me."

God certainly has no intention of removing His Spirit from obedient believers. But still this aspect of confession is important. It is a renewed affirmation that we cannot accomplish anything apart from the direct spiritual aid of the Holy Spirit. It is to admit that without God's Spirit operating in and through us all efforts will be hopelessly ineffective.

TEMPLE-CLEANSING TIME

To a great degree, confession in prayer is a time of spiritual cleansing. In ancient Bible days it was often necessary to clean and restore God's temple. Concerning the revival and restoration of the temple under Hezekiah, the Bible tells us, "And the priests went into the inner part of the house of the

Lord, to cleanse it, and brought out all the uncleanness that they found in the temple of the Lord into the court of the house of the Lord'' (II Chron. 29:16).

Today, the dwelling place of God is not a temple of brick and mortar but the inner soul of man. Scripture declares, ''What? know ye not that your body is the temple of the Holy Ghost . . . ?'' (I Cor. 6:19).

Confession is necessary to private prayer because it initiates the process of cleansing our spiritual temple. Allow enough time during prayer for a thorough cleansing. Remember, confession in prayer is that final step that leads to confident praying. . .

Lord, teach me to confess!

CONFESSION
THE THIRD STEP IN WORLD-CHANGING PRAYER

1. Following your time of silent waiting, immediately ask God to search your heart for any unconfessed sin.

2. Mentally examine your recent activities to discover possible areas of spiritual failure that need confessing.

3. Confess any specific sins you may be guilty of, either against God or your fellow man.

4. Confess your need for specific divine guidance and supernatural unction.

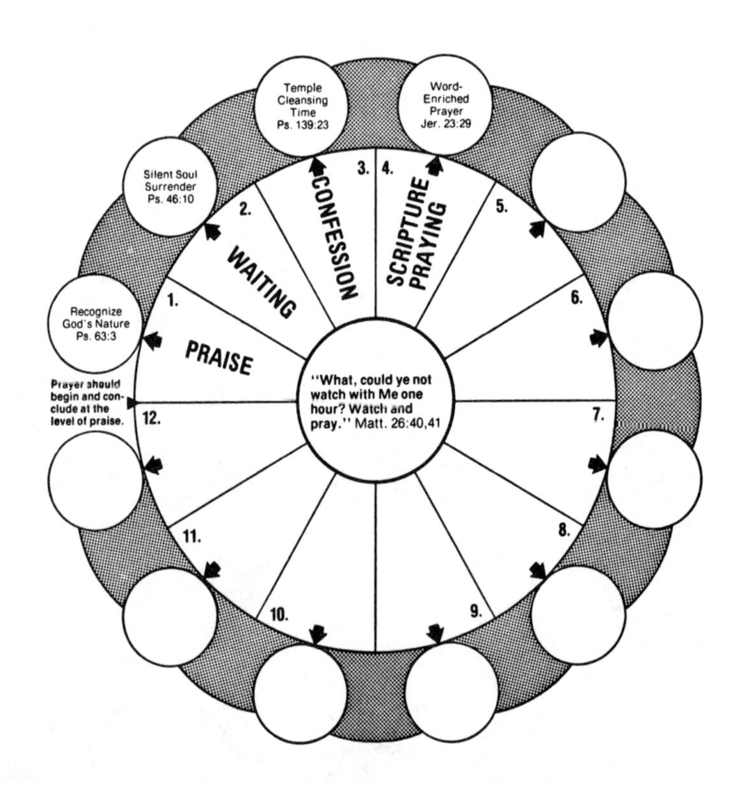
Temple
Cleansing
Time
Ps. 139:23
Word-
Enriched
Prayer
Jer. 23:29
Silent Soul
Surrender
Ps. 46:10
Recognize
God's Nature
Ps. 63:3
1.
2.
3.
4.
5.
6.
7.
8.
9.
10.
11.
12.
PRAISE
WAITING
CONFESSION
SCRIPTURE
PRAYING
"What, could ye not watch with Me one hour? Watch and pray." Matt. 26:40,41
Prayer should begin and conclude at the level of praise.

SCRIPTURE PRAYING 4

THE ACT OF FAITH APPROPRIATION

"There are only three classes of people in the world today," an unknown preacher confessed. "Those who are afraid, those who do not know enough to be afraid, and those who know their Bibles."

Although the Word of God is essential to the whole of our Christian experience, it is especially crucial to prayer. The degree to which we believe in God's Word and apply it to prayer is the degree to which God will pour out His power during our prayer.

We can never expect to grow in spiritual confidence if we spend little or no time getting to know God through His Word. Thus, God's Word must become an actual part of the devotional life. We may study the Bible throughout the week, but we should also seek to bring God's Word directly into our daily prayer.

Only as we systematically apply God's Word during prayer will we come to a full understanding of how much power God has available to us. Leonard Ravenhill preached, "One of these days some simple soul will pick up the Book of God and read it, and believe it. The rest of us will be embarrassed. We have adopted the convenient theory that the Bible is a Book to be explained, whereas first and foremost, it is a Book to be believed (and after that to be obeyed)."[1]

DIVINE NOURISHMENT

"Prayer," said E. M. Bounds, "projects faith on God, and God on the world. Only God can move mountains, but faith and prayer move God."[2]

It is true that faith combined with prayer moves mountains, but where do we gain this mountain-moving faith? Paul reminded the Roman believers, "Faith cometh by hearing, and hearing by the word of God" (Rom. 10:17). In no other way is our faith strengthened as in familiarity with the Word of God.

"Fasting and long hours of prayer do not build faith," E. W. Kenyon wrote. "Reading books about faith and men of faith and their exploits stirs in the heart a deep passion for faith, but does not build faith. *The Word alone is the source of faith*."[3]

Few writers have had as much impact on the lives of praying Christians as Andrew Murray. Like so many noted saints of God, Andrew Murray developed an intense prayer life heavily saturated with the Word of God. He once explained, "Little of the Word with little prayer is death to the spiritual life. Much of the Word with little prayer gives a sickly life. Much prayer with little of the Word gives more life, but without steadfastness. A full measure of the Word and prayer each day gives a healthy and powerful life."[4]

Our prayer time, no matter how intense, is never truly complete without the divine nourishment available only from God's Word. Indeed, the Word of God is the Christian's true prayer book. It is our guide and foundation for all effective praying. To neglect God's Word is to neglect God's power. Lehman Strauss adds, "When we neglect the daily, quiet, meditative reading of God's Word, we block the lifeline to God's throne of grace. Our abiding in Christ through the Word is a life process that must never cease."[5]

G. Campbell Morgan was another gifted minister who considered his devotional hour useless without a good helping of God's Word. The preacher cautioned, "My brothers, see to it that when morning breaks you go to God for sustenance for your spiritual life. That will make you strong against the allurements of the Devil. So many people turn out to face the temptations of the day spiritually unfed, spiritually hungry, and therefore they are attacked by all kinds of enticements of the enemy. It is the man fed by God, spiritually and physically, who is likely to overcome in the hour of temptation."[6]

PLEADING GOD'S PROMISES

Few leaders of the previous century were known as much for their deep confidence in God and effectiveness in prayer as was George Mueller. At ninety years of age Mueller was able to declare, "I have never had an unanswered prayer." He claimed the secret to receiving answers to prayer lies in how the Christian applies God's Word during prayer.

For example, George Mueller always prayed with an open Bible. He constantly filled his petitions with God's Word. Friends said the orphanage leader would not voice a petition without a "word from God" to back that petition. In fact, Mueller never started petitioning God until *after* he nourished himself in God's Word.

Describing his devotional hour, George Mueller wrote, "The first thing I did, after having asked in a few words the Lord's blessing upon His precious Word, was to begin to meditate on the Word of God, searching as it were into every verse to get a blessing out of it; not for the sake of the public ministry of the Word, nor for the sake of preaching on what I meditated upon, but for the sake of obtaining food for my own soul. The result I have found to be almost invariably this, that after a very few minutes my soul has been led to confession, or to thanksgiving, or to intercession, or to supplication; so that, though I did not, as it were, give myself to prayer, but to meditation, yet it turned almost immediately more or less into prayer."[7]

George Mueller had learned the important secret of transforming God's Word into faith-filled petitions. He literally "prayed" the Word of God.

Charles Spurgeon was another noted leader who understood this secret. He expressed, "Every promise of Scripture is a writing of God, which may be pleaded before Him with this reasonable request, 'Do as Thou hast said!' The Creator will not cheat the creature who depends upon His truth; and far more, the Heavenly Father will not break His Word to His own child."[8]

WORD-ENRICHED PRAYER

The Word of God is more than a mere foundation for effective praying; it is the actual substance for effective praying. Just as the Word of God brings life to the believer's daily walk, God's Word brings life into our praying.

Concerning the power of Scripture, Paul declared, "For this cause also thank we God without ceasing, because, when ye received the word of God which ye heard of us, ye received it not as the word of men, but as it is in truth, the word of God, which *effectually worketh* also in you that believe" (I Thess. 2:13; italics added). Another translation declares that God's Word has "living power in you who have faith" (*The New Testament in Basic English*).

Only recently have I discovered the amazing secret of prayer called "Scripture Praying." In Paul's words to the Thessalonians we find the basis for this mode of praying. If God's Word "effectually worketh" in those who believe, it should carry the same impact *within our prayers*. By bringing God's Word directly into our praying, we are bringing God's power directly into our praying.

The psalmist said, "I will never forget thy precepts: for *with them thou hast quickened me*" (Ps. 119:93; italics added). Note God's promise given through Jeremiah: "Is not my word like as a fire? saith the Lord; and like a hammer that breaketh the rock in pieces?" (Jer. 23:29).

E. M. Bounds was a saint of God known for his extraordinary prayer life. A lawyer during the Civil War, Bounds spent an average of four hours in prayer every morning. Immediately following prayer he would write his most intimate prayer experiences. Like other spiritual leaders of his generation, Bounds discovered the tremendous value of applying God's Word to prayer. He once testified, "The Word of God is the fulcrum (support) upon which the lever of prayer is placed, and by which things are mightily moved. God has committed Himself, His purpose, and His promise to prayer · His Word becomes the basis, the inspiration of our praying, and there are circumstances under which by importunate prayer, we may obtain an addition or an enlargement of His promises."[9]

THE METHOD OF SCRIPTURE PRAYING

My experiences with Scripture Praying began with a Christmas gift of Bible cassettes. Daily I would listen to passages from Psalms and Proverbs during my hour of prayer. As in the case of George Mueller, I quickly discovered that certain passages of Scripture prompted me to pray for specific needs. Before long I found that a definite plan for enriching my prayer with God's Word was developing.

Although I continue to use the cassettes of Scripture in my daily devotional hour, using an open Bible will accomplish the same purpose. If possible, you may wish to use both cassettes and an open Bible.[10]

Following is a simple three-step plan for Scripture Praying that emerged in my daily program.

First, listen to (or read) a passage from the Word of God. Try to include approximately *one chapter during each devotional hour*. Of course, you may listen to considerably more than one chapter, but too lengthy a portion of Scripture may dilute the impact of Scripture Praying.

Remember, in using this method of praying you are not actually studying the Bible for the sake of Bible study, but you are searching the Scripture for actual power that might be applied to your petitions.

Second, while listening to the Bible cassettes, keep your finger near the stop button of your recorder. (If you are reading Scripture allow your finger to move slowly from verse to verse.) The moment you discover a verse (or two) that impresses a particular truth upon your heart, stop the cassette recorder, or close your Bible, and *quietly meditate on what that verse is saying to you*. Ponder every aspect of this passage. This will usually happen in a matter of a few seconds. Carefully evaluate how the passage might be transformed into a specific petition.

Ask yourself several questions. Does this verse prompt me to pray for something specific? How can this passage be directly applied to my petition? Is it possible to use some of the words of this scripture, verbatim, as I pray?

Third, with these moments of meditation as a base, *form a personal prayer "enriched" by that promise from God*. In some cases the prayer warrior may listen to an entire chapter before receiving a specific thought that will directly apply to a particular petition. But when that thought comes, use it to enhance your request. Mentally develop an actual prayer based on what you have read or heard in the passage and offer that prayer to the Lord.

As you develop this method of praying, keep in mind that it is not necessary to form a prayer for every verse of a chapter. In fact, some passages of Scripture are somewhat difficult to use in Scripture Praying. For the most part, Psalms, Proverbs, the Gospels, or Epistles provide the best setting for this method of praying.

Beyond Word-enriched prayer the intercessor will find equal excitement in "Word-enriched praise." J. Oswald Sanders, in his excellent book *Prayer Power Unlimited,* explains, "The Scriptures are rich in material to feed and stimulate worship and adoration—especially the Psalms, which are God's inspired prayer books. As you read them, turn them into prayer. Vast tracts of truth await our exploration. Great themes abound—God's holiness, sovereignty, truth, wisdom, faithfulness, patience, love, mercy—all of which will call forth our worship."[11]

A FINAL CAUTION

As you begin to implement Scripture Praying be careful not to neglect other important aspects of prayer. Remember, our goal as prayer warriors is to develop a devotional habit that is complete and well-balanced. Some may find the excitement of Word-enriched prayer so fulfilling that little time is given for other serious prayer matters. Be careful not to neglect intercession, listening, praise, thanksgiving, and the other vital elements so essential to "complete" prayer. Yet, strive to give the Word of God its rightful place . . .

Lord, teach me to plead your promises!

SCRIPTURE PRAYING
THE FOURTH STEP IN WORLD-CHANGING PRAYER

1. When bringing Scripture into your devotional hour, ask God to bless His Word to your spiritual body, just as He blesses natural food to your physical body.
2. Examine a passage from either the Gospels, the Epistles, Psalms, or Proverbs. Look carefully for specific ways to apply each verse to prayer.
3. As you study a verse (or verses), ask yourself what petition this passage prompts you to make, or what promise this passage contains that stands directly behind a specific petition.
4. Develop actual prayers based on the thoughts and phrases included in a verse (or verses) of Scripture and offer those prayers confidently to the Lord.

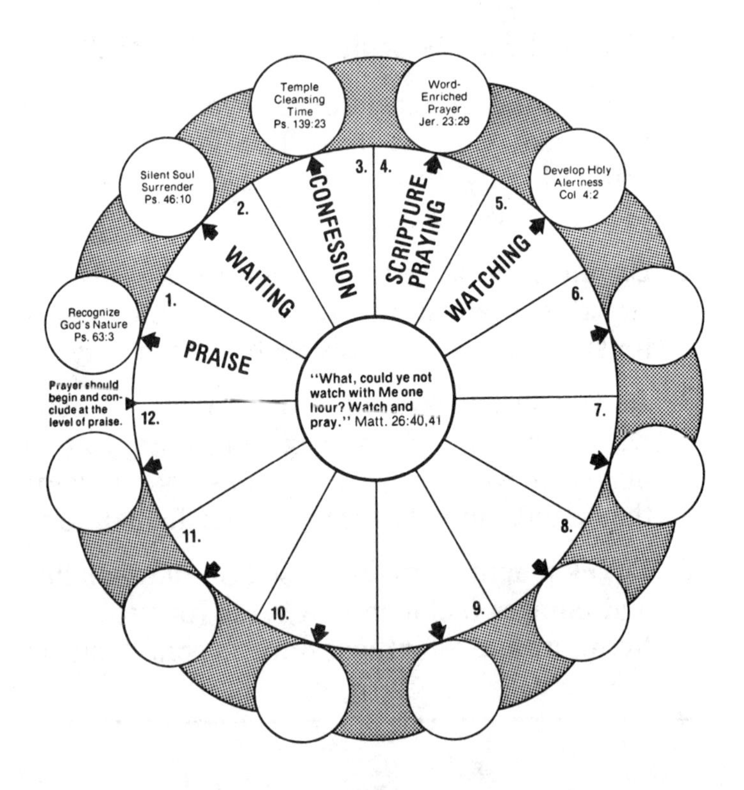
Temple
Cleansing
Time
Ps. 139:23
Word-
Enriched
Prayer
Jer. 23:29
Silent Soul
Surrender
Ps. 46:10
Develop Holy
Alertness
Col 4:2
Recognize
God's Nature
Ps. 63:3
Prayer should
begin and con-
clude at the
level of praise.
1.
2.
3.
4.
5.
6.
7.
8.
9.
10.
11.
12.
PRAISE
WAITING
CONFESSION
SCRIPTURE
PRAYING
WATCHING
"What, could ye not
watch with Me one
hour? Watch and
pray." Matt. 26:40,41

WATCHING 5

THE ACT OF MENTAL AWARENESS

Books on prayer seldom discuss, or even mention, the importance of "watching" in prayer. Yet Jesus commanded us to "watch and pray!" (Matt. 26:41; Mark 14:38). Paul also challenged believers to "continue in prayer, and *watch in the same* with thanksgiving" (Col. 4:2; italics added). He made it clear that watching was to be a *specific* element of prayer, something as important to prayer as thanksgiving.

BE ON THE ALERT

What did Jesus and His chief apostle mean when they challenged us to "watch" in prayer? The Greek word for our word *watch* is *gregoreo*, "to be awake or vigilant." The dictionary defines *watch* as "keeping awake in order to guard." It can also mean "a close observation" or "to be on the alert."

When Jesus and Paul used the expression *watch* they principally meant that believers should stay awake spiritually and keep guard. Since both

Jesus and Paul linked watching with prayer, they were referring to staying alert during prayer. As one writer suggests, "Watching in prayer and supplication bespeaks having spiritual insight to discern the wiles of Satan and to discover the latter's end and means."[1]

When the apostle Peter warned us to be "vigilant" because Satan seeks to devour us (I Peter 5:8), he used the very word *gregoreo* (translated "watch") which both Jesus and Paul used in conjunction with prayer.

After Paul spoke to the Ephesian Christians about putting on the full armor of God, he again stressed watching. Paul suggested they establish everything by "praying always with all prayer and supplication in the Spirit, and watching thereunto with all perseverance and supplication for all saints" (Eph. 6:18; italics added).

Dr. Curtis Mitchell of Biola College explains, "To pray correctly one must be mentally alert and vigilant. Much praying is hampered by a dull, drowsy frame of mind."[2]

During this activity of watching our spiritual function is somewhat similar to the ministry of the "watchmen" in ancient Bible days. Concerning the city of Jerusalem God said, "I have set watchmen upon thy walls, O Jerusalem, which shall never hold their peace day nor night: ye that make mention of the Lord, keep not silence" (Isa. 62:6).

Appointing watchmen to guard walled cities was a common custom in Bible days. The watchman's chief responsibility was to warn the inhabitants of approaching enemies. The thought in Isaiah 62:6 is that God's prophets were like these watchmen. They could not hold their peace until the prophecy of God was fulfilled in the full restoration of Jerusalem. These watchmen stood alert to warn of impending spiritual conflict.

A SPIRIT OF WATCHFULNESS

Our first order of business during the watching phase of prayer is to make ourselves *aware* of the various ways Satan seeks to hinder the effectiveness of our prayer. From the earliest moments of prayer he comes on the attack, trying to draw our minds from the key issues of prayer. To watch in prayer is to become aware of these attacks and stand firmly against them.

We should especially guard against prayer that lacks purpose. Suddenly the many items on our prayer list seem empty or vague. Prayer becomes shallow. We find ourselves making statements about prayer, instead of claiming specific things in prayer.

Only as we develop a spirit of watchfulness can we recognize Satan's plan of attack and block his efforts. As a perceptive prayer warrior suggests, "Always be on the alert to travel toward the goal of prayer, to disallow any unwanted words from mixing in, and to keep yourselves from praying prayers that are not prayers at all."[3]

But watching in prayer goes beyond developing an alertness to the manner in which Satan may attack. From a practical standpoint, time should be allocated during prayer for a mental reflection concerning what is happening beyond our immediate world. Not only must we be *alert* to per sonal satanic attacks, but we must become *aware* of the "wiles of the devil" as they pertain to God's plan throughout the world.

STEPS FOR WATCHING

There are two essential questions the prayer warrior should ask himself as he goes about the ministry of intercession. They are: "How much awareness do I have relative to the problems of world evangelism?" and, "Am I aware of how Satan is working to hinder God's workers?"

Because watching means "a close observation," we must develop a plan for prayer that helps us observe the needs around us much more specifically. Following are several suggestions that should help intercessors develop just such a plan.

First, endeavor to read material that makes you spiritually "aware" of specific world needs. Missionary journals and denominational reports can be of great assistance in developing this awareness. World Literature Crusade is a ministry that engages several staff members around the world who do nothing but research specific needs of world evangelism. Such research is of enormous value in helping to inform concerned intercessors. A good deal of "prayer fuel" is available to help Christians pray intelligently.[4] The tragedy is that so much of it is neglected due to a lack of awareness or outright unconcern.

Second, during prayer strive to reflect mentally about "news" of the day. Daily newspapers, as well as radio or television news broadcasts, contain certain items that have a definite bearing on God's work throughout the world. Economic problems, civil unrest, political changes, and even weather conditions can enter into the fulfillment of the Great Commission. Ask God to refresh your mind concerning current events that deserve special prayer attention.

Finally, and certainly *most* important, ask the Holy Spirit to show you exactly what you should claim in prayer and how you should claim it. None of the suggestions discussed in this book can be put fully to use apart from concentrated direction from the Holy Spirit. In fact, without the Holy Spirit guiding us, effectiveness in prayer is an impossibility.

SPIRITUAL PRAYER

Speaking on "spiritual prayer," Bishop J. C. Ryle expressed, "I commend to you the importance of praying spiritually. I mean by that, that we should labor always to have the help of the Spirit in our prayers, and be aware above all things of formality. There is nothing so spiritual but that it may become a form, and this is especially true of private prayer."[5]

There is nothing wrong with developing a consistent, systematic habit of prayer, as long as we carefully "watch" that our praying remains truly spiritual. Bishop Ryle adds, "If the skeleton and outline of our prayers be by habit, almost a form, let us strive that the clothing and filling up of our prayers be as far as possible of the Spirit."[6]

No discussion of the subject of watching in prayer can be complete without emphasizing the value of the Holy Spirit in prayer. Paul told Roman believers, "Likewise the Spirit also helpeth our infirmities: for we know not what we should pray for as we ought: but the Spirit itself maketh intercession for us with groanings which cannot be uttered. And he that searcheth the hearts knoweth what is the mind of the Spirit, because he maketh intercession for the saints according to the will of God" (Rom. 8:26, 27).

It is clear from this passage that a prayer warrior is not left to himself in understanding the "how" of prayer. Each has been given the help of the Holy Spirit to guide and direct. This guidance is best cultivated in the watching aspect of prayer.

Twice in Scripture believers are admonished to "pray in the Spirit" (Eph. 6:18; Jude 20). Of course, praying in the Spirit, as I have discovered, means vastly different things to different Christians. The purpose here is not to evaluate this expression from a theological standpoint. Numerous books have exhausted this subject quite well. However, I do suggest the reader seek to develop a much enlarged recognition of the Holy Spirit's power as it relates to personal prayer.

No doubt the majority of Christians, no matter their theological persuasions, would agree with the statement of Lehman Strauss: "If anyone were to ask me what is the first truly great secret of a successful prayer life, I would say in answer, 'Praying in the Holy Spirit.' " The writer adds, "Human wisdom and human desire can achieve human results. But praying in the Spirit produces divine results."[7]

In reading biographies of past spiritual leaders it is obvious that praying in the Spirit was not treated lightly. Samuel Chadwick, a saint mightily used of God, spoke of a powerful encounter with the Holy Spirit in 1882. He called it "the key to all of my life." Of his experience Chadwick testified, "It awakened my mind as well as my heart. It gave me a new Bible and a new message. Above all else, it gave me a new understanding and a new intimacy in the communion and ministry of prayer; it taught me to pray in the Spirit."[8]

Let the reader especially note that Chadwick's spiritual encounter "awakened" his mind. The preacher immediately discovered truths about prayer he had never observed before. A new intimacy was experienced in daily prayer, something every believer should earnestly covet.

Perhaps the reason much of our praying becomes dull and lifeless is that we lack spiritual intimacy with the only Being who can add life to our praying. John Bunyan wrote, "It is the easiest thing in a hundred to fall from power to form, but it is the hardest thing of many to keep in the life, spirit and power of any one duty, especially prayer. It is such a work that a man *without the help of the Spirit* cannot do so much as pray once, much less continue without, in a sweet praying frame, and in praying, so to pray as to have his prayer ascend unto the ears of the Lord of the Sabbath."[9]

SEEING THINGS INVISIBLE

God earnestly desires to reveal special secrets during prayer, to help us pray more specifically for particular needs. To "watch" in prayer is to open our spiritual eyes to perceive these secrets. We must permit the Holy Spirit to "enlighten" us during prayer. Professor Hallesby taught, "The spirit of prayer throws light upon every phase of our prayer life. Not only theoretical light, enlightening our minds, but practical light for our use in praying and for training in prayer."[10]

As we "watch" in prayer, those needs hiding in the shadows of human awareness come alive through the light of God's Spirit. We see each need with a supernatural clarity. What was once a blur is now in focus.

An entirely new dimension will soon be added to our praying. We will see what is not possible to see. Jonathan Swift said, "Vision is the art of seeing things invisible." Our praying suddenly has this unique, God-given "vision." Our imagination comes alive. By God's Spirit the mission field is not across the world, *we* are across the world—on that very mission field. We actually begin to feel the suffering being experienced by those for whom we pray.

Anne Townsend expressed this in her thought, "If I can imagine what it must be like to be the one for whom I am praying, then I find that I can begin to intercede for that person. My imagination leads me on to want to be more deeply involved with him in his own life. This involvement leads to caring, caring leads to love, and love leads to intercession."[11]

As we seek to "watch" in prayer God will enlarge the capacity of our imagination to see certain needs even more clearly. Scripture says, "But, as it is written, 'What no eye has seen, nor ear heard, nor the heart of man conceived, what God has prepared for those who love Him,' God has revealed to us through the Spirit . . ." (I Cor. 2:9, 10; RSV).

Paul is reminding us that spiritual insight does not emerge from the inner resource of man's ability *unless* it is illuminated through the power of the Holy Spirit. This is why we must earnestly covet more of God's Spirit in our praying.

INNER VISION

As we develop the ministry of "watching" in prayer, whether we set aside two minutes or ten, soon God will call upon us to pray very special prayers. We should expect to see things that startle us.

Professor Hallesby shared an account that illustrates this thought. He spoke of an ordinary country girl, Bolette Hinderli, who had a most unusual prayer experience that ultimately brought thousands to Christ.

While in prayer the young girl experienced an inner vision of a man in a prison cell. She observed his face as plainly as the print on this page. Accompanying the vision was an inner voice that urgently declared, "This man will share the same fate as other criminals if no one takes up the work of praying for him. Pray for him, and I will send him out to proclaim my praises among the heathen."

Bolette Hinderli was obedient to the heavenly call. For months she prayed earnestly that the prisoner would learn of God. She carefully searched news articles and listened to testimonies of converted Christians. She hoped to hear of someone converted while in prison and now proclaiming the gospel.

Finally, during a trip to a distant city in Norway, Bolette Hinderli heard that a former prisoner, now converted to Christ, was scheduled to share the evening message in a local church. With quiet excitement Miss Hinderli sat in a pew, awaiting the message. Then, Lars Olsen Skrefsrud, the guest speaker for the evening, walked to the small pulpit. Bolette's heart exploded for joy. She immediately recognized the face of the man who preached. It was, without question, the very man for whom she had been praying.

We must depend daily on the Holy Spirit to enlarge our awareness in all matters of prayer. Let us follow the suggestion of Andrew Murray who challenged, "The great lesson for every time of prayer is—to see to it, first of all, that you commit yourself to the leading of the Holy Spirit, and with entire dependence on Him, give Him the first place; for through Him your prayer will have a value you cannot imagine, and through Him also you will learn to speak out your desires in the name of Christ."[12] . . .

Lord, teach me to watch!

WATCHING
THE FIFTH STEP IN WORLD-CHANGING PRAYER

1. Take a few moments during prayer to become spiritually alert. Watch for the methods Satan may try to use to hinder your Christian walk that day. Prayerfully claim power to defeat Satan in each of these areas.
2. Read denominational or missionary-evangelism magazines to help become alert to specific needs in God's work around the world.
3. Prayerfully recall various international news developments that deserve special prayer.
4. Ask the Holy Spirit to reveal further spiritual facts about these needs. This will aid you in praying more intelligently for these needs.

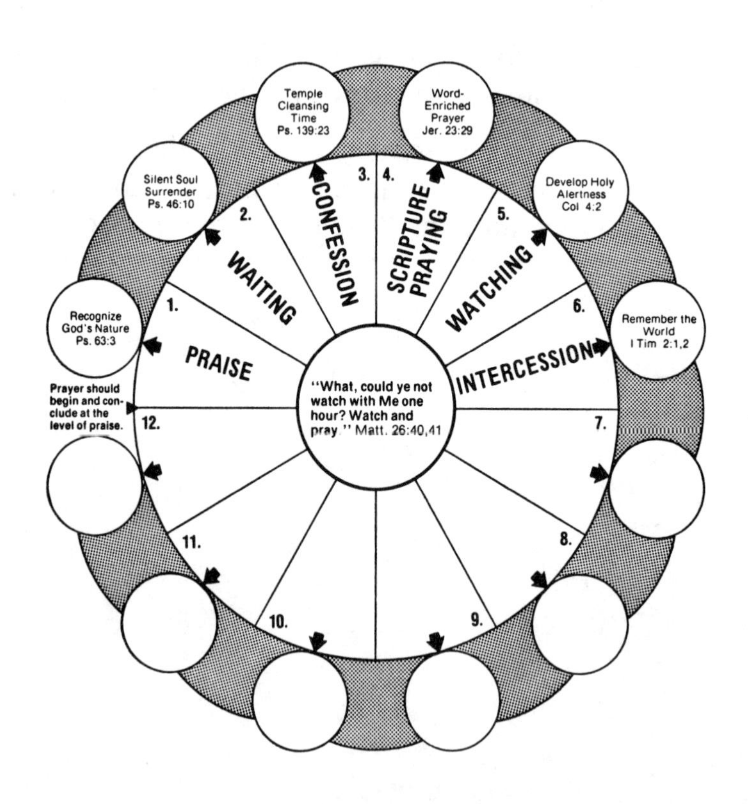
Temple
Cleansing
Time
Ps. 139:23
Word-
Enriched
Prayer
Jer. 23:29
Silent Soul
Surrender
Ps. 46:10
Develop Holy
Alertness
Col 4:2
Recognize
God's Nature
Ps. 63:3
Remember the
World
I Tim 2:1,2
1.
2.
3.
4.
5.
6.
7.
8.
9.
10.
11.
12.
PRAISE
WAITING
CONFESSION
SCRIPTURE
PRAYING
WATCHING
INTERCESSION
"What, could ye not
watch with Me one
hour? Watch and
pray." Matt. 26:40,41
Prayer should
begin and con-
clude at the
level of praise.

INTERCESSION 6

THE ACT OF EARNEST APPEAL

André Maurois, a French biographer, said, "The universe is indifferent. Who created it? Why are we here on this puny mud heap spinning in infinite space? I have not the slightest idea and I am quite convinced that no one has!"[1]

Fortunately, the follower of Christ knows his reason for being. We have both a divine task and a divine purpose. Our supreme "purpose" is to glorify God. Our supreme "task" is to evangelize the lost. In the truest sense, the latter most faithfully fulfills the former. To evangelize the lost glorifies God on the highest level.

This is why intercession (prayer for others) is so essential to the devotional habit. It might be labeled "the heart of prayer." Although intercession is only one aspect of prayer, because of its importance I have included an appendix on page 155 to help the reader further develop this essential aspect of prayer.

NO HIGHER PLANE

What is intercession? It is God's method for involving His followers more completely in the totality of His plan. In no other way can the believer become as fully involved with God's work, especially the work of world evangelism, as in intercessory prayer.

Basically, intercession is prayer offered on behalf of another. When the prayer warrior intercedes he forgets his personal needs and focuses all of his faith and prayer-attention on others.

To intercede is to mediate. It is to stand between a lost being and an almighty God, praying that this person will come to know about God and His salvation. As Edward Bauman explains in *Intercessory Prayer*, "When we pray for others we do not stand with outstretched hands hoping to receive something for ourselves. We stand at God's side, working together with Him, in the task of redeeming others."[2]

Surely there is no higher plane for prayer than intercession. What could be more important than participating in the redemption of another being through prayer? True, our prayer does not save the sinner, but somehow it serves to prepare his heart for the moment word reaches him of Christ's love. Search for a person who claims to have found Christ apart from someone else's prayer, and your search may go on forever.

The ministry of intercession, that of earnestly appealing on behalf of another, is especially important because it is the believer's common ground for Christian service. Spiritually speaking, prayer is the divine equalizer. Some preach, others teach, a few sing publicly, but all can pray. Paul Billheimer reminds us, "Many people grieve because they have been denied service on the mission field or in some other chosen endeavor. But through faithful intercession they may accomplish as much and reap as full a reward as though they had been on the field in person."[3]

THE HALLMARK OF PRAYER

Intercession is the broadest scope of prayer. There is no other mode of prayer that reaches out to *all* the world as does intercessory prayer. E. M. Bounds explains, "Prayer must be broad in its scope—it must plead for others. Intercession for others is the hallmark of all true prayer. . . . Prayer is the soul of a man stirred to plead with God for men."[4]

In intercessory prayer we find the key to freedom for those in bondage. Note the promise God gave Abimelech: "He [Abraham] is a prophet, and he shall pray for thee, and thou shalt live" (Gen. 20:7).

Could it be that our very prayers hold "life" for the unevangelized? Those directly involved in world evangelism would answer a resounding yes. Ask almost any missionary if prayer is important in his labor and be prepared to hear a sermon.

Dr. Yohann Lee, overseas director of World Literature Crusade, is a Korean Christian who was born in China where his family once served as missionaries. Directing the overseas aspects of a ministry that has seen more than eight million written decisions for Christ, Lee could well be considered an authority on successful evangelism.

To what does Lee attribute these extraordinary results? Speaking specifically on the steadfastness of these many converts, Lee says, "The prayers of the saints directly affect the proportion and degree of the Holy Spirit's power over a newborn babe in Christ. *Prayer is where it all begins and where it all ends.*" A. T. Pierson adds, "Every step in the progress of missions is directly traceable to prayer. It has been the preparation for every new triumph and the secret of all success."

THE GREAT CRY

But intercession is much more than merely praying for others. Interceding is engaging in actual battle.[5] There is a certain spirit of authority that must accompany a good deal of intercession. This thought is amplified by A. J. Gordon, "We have authority to take from the enemy everything he is holding back. The chief way of taking is by prayer, and by whatever action prayer leads us to. The cry that should be ringing out today is the great cry, 'Take, in Jesus' great Name!' "[6]

While visiting Communist China and walking the dusty paths of a rural commune, I was vividly reminded that Christ gave His life for those in the most remote places on earth. As I gazed across vast acres of Chinese farm land my heart recited, "The earth is the Lord's, and the fulness thereof" (Ps. 24:1).

I reminded myself that China really belongs to God. Satan has staged only a temporary invasion.

Intercessors hold the power and authority to claim back what rightfully belongs to God, including all of China's billion souls.

True, God could save China's masses in a moment, but He waits for praying saints to join Him in the battle. This is *His* plan, and those who believe God answers prayer must be at the heart of it.

But to be at the heart of God's plan for world evangelization requires much more than mere lip service. As intercessors we must go beyond the simple act of "praying for others" to the point of manifesting a genuine spirit of concern for others. Consider the example of Christ. Before our Lord ascended to heaven for the purpose of interceding on our behalf (Rom. 8:34), He first *gave* Himself to die on a lonely cross.

Thus, intercession begins with a spirit of giving before it becomes a spirit of praying. Francois Coillard explains, "Our prayers for the evangelization of the world are but a bitter irony so long as we give only of our superfluity, and draw back before the sacrifice of ourselves."[7]

PRAYER CENTERED ON OTHERS

When Jesus taught His disciples to pray it was clear the emphasis was to be on others (Matt. 6:9-13). His prayer began with the plural possessive pronominal adjective—"our." We were not taught to pray, "*My* father, but, "*Our* Father!" Further in the prayer we see statements like "give *us*," "lead *us*," and "forgive *us*." In the deepest sense, the prayer is a love prayer. Every word is self-less. It cannot be prayed without deep compassion.

John Calvin declared, "Our prayer must not be self-centered. It must arise not only because we feel our own need as a burden which we must lay upon God, but also because we are bound up in love for our fellow men that we feel their need as acutely as our own. To make intercession for men is the most powerful and practical way in which we can express our love for them."[8]

To keep our praying always centered on others, intercession should come before petition. "We are all selfish by nature," explained J. C. Ryle, "and our selfishness is very apt to stick to us, even when we are converted. There is a tendency in us to think only of our own needs, our own spiritual conflicts, and our own progress in religion, and forget others."[9]

Because Jesus realized we would periodically lapse into a spirit of selfishness, He taught us to pray, "Thy kingdom come," before praying, "Give us this day our daily bread." Jesus wanted us to become "soul conscious" instead of "thing conscious." E. M. Bounds advises, "So also prayers for men are far more important than prayers for things because men more deeply concern God's will and the work of Jesus Christ than things."[10]

THE QUESTION OF REPETITION

When believers begin praying daily for unevangelized nations, it is not uncommon for their praying to sound strangely similar. After several weeks, or even just a few days, questions may arise concerning the matter of repetition in prayer. Is it wrong to repeat a prayer that is exactly the same as or similar to a prayer we have prayed previously? What did Jesus mean when He cautioned His followers concerning "vain repetition" in prayer?

Look carefully at the passage in question. Jesus said, "But when ye pray, use not vain repetitions, as the heathen do: for they think that they shall be heard for their much speaking" (Matt. 6:7).

It is not uncommon to hear some Bible teachers use this verse to suggest that all repetition in prayer is unscriptural. But look again at our Lord's exact words. Jesus did not actually condemn *all* repetition in prayer. Instead, He instructed His followers to avoid "vain" or "empty" repetition. He further qualifies the term *vain* by adding, "as the heathen do." These four words reveal what kind of repetition is meaningless in prayer.

Various heathen cultures have strange and unique forms of prayer that are clearly empty and repetitious. The Tibetan Buddhist prayer wheel is most notable. Chiseling prayers to heathen gods on a clay wheel, and assuming that spinning the wheel causes these hundreds of prayers to rise simultaneously during each revolution, is a perfect example of "vain" repetition.

On the other hand, the Christian in right standing with Jesus, who brings before his Lord a similar petition from day to day, hardly finds himself in the same category as a wheel-spinning Buddhist. To pray similar prayers daily for various nations of rld cannot be classified as "vain" repeti- True, it may appear repetitious, but it is not vain.

The reader may be surprised to discover that repetition in prayer is even scriptural. In fact, Abraham failed in prayer because he gave up in his petitioning (Gen. 18:16-33). However, Elijah pleaded with God seven times and witnessed a remarkable outpouring from God (I Kings 18:42-45). Commenting on these passages Jack Taylor asks, "Is it without significance that Elijah prayed seven times—the number of perfection and fullness—while Abraham stopped at six times, the number of human frailty?"[11]

Further, it is interesting to note that even our Lord repeated a prayer. In Gethsemane Christ offered a petition three times, "saying the same words" (Matt. 26:44). Twice Jesus prayed for a blind man (Mark 8:24, 25). King David repeated a "prayer of praise" twenty-six times in Psalm 136.

MAKING MENTION IN PRAYER

Becoming closely acquainted with Jack McAlister of World Literature Crusade has introduced the author to various qualities concerning personal prayer that have previously proven difficult. While sharing with Dr. McAlister in a memorable visit to the People's Republic of China, I had the opportunity to observe his prayer life from close range. During the trip one long-standing question about repetition in prayer was answered.

After spending numerous times in prayer with McAlister, I was amazed to find that he prayed for every person on the World Literature Crusade headquarter's staff by name. He also prayed for each overseas leader associated with the ministry. Quietly and confidently he would appeal for compassion, wisdom, and strength for each of the more than two hundred workers on his list. Wives of these workers were also included.

Then, with continuing confidence, McAlister prayed for every major Christian leader even vaguely familiar to me. And there was more. He proceeded to intercede for every king, president, and political leader of the almost fifty Islamic and Communist nations. He did not pray for the leaders collectively, but for each separately, *by name*.

Although the intensity and confidence of this praying blessed me, I realized some believers are troubled by the thought of lengthy prayer lists. They feel they are shortchanging a need by simply "mentioning" the need briefly in prayer. Fortunately for my own prayer life, God directed my attention to a firm scriptural foundation for this very method of praying.

Not once, or twice, but four specific times the apostle Paul spoke of "making mention" of his fellow Christians in prayer. To Roman believers he wrote, "For God is my witness . . . that *without ceasing* I make mention of you always in my prayers" (Rom. 1:9; italics added).[12]

Surely the apostle did not spend his entire waking time praying for every specific need of each fellow Christian. Instead, he confidently lifted their names before God, fully trusting God to bless each of them.

After observing this confident praying of Jack McAlister, and discovering the scriptural basis for making mention in prayer, I was pleased to note that other prayer warriors have also witnessed great results through this type of praying. According to R. E. Speer in his book *Paul, the All-Round Man*, Bishop Handley Moule told of a dedicated Sunday school teacher who helped bring numerous students to a saving knowledge of Jesus. Following her death, the teacher's diary was found to contain, among other entries, these resolutions: "Resolved to pray for each scholar *by name*." "Resolved to wrestle in prayer for each scholar *by name*." "Resolved to wrestle for each *by name* and to expect an answer."[13]

Never be troubled by the fact that your knowledge of a need is somewhat limited. True, you should ask the Holy Spirit to aid you in prayer so that your praying is as meaningful and intelligent as possible. But don't become discouraged solely because your prayers lack the depth of understanding you desire. Above all, remember that all of prayer, especially intercession, is a learning experience. Professor Hallesby preached, "As far as my understanding of these things goes, intercessory prayer is the finest and most exacting kind of work that is possible for men to perform." This perceptive Bible teacher concluded, "Since intercessory prayer is such a fine and difficult art, it is not at all remarkable that it should require a long and rigorous period of training."[14] . . .

Lord, teach me to intercede!

INTERCESSION
THE SIXTH STEP IN WORLD-CHANGING PRAYER

1. Carefully prepare for intercession by developing a specific plan that includes special prayer for God's work around the world.

2. Summon a new compassion for these moments of intercession, so your praying will reach out to the lost with genuine concern.

3. Fill your intercession with the four key scriptural claims: Ask God to give more laborers to the harvest, to open doors for these workers, to bless them with fruit as the result of their efforts, and with finances to expand their work. *(See Appendix on page 155 for an explanation of these claims.)*

4. Always endeavor to include specific countries and their leaders during your time of intercession.

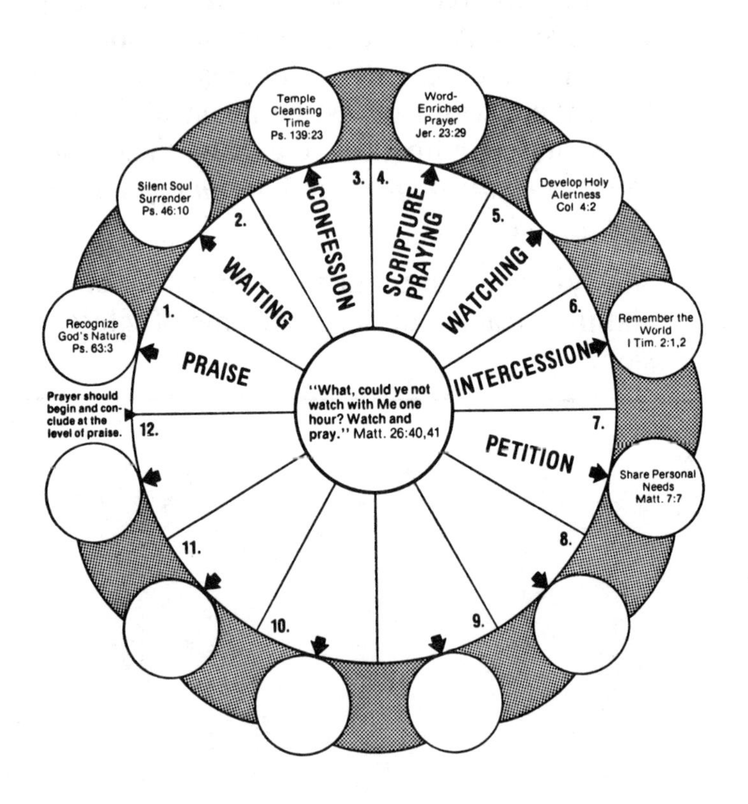
Temple Cleansing Time Ps. 139:23
Word-Enriched Prayer Jer. 23:29
Silent Soul Surrender Ps. 46:10
Develop Holy Alertness Col 4:2
Recognize God's Nature Ps. 63:3
Remember the World I Tim. 2:1,2
Share Personal Needs Matt. 7:7
Prayer should begin and conclude at the level of praise.
1. PRAISE
2. WAITING
3. CONFESSION
4. SCRIPTURE PRAYING
5. WATCHING
6. INTERCESSION
7. PETITION
8.
9.
10.
11.
12.
"What, could ye not watch with Me one hour? Watch and pray." Matt. 26:40,41

PETITION 7

THE ACT OF PERSONAL SUPPLICATION

"Asking is the symbol of our desire," related E. Stanley Jones. "Some things God will not give until we want them enough to ask."[1]

Petition is that aspect of prayer given over to asking God for specific personal things. To seek an unselfish spiritual or material blessing is not unscriptural. An obscure Old Testament passage illustrates. The passage is found amid a lengthy list of "begats." Commentaries declare that more than five hundred individual names are mentioned in the "begats" of I Chronicles. Yet, amid this somewhat exhaustive genealogy, God pauses to provide a brief look at one of these individuals, a man named Jabez.

The Bible says, "And Jabez was more honourable than his brethren: and his mother called his name Jabez, saying, Because I bare him with sorrow. And Jabez called on the God of Israel, saying, Oh that thou wouldest bless me indeed, and enlarge my coast . . . and that thou wouldest keep me from evil, that it may not grieve me! And God granted him that which he requested" (I Chron. 4:9, 10).

Nothing is mentioned about Jabez in Scripture other than that he sought a personal blessing of God and that it was granted. Such a testimony is not recorded of anyone else on this list of five hundred. Jabez was bold enough to entreat of God a blessing. God not only honored the request, but chose to use Jabez as an eternal example of how He longs to answer our sincere petitions.

THE RULE OF GOD

It is well said that "asking is the rule of the kingdom." The author of this phrase, Charles Spurgeon, adds, "It is a rule that will never be altered in anybody's case. If the royal and divine Son of God cannot be exempted from the rule of asking that He may have, you and I cannot expect to have the rule relaxed in our favor. God will bless Elijah and send rain on Israel, but Elijah must pray for it. If the chosen nation is to prosper, Samuel must plead for it. If the Jews are to be delivered, Daniel must intercede. God will bless Paul, and the nations shall be converted through him, but Paul must pray. Pray he did without ceasing; his epistles show that he expected nothing except by asking for it."[2]

In the same sense that our Christian experience is a "personal" experience, prayer, too, must become very personal. We must not hesitate to declare as Jabez, "Bless me, indeed!" When Jesus faced the blind man, He asked, "What wilt thou that I should do unto thee?" (Mark 10:51). Certainly our Lord knew the man's infirmity, but He wanted him to declare it.

This is petition. It is the confession of helplessness in a specific matter. As E. M. Bounds reminds us, "Prayer is the language of a man burdened with a sense of need. Not to pray is not only to declare that there is nothing needed, but to admit to a non-realization of that need."[3]

In a practical sense, petition is not the prayer of a man opening heaven's doors to release God's power. Rather, it is man opening his heart's door to receive power already appropriated by God. Expressed helplessness is the key to opening that door, thus giving God access to our need. *We must define the need.*

EXPRESSED DEPENDENCE

Because petition is an expression of helplessness, it should be present each day in the devotional hour. Jesus taught us to pray, "Give us *this day* our *daily* bread" (Matt. 6:11; italics added).

E. M. Blaiklock explains that the Greek word for "daily" in Matthew 6:11 occurs almost nowhere else in any extant Greek text. According to Blaiklock, it appears only in a papyrus document, and there without a particular context. From its derivation the word seems to mean "of the morrow" or "of the coming day." The writer concludes, "The translation could well be: 'Give us today the bread of tomorrow.' "[4]

No matter what the full interpretation of Matthew 6:11 is, it is evident we are to express our dependence on Christ for every need. Personal petition is our means of such expression. During this aspect of prayer we are able to do as Job did when he "ordered" his cause before the Lord (Job 23:3, 4). We go before God as an attorney with a carefully prepared argument upon which to base our case. We have a sincere, unselfish basis for our requests. Our motive is pure and our arguments well ordered. Spurgeon said, "The best prayers I have heard in our prayer meetings have been those which have been fullest of argument."[5]

Of course, to bring our arguments before God in prayer does not mean we are twisting God's arm in order to obtain a particular blessing. God desires that we present these "arguments" because we will learn the principles of prayer only by the actual practice of prayer. This may also be the reason God sometimes delays an answer to our prayers. He longs to answer our petitions, but He also desires to teach us much more about matters of true spiritual warfare. This prepares us for the really serious battles that lie ahead.

KEYS TO PETITION

When offering personal petitions there are several principles that should be remembered.

First, *a petition should be specific*. Prayer must never be so vague that within minutes of our praying we have forgotten why we prayed. Andrew Murray suggests, "Let your prayer be so definite that you can say as you leave the prayer closet, 'I know what I have asked from the Father, and I expect an answer.' "[6]

To forget our purpose for praying is a sure indication of an absence of desire. The greater the intensity of our desire for a blessing, the greater the difficulty to blot the desire from our mind. If we can't remember what we asked for after we asked for it, perhaps we really didn't need.

Next, *a petition should be complete*. Each request ought to be carefully thought through before it is presented. Avoid shallow petitions like, "Lord, bless me," or, "Lord, help the missionaries today." Instead, pray carefully through each request. It is spiritually healthy to take a need apart, piece by piece, during prayer. Analyze the problem from every angle and then express it as a petition. The more specific and complete the petition, the more faith is generated when we bring it to God.

Especially be careful that your petitions do not become sermons pointed heavenward. D. L. Moody said, "We hear a good deal of praying that is just exhorting God, and if you did not see the man's eyes closed, you would suppose that he was preaching. Much that is called prayer is not prayer at all. There needs to be more petition in our prayers."[7]

Third, *a petition should be sincere*. Personal attitudes are important in the matter of petition. It is true Jesus promises blessings to those who ask, seek, and knock, but we must strive to bring our claims before God with a right spirit. An unknown preacher expressed, "We are to ask with a beggar's humility, to seek with a servant's carefulness, and to knock with the confidence of a friend."

How sincere are we when we seek a specific blessing of God? Insincere praying is selfish praying. Andrew Murray cautioned, "One of the great reasons why prayer in the inner chamber does not bring more joy and blessing is that it is too selfish, and selfishness is the death of prayer."[8]

Finally, *a petition should be simple*. Although it was suggested earlier that we should analyze a problem, piece by piece, our manner of petition ought to be simple and informal. Long before an infant expresses its inner feelings in words, it cries out from within expressing needs in the simplest of terms. The offering of a petition should be complete enough to build faith, but simple in its expression. Eloquence is not necessary for effective praying.

A CHILD'S PETITION

Charles Spurgeon shared the account of a young lad who refused to doubt that God would answer even the simplest of petitions. At the start of the school term the local schoolmaster had repeatedly urged the children to be punctual. Hc promised to punish any child who was late.

Unfortunately, the parents of the boy made no effort to help the lad in these matters of discipline, and one day the child was considerably late for school. Just as his mother sent him through the door, the clock struck the very hour school was to begin.

A friend, standing nearby, saw the youngster running and heard his simple petition: "Dear God, do grant that I may be on time for school."

It occurred to the friend that for once the child had offered a prayer that was impossible for God to honor. Indeed, one cannot change the time. Still, he was curious to see what might result.

Interestingly, it also happened that this very morning the schoolmaster, in trying to open the schoolhouse door, turned the key the wrong way and jammed the bolt. Unable to force it loose, he sent for the local locksmith. Precisely the moment the locksmith fixed the bolt, the lad arrived.

Even the simplest petition, when offered in faith, opens doors to the miraculous. God is greatly pleased when we come before His presence ready to ask of Him those petitions that will honor His name . . .

Lord, teach me to ask!

PETITION
THE SEVENTH STEP IN WORLD-CHANGING PRAYER

1. Begin your petition by asking the Holy Spirit to help you claim only those desires that will bring special honor to the Lord.

2. Make a mental list of specific needs you have for that very day and offer each need to God.

3. Enlarge a petition carefully, taking time to explain to God why you desire an answer for that request.

4. Frequently examine your motives for claiming a petition. Be certain they are pure in the sight of God.

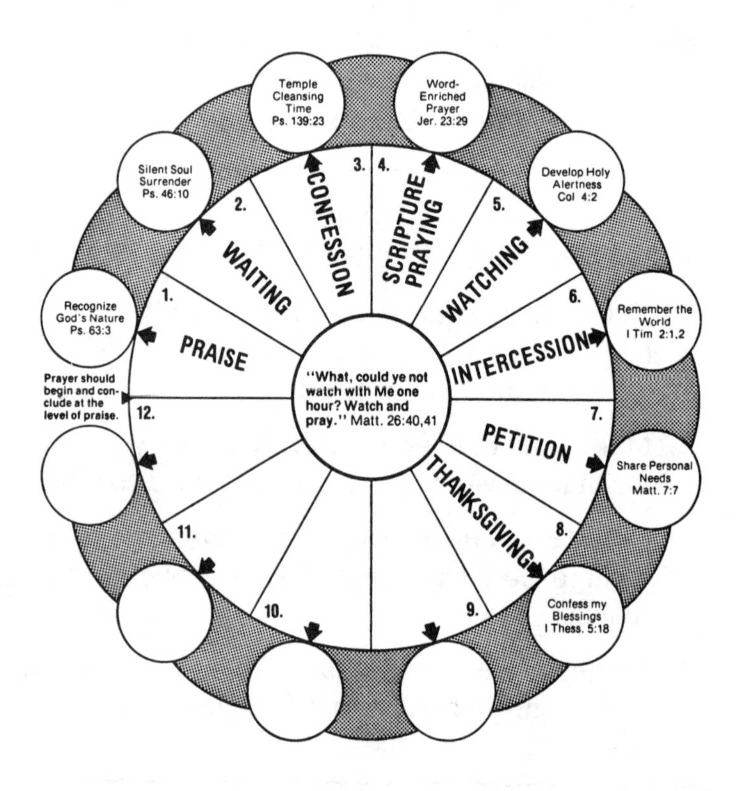
Temple
Cleansing
Time
Ps. 139:23
Word-
Enriched
Prayer
Jer. 23:29
Silent Soul
Surrender
Ps. 46:10
Develop Holy
Alertness
Col 4:2
Recognize
God's Nature
Ps. 63:3
Remember the
World
I Tim 2:1,2
Share Personal
Needs
Matt. 7:7
Confess my
Blessings
I Thess. 5:18
Prayer should
begin and conclude at the
level of praise.
1. PRAISE
2. WAITING
3. CONFESSION
4. SCRIPTURE PRAYING
5. WATCHING
6. INTERCESSION
7. PETITION
8. THANKSGIVING
9.
10.
11.
12.
"What, could ye not
watch with Me one
hour? Watch and
pray." Matt. 26:40,41

THANKSGIVING 8

THE ACT OF EXPRESSED APPRECIATION

Although closely related to praise, thanksgiving itself is an important element that deserves careful attention during prayer. Basically, thanksgiving is the act of expressing specific gratitude to God for blessings He has bestowed upon us. These expressions may be mental or vocal.

Thanksgiving differs from praise in that praise focuses on *who* God is, whereas thanksgiving focuses on *what* God has specifically done *for us*. As one writer explains, "When we give thanks we give God the glory for what He has done for us; and when we worship or give praise, we give God glory for what He is in Himself."[1]

THE ATTITUDE OF THANKSGIVING

The precise position for thanksgiving on our prayer schedule may vary. I have chosen to place it toward the end of my devotional hour as an expression of appreciation to God following my time of petition. Thanksgiving helps me focus on God's faithfulness.

However, a look at Scripture seems to suggest thanksgiving could be sprinkled throughout our praying. Paul told the Colossians, "As ye have therefore received Christ Jesus the Lord, so walk ye in him: Rooted and built up in him, and stablished in the faith, as ye have been taught, abounding therein with thanksgiving" (Col. 2:6, 7). Later, he added, "Devote yourselves to prayer, keeping alert in it with an attitude of thanksgiving" (Col. 4:2; NASB).

Paul had a similar message for the church at Philippi. He instructed these believers: "Be careful for nothing; but in every thing by prayer and supplication with thanksgiving let your requests be made known unto God" (Phil. 4:6). According to Paul, all prayers should be filled with a "spirit of thanksgiving."

A CONFESSION OF BLESSINGS

Thanksgiving might well be labeled "a confession of blessings." It is during this aspect of prayer that we recognize all of life's blessings and confess them before God. This is essential to prayer because it draws the heart to God, keeping it entirely centered on Him. Like praise, thanksgiving takes the believer's attention from self and places it where it must be centered to make prayer effective.

Thanksgiving is also important because it is the prayer warrior's special gift to God for His kindnesses. What else can we possibly give God other than praise and thanksgiving? The psalmist declared, "What shall I render unto the Lord for all his benefits toward me?'' (Ps. 116:12). Later, he answers, "I will offer to thee the sacrifice of thanksgiving, and will call upon the name of the Lord'' (Ps. 116:17).

In looking at the life of Christ it is evident that a spirit of thanksgiving was important to Him. In the Gospels we frequently see our Lord expressing gratitude. Describing the resurrection of Lazarus, the apostle John records, "Then they took away the stone from the place where the dead was laid. And Jesus lifted up his eyes, and said, Father, *I thank thee* that thou hast heard me'' (John 11:41; italics added). Note Mark's description of Jesus feeding the multitude: "And he took the seven loaves, *and gave thanks*'' (Mark 8:6; italics added).

On yet another occasion, after sharing important teaching with His disciples, Jesus paused to pray, "*I thank thee, O Father*, Lord of heaven and earth, because thou hast hid these things from the wise and the prudent, and hast revealed them unto babes'' (Matt. 11:25; italics added). Surely that which was so important to our Savior should be considered essential to our devotional habit.

THANK OFFERINGS

A wandering mind normally hinders effective praying, but if properly channeled it actually can prove helpful during your time of thanksgiving. Allow your mind to wander through the previous day's activities. This will lead you to many points of concentration for specific thanksgiving.

Also, become aware of all that exists around

you. What do you see worthy of thanksgiving? In the same sense that we need to "watch" in prayer, or become alert to certain needs, we need to "watch" in thanksgiving. Become more aware of those specific things Jesus has done for you. Then verbalize these blessings.

Remember, thanksgiving begins when you mentally catalog the specific things God has done for you so you can put these blessings into words.

Following is a brief list of several "thank offerings" you might give God during your devotional hour:

First, *confess spiritual blessings*. What specific spiritual blessings has God given you recently? Perhaps He has bestowed a special blessing during this very devotional hour that is worthy of a word of appreciation. Take time during prayer to offer these blessings back to God in the form of vocal thanksgiving.

Second, *confess material blessings*. A moment should be given to consider the many material blessings God has generously provided. Be very specific, remembering even the little things. Thank Him for the chair in which you sit, or the warmth of the room. The more specific thanksgiving becomes, the more meaningful a role it will play in your devotional life.

Third, *confess physical blessings*. We should thank God specifically for good health. If we are free of pain or sickness, it is a blessing worthy of thanksgiving. If we are experiencing pain in one leg, we can express appreciation for strength in the other. We may thank God for good eyesight, or for the ability to hear. Each heartbeat or breath of air can be reason for thanksgiving. Like praise, thanksgiving is truly limitless.

Finally, *confess external blessings*. Some blessings are not directly related to us, but still they deserve an expression of appreciation. These might be termed external blessings. For example, thank God for kindnesses rendered to your friends, community, or nation. Above all, thank Him for His blessings on the work of evangelism around the world.

But especially strive to escape the tendency of generalized thanksgiving. Rather than declaring, "God, I thank you for blessing our church service last Sunday," magnify your thanksgiving. Let it include specific reasons why you are thankful.

THANKS FOR PAST BLESSINGS

An especially meaningful goal of thanksgiving is to thank God each day for at least one blessing you cannot remember thanking Him for previously. This will require a moment of quiet contemplation concerning God's goodness.

In seeking a point of focus for this type of thanksgiving, you may wish to look at past experiences. Perhaps God granted you specific favor or some particular blessing decades ago for which you never expressed thanks.

Do you recall ever thanking God specifically for the person who first told you about Jesus? Have you thanked God for your first Bible, or for the Sunday school teachers who encouraged you in your early years of faith?

Thanksgiving is further described as limitless by Paul's admonition to Ephesian believers, "Be filled with the Spirit . . . Giving thanks always for all things unto God" (Eph. 5:18, 20). To the Thessalonians Paul adds, "In every thing give thanks: for this is the will of God in Christ Jesus concerning you" (I Thess. 5:18). John Wesley wrote in his journal that it was because of this attitude that he was able to thank God that he broke only his arm in an accident, and not his head.

In each situation of life, no matter the difficulty it presents, focus for thanksgiving can be discovered. Even the death of a loved one reminds us of the knowledge of eternal life, something for which we are truly thankful.

Let us carefully seek to develop this ministry of expressing appreciation to God during prayer. For every specific prayer of petition may we share two or three specific expressions of thanksgiving. God grant that we never cease to be grateful for His bountiful provisions. . .

Lord, teach me to give thanks.

THANKSGIVING
THE EIGHTH STEP IN WORLD-CHANGING PRAYER

1. Begin thanksgiving by thinking about all God has given you in recent days.

2. Use these moments of reflection as a basis for offering specific thanksgiving for spiritual, material, physical, and external blessings.

3. Frequently thank God "in advance" for blessings you expect Him to bestow on you in the future.
4. Thank God for at least one particular blessing you have not thanked Him for previously.

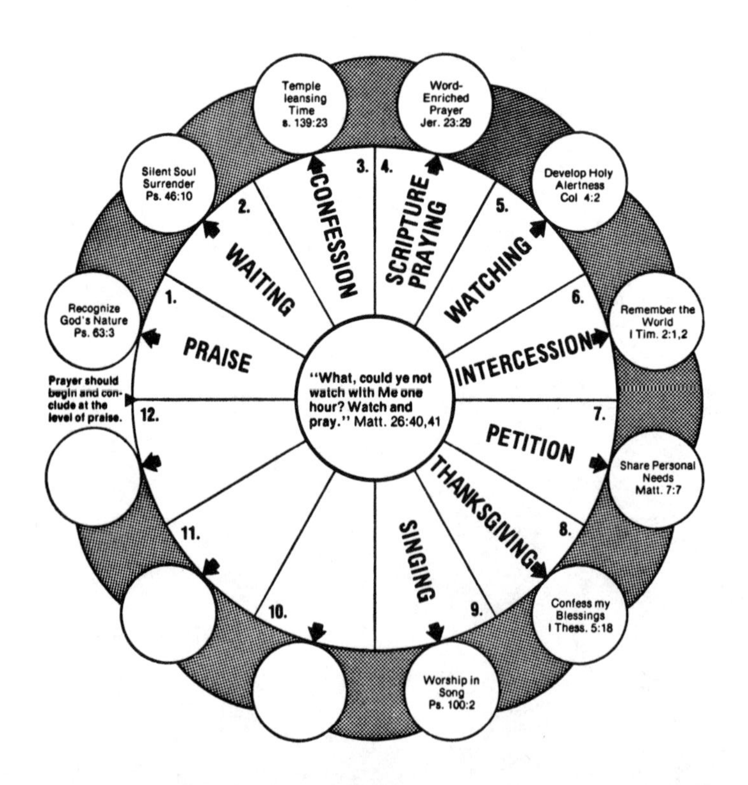
Temple
leansing
Time
s. 139:23
Word-
Enriched
Prayer
Jer. 23:29
Silent Soul
Surrender
Ps. 46:10
Develop Holy
Alertness
Col 4:2
Recognize
God's Nature
Ps. 63:3
Remember the
World
I Tim. 2:1,2
Prayer should
begin and con-
clude at the
level of praise.
Share Personal
Needs
Matt. 7:7
Confess my
Blessings
I Thess. 5:18
Worship in
Song
Ps. 100:2
1. PRAISE
2. WAITING
3. CONFESSION
4. SCRIPTURE PRAYING
5. WATCHING
6. INTERCESSION
7. PETITION
8. THANKSGIVING
9. SINGING
10.
11.
12.
"What, could ye not watch with Me one hour? Watch and pray." Matt. 26:40,41

SINGING 9

THE ACT OF MELODIC WORSHIP

Words of adoration combined with a melody from the heart lead to praise in its most beautiful form. Martin Luther expressed it thus, "The gift of language combined with the gift of song was given to man that he should proclaim the Word of God through music."

Here we discover one of the most neglected aspects of personal worship—singing alone in God's presence. The psalmist enjoined, "Serve the Lord with gladness: come before his presence with singing" (Ps. 100:2).

While many believers freely participate in congregational singing, few have discovered the joy of singing songs unto the Lord *during* prayer. The author was amazed to discover that only a few books on prayer from a collection exceeding 150 even mentioned singing, and then only in passing. Yet, no fewer than forty-one of the Psalms specifically refer to "singing praises" unto the Lord. In several of these Psalms the student of prayer can find three or four separate injunctions to "sing." Surely there must be power in giving a personal "song offering" to the Lord in private prayer.

The godly missionary, Mary Slosser, who worked with great diligence among the Chinese, spoke of the importance of music in her prayer life. She explained, "I sing the doxology and dismiss the devil!" Concerning the power of song, Amy Carmichael adds, "I believe truly that Satan cannot endure it and so slips out of the room—more or less!—when there is a true song. Prayer rises more easily, more spontaneously, after one has let those wings, words, and music, carry one out of oneself into that upper air."[1]

What should we sing during prayer? On two different occasions Paul spoke of "making melody" in our hearts unto the Lord with "spiritual songs" (Eph. 5:19; Col. 3:16). When Paul spoke of a spiritual song he was speaking of a song that originated in the believer's heart. The word *spiritual*, as used in these verses, means "inspired by the Spirit." Paul could not have been referring to the use of hymnbooks in public or private worship since hymnbooks were centuries away from publication when he wrote these words. Undoubtedly, hand-copied Psalters were extremely scarce.

We recall also that Paul and Silas "sang praises" unto God while they were in prison (Acts 16:25). Surely there were no hymnbooks present in this damp cell. Their songs of praise were most certainly based on melodies created in their hearts. To these melodies were added personal words of praise.

THE WEAPON OF SONG

Singing unto the Lord during prayer is more than merely a fresh and exciting way to minister unto the Lord. It is actually a weapon of warfare that adds immense power to our praying. Note an Old Testament passage that supports this claim:

In II Chronicles 20 we read that Moab, Ammon, and the inhabitants of Mount Seir conspired to wage war on King Jehoshaphat of Judah. Upon hearing of the conspiracy, Jehoshaphat called the people of Judah to repentance. From across the nation they gathered for a time of prayer and fasting.

Through Jahaziel the prophet, God promised Jehoshaphat that Judah would see victory in battle. Full details of the battle are described in verses 20-22: "And they rose early in the morning, and went forth into the wilderness of Tekoa: and as they went forth, Jehoshaphat stood and said, Hear me, O Judah, and ye inhabitants of Jerusalem; Believe in the Lord your God, so shall ye be established; believe his prophets, so shall ye prosper. And when he had consulted with the people, he appointed singers unto the Lord, and that should praise the beauty of holiness, as they went out before the army, and to say, Praise the Lord; for his mercy endureth for ever. *And when they began to sing and to praise*, the Lord set ambushments against the children of Ammon, Moab, and mount Seir, which were come against Judah; and they were smitten" (italics added).

Later, the narrative relates that Judah's troops arrived at the front lines of battle only to discover the enemy was already defeated. God may have sent angelic hosts to fight the battle since there is no evidence of other troops helping Judah win the campaign.

Key to this account are the words of verse 22, "And when they began to sing and to praise, the Lord set ambushments. . . ." The victory *began* and *ended* with musical worship. So great was the blessing of victory that Scripture declares, "And when Jehoshaphat and his people came to take away the spoil of them, they found among them in abundance both riches . . . and precious jewels . . . *more than they could carry away*" (II Chron. 20:25; italics added).

When the campaign was fully concluded Jehoshaphat and the people of Judah named the valley *Berachah*, which means "blessing." Indeed, the ministry of song when properly used in the devotional habit is a weapon that always leads to blessing.

THEMES FOR SONG

How do we make singing unto the Lord practical in the daily devotional habit? Of course, the singing of well-known hymns, from memory or with the aid of a hymnbook, is a possibility. However, this may tend to add unwanted form to this aspect of prayer, in the same sense that reading someone else's prayers often drains life from our praying.

Rather, ask the Holy Spirit to create "new" melodies within your heart. With these melodies you will be able to sing songs based on a variety of themes.

The Bible lists at least six distinct themes that might be used in ministering unto the Lord with song. You need not sing songs based on all of these themes during every prayer time, although the list does reveal the vast scriptural foundation for such worship.

SONGS OF PRAISE

First, *sing praises unto the Lord*. Such was the worship of Paul and Silas in jail (Acts 16). The psalmist declared, "Praise the Lord; for the Lord is good: *sing praises unto his name*; for it is pleasant" (Ps. 135:3; italics added). During this singing phase of prayer, you may wish to *sing* praises to God instead of speaking them. As suggested, allow the melody to flow from your heart. Do not be concerned if your voice seems somewhat unpleasant.

On a number of occasions when my daughters were younger, they would sing songs to their father. Often these songs were actually composed *while* they were being sung. Equally often, the presentation was slightly off key. Yet, I was always delighted when they came to me with their special songs. Each song was special because of the sincerity of heart behind it, and because the singers were objects of their father's affection.

So it is with our "spiritual" singing. To sing praises unto the Lord brings great joy to God's heart because of His intense love for us.

SONGS OF POWER AND MERCY

Second, *sing of God's power and mercy*. "But I will sing of thy power," declared the psalmist.

"Yea, I will sing aloud of thy mercy in the morning: for thou hast been my defense and refuge in the day of my trouble" (Ps. 59:16). Note the psalmist not only speaks of singing, but of singing *aloud*. The thought is that our song is not to be confined only to the heart. It is to be a vocal praising of God with melody.

To sing of God's *power* is to put into song all that God has accomplished with His power. To sing of His *mercy* is to sing of His faithfulness and justice. It is to sing the attributes of His divine nature. Indeed, all that God is can become a theme for a personal "spiritual" song.

SONGS OF THANKSGIVING

Third, *sing a song of thanksgiving*. Look again at the words of the psalmist: "Sing unto the Lord *with thanksgiving*; sing praise upon the harp unto our God" (Ps. 147:7; italics added). As suggested in earlier chapters, praise is to recognize God for who He is. Thanksgiving, on the other hand, is to recognize God for what He has done for us. In singing "with thanksgiving" we create a song based on those specific gifts or blessings God has provided.

Sadly, few believers have ever experienced the joy of thanking God in song for little things like food and raiment. Anything we can thank God for verbally, we can thank God for musically.

Do not hesitate to combine the aspects of thanksgiving and singing periodically during your devotional hour. Sing specific "thank-you's" to the Lord for His generous gifts.

SONGS OF GOD'S NAME

Fourth, *sing the name of God*. To sing the name of the Lord in a song is scriptural. The psalmist testified, "I will praise the name of God with a song, and will magnify him with thanksgiving" (Ps. 69:30).

As suggested in our earlier discussion of praise, the "name" of the Lord in the Old Testament may be a direct reference to the name God took upon Himself when coming to earth in the form of His Son. The Bible says, "God was in Christ" when He reconciled the world (II Cor. 5:19). This makes it possible to praise the name of the Lord Jesus Christ in song. All that Jesus is or did can become the theme of our singing during our time alone in God's presence.

SONGS OF GOD'S WORD

Fifth, *sing God's Word*. The psalmist speaks once again of the power of song: "Thy statutes have been my songs in the house of my pilgrimage" (Ps. 119:54). To put melody to God's Word is another excellent way to worship God in song. We know that Christians of the early church were admonished to sing Scripture. James advised, "Is any among you afflicted? let him pray. Is any merry? let him sing psalms" (James 5:13). Surely this admonition does not apply only to singing in a gathering of believers. A person can be afflicted alone as well as with the congregation. If he is alone and afflicted, he is to pray. Similarly, if *any* (note the emphasis on the singular) *is merry, let him sing*. Any believer who is happy in Christ has at least one theme for a personal song during prayer. He can express his joy in a spiritual song.

SONGS OF MY HEART

Finally, *sing a new song*. The psalmist shared, "I will sing a new song unto thee, O God: upon a psaltery and an instrument of ten strings will I sing praises unto thee" (Ps. 144:9).

"New" refers to something fresh. "A new song" means "my own song," not someone else's. It refers to a song from my heart that I have never sung before. Yesterday's song does not qualify under this category of singing. The theme may be similar but the song will be new. Of course, all the various themes for singing may fall under this category if we have never sung the melody or words previously. Even the singing of a scripture in a new way can be a "new song" from my heart.

SING AMONG THE NATIONS

Only the imagination can limit our singing "new songs" unto the Lord. A friend shared with me how God led her to use a map of the world during her time of singing. For more than two hours she sang through a listing of all 210 countries on the map. Her song was simple. She sang of God's glory flowing into each nation. The melody was created "new" in her heart.[2]

She explained this was one of the most beautiful times of worship that she remembers. The song was one she had never sung before. Perhaps, by the Holy Spirit, she was fulfilling the expression of the psalmist, "I will sing unto thee among the nations'' (Ps. 57:9). Through singing her special song this friend experienced a new joy in her devotional life.

Indeed, singing unto the Lord is especially important because it trains us in many new areas of worship. Ultimately, worship will be our *eternal purpose* in heaven, and singing will be a great part of this eternal purpose. In fact, note the description Isaiah gives of believers entering Zion, ''Therefore the redeemed of the Lord shall return, and come with singing unto Zion; and everlasting joy shall be upon their head: they shall obtain gladness and joy; and sorrow and mourning shall flee away'' (Isa. 51:11).

If singing is to play so vital a role in heaven's worship, surely it would do the believer well to ''practice up'' for the day we unite together in heavenly song to minister unto the Lord in our eternal Zion . . .

Lord, teach me to sing!

SINGING
THE NINTH STEP IN WORLD-CHANGING PRAYER

1. Pause in your devotional hour to sing a specific song unto the Lord.

2. Select a special theme for your song, such as praise, thanksgiving, or a favorite passage of Scripture.

3. Ask the Holy Spirit to create an original melody in your heart so your song is truly ''a new song.''

4. Don't hesitate to sing "songs of thanksgiving" for specific blessings or victories you believe God will give you in the days ahead.

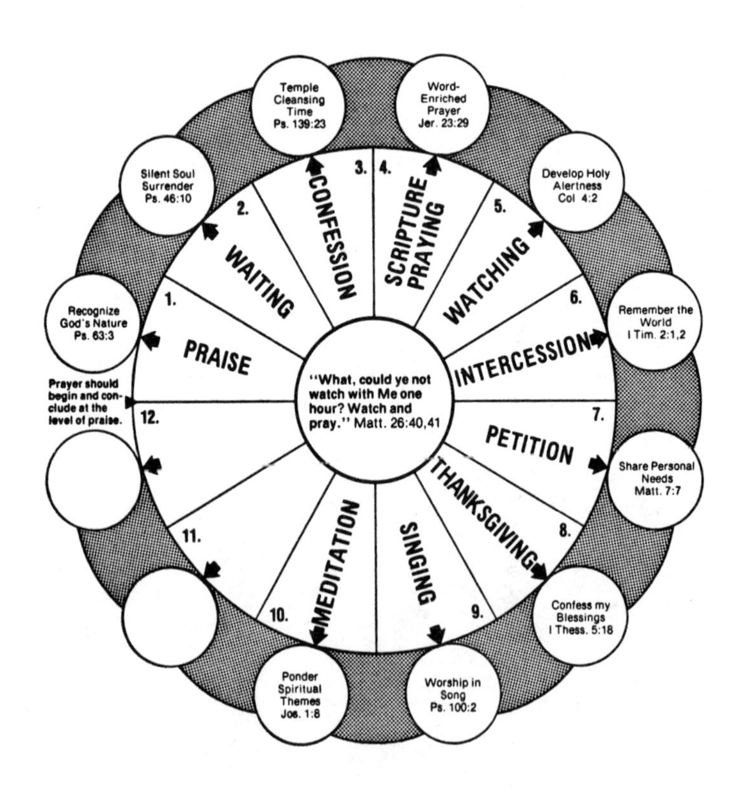
Temple
Cleansing
Time
Ps. 139:23
Word-
Enriched
Prayer
Jer. 23:29
Silent Soul
Surrender
Ps. 46:10
Develop Holy
Alertness
Col 4:2
Recognize
God's Nature
Ps. 63:3
Remember the
World
I Tim. 2:1,2
Prayer should
begin and con-
clude at the
level of praise.
Share Personal
Needs
Matt. 7:7
Confess my
Blessings
I Thess. 5:18
Ponder
Spiritual
Themes
Jos. 1:8
Worship in
Song
Ps. 100:2
1. PRAISE
2. WAITING
3. CONFESSION
4. SCRIPTURE PRAYING
5. WATCHING
6. INTERCESSION
7. PETITION
8. THANKSGIVING
9. SINGING
10. MEDITATION
11.
12.
"What, could ye not
watch with Me one
hour? Watch and
pray." Matt. 26:40,41

MEDITATION 10

THE ACT OF SPIRITUAL EVALUATION

The devotional hour is greatly strengthened when the believer takes time to ponder a spiritual theme in reference to God. This act of spiritual evaluation, called meditation, helps the believer discover how to apply all the truths God has revealed during prayer.

A century ago the wife of a Presbyterian minister, Bridgid E. Herman, wrote this meaningful description of meditation, "Meditation is a spiritual act as definite and purposeful as a business engagement, a pledge of friendship, or a solemn undertaking. In it we apply spiritual facts and principles to ourselves as individuals and as citizens of the Kingdom of God. Having pondered them, we seek to appropriate their value by an outgoing of our loving desires toward God, and by exercising our will in the formation of resolutions. No meditation is really valid unless it leaves us with something to which we can return during the day's business and find it helpful there."[1]

THE GIFT OF ATTENTION

While studying scores of books on prayer I was greatly disappointed to discover that almost as little is said about meditation as singing, although both aspects are thoroughly scriptural.

The Old Testament definition for the word *meditation* is "to mutter" or "to muse." This suggests a silent inner study of some spiritual matter. This is the essence of the meaning of "meditate" in Joshua 1:8: "This book of the law shall not depart out of thy mouth; but thou shalt meditate therein day and night, that thou mayest observe to do according to all that is written therein: for then thou shalt make thy way prosperous, and then thou shalt have good success." Here, the Hebrew word for "mediate" (*hagah*) means "to mutter upon."

Another Hebrew expression translated "meditate" is *sicah*, which means "to bow down." The psalmist used this word when declaring, "I will meditate in thy precepts, and have respect unto thy ways" (Ps. 119:15). The thought is that we render special "mental attention" by bowing down in respect of God's Word.

In the New Testament *meditation* is emphasized in Paul's admonition to Timothy, "Meditate upon these things; give thyself wholly to them; that thy profiting may appear to all" (I Tim. 4:15). In this verse the Greek word for "meditate," *meletao*, means "to be careful," or "to show care" in a matter. This suggests meditation is more than merely thinking good thoughts. It is the giving of attention to how we might specifically apply these ponderings after the devotional hour has ended.

THE VALUE OF MEDITATION

Scriptural meditation provides the believer with spiritual benefits received through no other means. Personal inner peace is but one of these benefits. The Bible promises, "Thou wilt keep him in perfect peace, whose mind is stayed on thee" (Isa. 26:3). Enlarging on this verse, E. M. Blaiklock explains, "Here the Hebrew is actually saying, 'peace, peace,' thus making up for its deficiency in adjectives by the repetition of the noun. It might well have been translated literally—'in peace, in peace, I repeat . . .' "[2]

Throughout Scripture frequent attention is given to this matter of meditation: "How precious also are thy thoughts unto me, O God! how great is the sum of them! If I should count them, they are more in number than the sand: when I awake, I am still with thee" (Ps. 139:17, 18).

Earlier the psalmist declared, "My meditation of him shall be sweet: I will be glad in the Lord" (Ps. 104:34). He also declared, "In the multitude of my thoughts within me thy comforts delight my soul" (Ps. 94:19).

The person who spends time thinking thoughts of God will find tremendous depth and understanding that will touch all areas of his life. It is, after all, in meditation that we rise above ourselves (and the world) for the purpose of seeing God's plan in proper perspective. Only from such a vantage point can we see the spiritual realm clearly. Bridgid E. Herman reminds us, "Self-regard is the slum of the soul, and the supreme function of meditation is to lift us out of its squalor into the clear, pure air of the spiritual world."[3]

Meditation is equally meaningful because it allows the believer to cultivate a harvest of fresh creative thoughts. As Oliver Wendell Holmes explained, "A man's mind stretched with a new idea can never go back to its original dimensions."

THE INTERIOR OF PRAYER

"To think well," Thomas Traherne said, "is to serve God in the interior court." Meditating with a solidly biblical foundation is the best thinking in which man can engage.

Bridgid Herman further explains, "The difference between the saints of old and ourselves is not one of inherent nature: it is simply that they took time to ponder God, to gaze upon Him in an act of supreme attention in which intelligent will and desire concurred in perfect harmony, while we are too greatly overrun with small activities and occupations to find leisure for such pondering."[4]

The author also advises, "To come to our own case. Behind all true Christian service—service, that is, springing from a sense of Divine vocation and sustained by a supernatural motive—lies the interior life of prayer. And if that prayer life, and therefore the service that springs from it, is feeble and ineffective, it is largely because it lacks the background of genuine honest thinking."[5]

Scripture provides the believer with a meaningful list of practical themes upon which to focus our meditation. Like other suggestions shared in these chapters, it is not necessary to implement all of these types of meditation during every devotional hour. However, the list is practical because it is scriptural. For a well-balanced devotional hour select at least one aspect each day as a focus for your meditation.

FOCUS ON GOD HIMSELF

First, *focus meditation on God Himself.* Speaking of meditation the psalmist declared, "My soul, wait thou only upon God; for my expectation is from him" (Ps. 62:5).

Earlier it was suggested that the believer take time to *wait* in prayer for the purpose of focusing love entirely upon God. Now, we return in prayer to enlarge that focus. At first glance it may appear that waiting and meditation overlap in their functions. However, *waiting* is an act of loving, while *meditation* is an act of thinking.

During this particular type of meditation ponder the nature of God with full intensity. Carefully probe everything you know about your heavenly Father, constantly asking the Holy Spirit to illuminate and stretch your thinking.

In the course of this type of meditation you will often find yourself asking many questions. What do I really believe about God? What does the Bible say about God that touches my life? How would I define my concept of God? What great attributes of God can I better appropriate in my daily life? As you answer these and other questions about God, your understanding of His nature and purpose increases dramatically, as does your confidence in His Word.

FOCUS ON GOD'S WORD

Second, *focus meditation on God's Word*. The first two verses of the Psalms lead us to this focus of meditation: "Blessed is the man that walketh not in the counsel of the ungodly, nor standeth in the way of sinners, nor sitteth in the seat of the scornful. But his delight is in the law of the Lord; and in his law doth he meditate day and night" (Ps. 1:1, 2).

Because meditation is the mental evaluation of any spiritual theme, the Bible becomes a tremendous source for meditation. Scripture is filled with thousands of brief phrases that inspire enormous power. Altogether, nearly thirty thousand promises await us in Scripture. Each promise is a focus for meditation. F. W. Faber expressed that one commonplace truth, seemingly tame and trivial to the beginner of meditation, will suffice a saint for hours of contemplation.

Speaking of the power of God's Word in meditation, Bridgid Herman enlarges, "The Book has a voice of its own—a message and a power that remain untouched by the passage of time. To listen to that voice and test that power for oneself is well worth all the labor and discipline involved."[6]

FOCUS ON GOD'S WORKS

Third, *focus meditation on the works of God*. The psalmist expressed, "I will meditate also of all thy work, and talk of thy doings" (Ps. 77:12). Here is another form of meditation that proves limitless. Every created aspect of the universe can become a focal point for effective meditation. But always, these ponderings must be in reference to God. We do not meditate on the beauty of a mountain stream simply because of the stream's beauty, but because of the stream's Creator.

An experience from the life of the sixteenth-century monk, Brother Lawrence, illustrates. "He told me," said an intimate friend, "that in the winter, seeing a tree stripped of its leaves, and considering that within a little time the leaves would be renewed and after that the flowers and fruit appear, he received a high view of the Providence and power of God which has never since been effaced from his soul. This view had set him perfectly loose from the world, and kindled in him such a love for God that he could not tell whether it had increased in above forty years that he had lived since."[7]

FOCUS ON PAST VICTORIES

Fourth, *focus meditation on past victories*. Here is a seldom-mentioned aspect of meditation that will provide an oasis of delight for your devotional hour. The psalmist shared succinctly, "I remember the days of old" (Ps. 143:5).

In times of distress and discouragement much spiritual relief can be found in looking at the many blessings God has given us in previous days.

Consider Jeremiah's difficult experiences as recorded in Lamentations. Indeed, the very word *lamentation* means brokenness, pain, or grief. Of the five painful chapters in the book, perhaps the most distressing is chapter 3. Here the prophet speaks of God pulling him in pieces and of all his bones being broken. A particularly graphic verse reads, "He hath also broken my teeth with gravel stones, he hath covered me with ashes" (Lam. 3:16).

But notice the pause in the narrative that transforms Jeremiah's desert experience into a garden of blessings. In the midst of his complaints the prophet declares, "*This I recall to my mind*, therefore have I hope. It is of the Lord's mercies that we are not consumed, because his compassions fail not. They are new every morning; great is thy faithfulness" (Lam. 3:21-23; italics added).

Jeremiah discovered the secret of retrospective meditation. "This I recall," the prophet wrote during his battle with depression. When he had reached the point of total defeat he reflected on the past faithfulness of God. Because of this, Jeremiah was able to testify, "Great is thy faithfulness!"

We can do little during prayer that will add more beauty and freshness to our daily experience than will a moment sanctified to ponder past victories in Jesus. Sometimes a former experience will come alive with such reality that we almost relive the experience. The end result is a new confidence to face even the most difficult future.

FOCUS ON POSITIVE THOUGHTS

Finally, *focus meditation on positive thoughts*. Paul told his Philippian friends, "Finally, brethren, whatsoever things are true, whatsoever things are honest, whatsoever things are just, whatsoever things are pure, whatsoever things are lovely, whatsoever things are of good report; if there be any virtue, and if there be any praise, think on these things'' (Phil. 4:8).

Anything worthy of praise is worthy of meditation. For example, some are lovers of little children. They may see the glory of God in a baby's eyes. Let them begin their time of meditation by setting a small child—perhaps the child they love best—in the midst of their many thoughts.

Any thought that meets the measure of Philippians 4:8 may serve as a focus for meditation. Teaching received in a Sunday school class or excerpts from a Christian periodical make excellent ''food for meditation.'' Even a distraction during prayer may serve as fuel to ignite the flames of meaningful meditation.

If, during your time of spiritual evaluation, a distressing thought repeatedly buffets the mind, make that thought a special point for meditation. With God's help, walk through the problem step by step until a solution is discovered. Soon, meditation will become a practical way to visualize new avenues for sound spiritual growth. . .

Lord, teach me to meditate!

MEDITATION
THE TENTH STEP IN WORLD-CHANGING PRAYER

1. Select a theme for your time of meditation,

applying full attention to that specific area of spiritual thought.

2. Allow your mind to wander within the framework of your chosen theme. Ponder all aspects of the theme carefully in reference to God.

3. Ask questions about this theme that might lead you into an even deeper mental study of the subject.

4. Bring Scripture into all phases of meditation. This strengthens your awareness that God's Word is the necessary foundation for all meaningful spiritual thought.

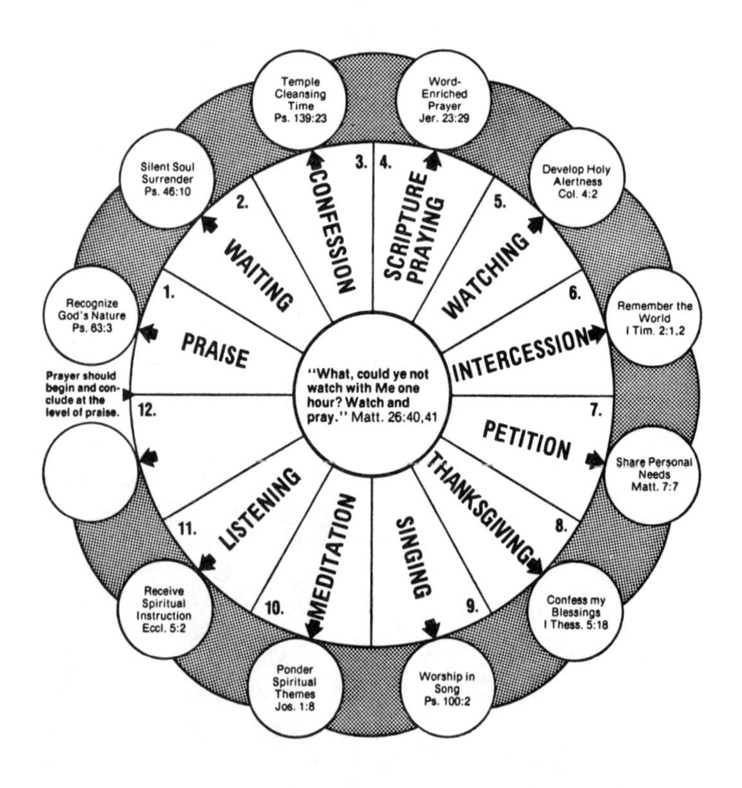
Temple Cleansing Time Ps. 139:23
Word-Enriched Prayer Jer. 23:29
Silent Soul Surrender Ps. 46:10
Develop Holy Alertness Col. 4:2
Recognize God's Nature Ps. 63:3
Remember the World I Tim. 2:1,2
Prayer should begin and conclude at the level of praise.
Share Personal Needs Matt. 7:7
Receive Spiritual Instruction Eccl. 5:2
Confess my Blessings I Thess. 5:18
Ponder Spiritual Themes Jos. 1:8
Worship in Song Ps. 100:2
1. PRAISE
2. WAITING
3. CONFESSION
4. SCRIPTURE PRAYING
5. WATCHING
6. INTERCESSION
7. PETITION
8. THANKSGIVING
9. SINGING
10. MEDITATION
11. LISTENING
12.
"What, could ye not watch with Me one hour? Watch and pray." Matt. 26:40,41

LISTENING 11

THE ACT OF MENTAL ABSORPTION

"Prayer is the soul's pilgrimage from self to God; and the most effectual remedy for self-love and self-absorption is the habit of humble listening."[1] These words, written almost a century ago, bring us to that element of prayer called *listening*. Many centuries earlier, Solomon penned, "Be not rash with thy mouth, and let not thine heart be hasty to utter any thing before God: for God is in heaven, and thou upon earth: therefore let thy words be few" (Eccles. 5:2).

In our study of the devotional hour it becomes evident that certain elements of prayer seem quite similar. Some might wonder how listening differs from either waiting or meditation.

As stated, waiting is to thoughtfully focus attention on God in a love relationship. It is a time of resting silently in God's love. On the other hand, meditation is a very careful exploration of a particular spiritual theme. Though closely related to both, listening is an element of prayer that stands alone. To listen in prayer is to mentally absorb divine instructions from God concerning specific matters for that day.

THE UNIVERSITY OF SILENCE

Best friends are always good listeners. If we truly desire to be friends with the Lord, we must learn the secret of listening. Not only did Jesus say He would enter the open door of a person's heart, but He promised to "sup" with that person as well (Rev. 3:20). To sup means to have fellowship. Much of our praying consists of *asking* instead of *supping*. Prayer often becomes one-sided and self-centered. Our prayer should be a conversation, one in which we listen as much as we speak.

Rosalind Rinker advises, "Instead of each of us making a prayer speech to Him, let's talk things over with Him, back and forth, including Him in it, as we do when we have a conversation."[2]

In a certain sense, listening is an actual ministry. Jesus ministered through listening. As Hope MacDonald explains in *Discovering How to Pray*, "Jesus listened to the cry of the blind man in the crowded noisy street. He listened to the story of Mary Magdalene when she came uninvited to a dinner party. He listened to the plea of the lepers when no one else would go near them. Jesus also listened to Nicodemus, who came to talk to Him late one night. Our Lord even listened to the thief hanging next to Him when He was dying on the cross."[3]

To be like Jesus is to be a listener, especially in prayer. The desire of Jesus was to do the will of

His Father. To find His Father's will Jesus spent whole nights listening.

We, too, must follow the example of Jesus and learn the art of listening in God's University of Silence. Paul told the Thessalonians, ". . .study to be quiet" (I Thess. 4:11). J. R. Miller explains, "Quietness in a man or a woman is a mark of strength. Noise is not eloquence. Loudness is not power. In all the departments of life, it is the quiet forces that effect most. Therefore, if we would be strong, we must learn to be quiet. A quiet heart will give a quiet life."[4]

THE GIFT OF LISTENING

To quiet our hearts for the specific purpose of receiving the day's guidance is an act of both dependence and faith. Listening implies confidence that God truly desires to speak to us. It also serves to move our devotional habit still further from an emphasis on self. Alan Redpath confesses, "Sometimes I wonder if our devotions are not the greatest barrier to spiritual growth, because they are so often just one-sided—it is our praying, it is our talking, our Bible study, our effort. How long is it since you sat down with great delight in His presence and were conscious that He was flooding your heart and speaking with you?"[5]

Only as we learn to hear the voice of the Father can we learn to dispel the voices of the world. As David Hubbard shares, "We are besieged by words in our society. Billboards blaze them into our minds as we go by. Headlines scream from the newspapers. Regular prayer builds into our lives those experiences of silence and concentration when the still, small voice of our Saviour can cut through life's howl and speak His words of peace and joy."[6]

Of necessity, much of prayer must take place in silence because much of prayer concerns the believer seeking divine guidance. Not only will God reveal how to pray effectively, if we will listen, but He will reveal how to *live* effectively.

Donald E. Demaray refers to this listening aspect of prayer as the law of the inner voice. He explains, "Individual guidance from God, received in prayer, is of vital importance. And how easy it is to listen to your own voice pressing you to do the selfish things! But it is the voice of God—the inner voice—we must learn to hear. The regular quiet time is the laboratory for developing that capacity to 'hear.' In the course of the busy day, too, we will hear His voice, but it is in the stillness of the prayer closet that the gift of listening is given and received."[7]

God, alone, knows the solution to every problem we will face. This listening phase of prayer allows the believer to tune in on God's solutions. Carefully guard your devotional hour from becoming a soliloquy of selfishness. We do not engage in prayer to tell God what to do. Our goal in prayer is to discover what God wants us to do so that He will be glorified.

THE PRICE OF SILENCE

God mightily used Moses because he was "very meek." More than this, as Scripture relates,

Moses was meek "above all the men which were upon the face of the earth" (Num. 12:3). Here was an old man, eighty years of age, and yet God chose Moses to lead an army of several million. Why? Because Moses was "meek," and the meek person is a listener.

John Anthony Hanne adds this insight: "There were men like Aaron who were eloquent preachers, men like Korah who were natural leaders, but only one man that recognized that he couldn't lead unless God first spoke to him and then spoke through him. Day after day for 40 years, dwelling upon what God had said, Moses listened and so spoke. Small wonder that through Moses came more of the Bible than any other man."[8]

Awesome power awaits the Christian who develops a listener's spirit. But because this spirit leads to such power the price to obtain it is high. Describing this spirit Peter relates, "A meek and quiet spirit . . . is in the sight of God of great price" (I Peter 3:4).

What is the price of silence, but the gift of self to God? It is to shut our eyes to what the world considers important and listen only to the Holy Spirit's call.

The price of silence is also time, much time given to the practice of listening. A praying saint wrote, "Prayer of positive, creative quality needs a background of silence, and until we are prepared to practice this silence, we need not hope to know the power of prayer."[9]

In an active world nothing seems more difficult

than "soul listening." The closer we come to the conclusion of our devotional hour the more our minds cry out for action. Let us listen carefully to be certain all of our plans for action originate in God.

THE WHISPERINGS OF GOD

Since the sounds of the world wreak havoc in our prayer, the secret of silence begins in conquering these undesirable sounds. F. W. Faber declares, "Whenever the sounds of the world die out in the soul, then we hear the whisperings of God. He is always whispering to us, only we don't always hear because of the noise, hurry and distractions which life causes as it rushes on."[10]

How will God speak during these times of stillness? Often His whisperings come in the form of a quiet impression on the heart. Elijah heard God speak with the "sound of a gentle whisper" (I Kings 19:12; LB). But His whispering was very specific, as God gave Elijah guidance for that particular moment in his experience.

On other occasions there is no inner voice to guide us, yet we sense God's presence gently leading. We know that to move in a certain direction will please God, and so we follow this quiet leading.

Most often God speaks through His Word. In fact, all forms of guidance must be measured by Scripture. Guidance contrary to God's Word is guidance originating from another source.

A PRACTICAL FUNCTION

During the listening aspect of prayer you may wish to keep a note tablet handy to record these impressions concerning your day. If a housewife asks God to help her plan the day's activities, she should be ready to jot down any divine promptings. The businessman who questions which important project demands the most careful attention for the day should ask God to give him specific wisdom for that specific day's responsibilities.

Always remember, listening serves a practical function. You are not merely listening for divine "niceties," but you are asking God to order your day. The value of having paper and pencil is that it displays faith. It says to God, "I believe you will truly speak to me, and I have come prepared to record your instructions."

True, there are dangers to be faced when we enter these deeper aspects of prayer. Much of prayer is an experiment in spiritual growth that involves both failure and success. But if we persevere, the blessings will transcend all disappointments. Our knowledge of God will increase and abound beyond measure. As Bridgid Herman so accurately states, "One hour of such listening may give us a deeper insight into the mysteries of human nature, and a surer instinct for Divine values, than a year's hard study or external intercourse with men."[11] . . .

Lord, teach me to listen!

LISTENING
THE ELEVENTH STEP IN WORLD-CHANGING PRAYER

1. In the "listening" time of prayer do not hesitate to ask God very specific questions about difficult problems or situations.
2. Search Scripture for specific answers to your questions. God most often speaks through His Word.
3. Mentally evaluate all circumstances that relate to a problem. Ask God to show you His plan through those circumstances.
4. Be prepared to write down any ideas God may share concerning the details of solving that particular problem.

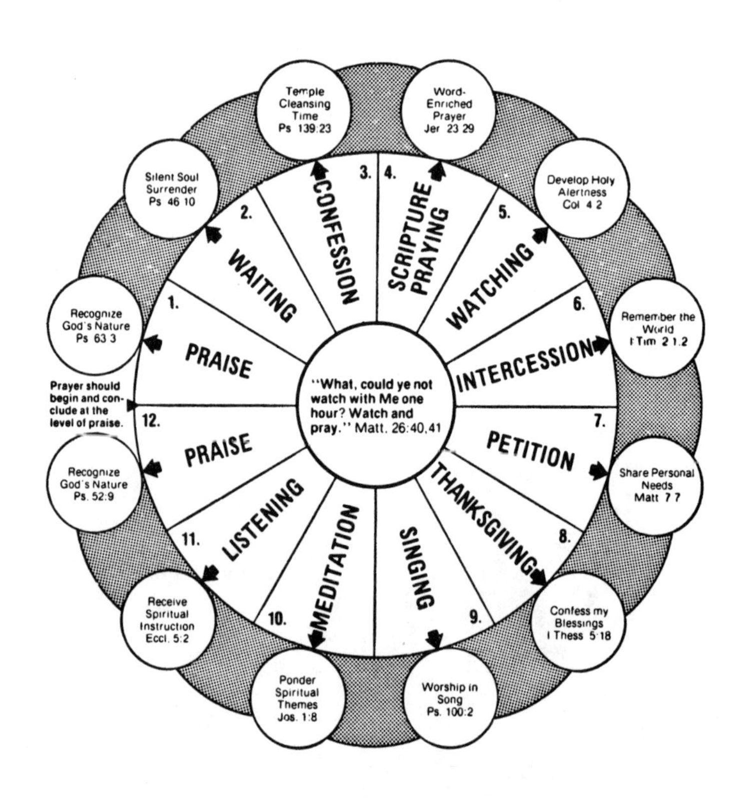

Temple Cleansing Time Ps 139:23
Word-Enriched Prayer Jer 23 29
Silent Soul Surrender Ps 46 10
Develop Holy Alertness Col 4 2
Recognize God's Nature Ps 63 3
Remember the World I Tim 2 1.2
Prayer should begin and conclude at the level of praise.
Recognize God's Nature Ps. 52:9
Share Personal Needs Matt 7 7
Receive Spiritual Instruction Eccl. 5:2
Confess my Blessings I Thess 5:18
Ponder Spiritual Themes Jos. 1:8
Worship in Song Ps. 100:2
1. PRAISE
2. WAITING
3. CONFESSION
4. SCRIPTURE PRAYING
5. WATCHING
6. INTERCESSION
7. PETITION
8. THANKSGIVING
9. SINGING
10. MEDITATION
11. LISTENING
12. PRAISE
"What, could ye not watch with Me one hour? Watch and pray." Matt. 26:40,41

PRAISE 12

THE ACT OF DIVINE MAGNIFICATION

Prayer has now come full circle, and we find ourselves again at praise. Worship should seal all praying. We began with an act of adoration, and we will end with an act of magnification.

When Mary received word she would give birth to the Son of God, divine worship exploded from her lips: "My soul doth magnify the Lord, and my spirit hath rejoiced in God my Saviour. . . . For he that is mighty hath done to me great things; and holy is his name" (Luke 1:46-49).

Jesus not only taught us to begin our prayer with praise—"Our Father which art in heaven, Hallowed be thy name," but He also taught us to end our praying with praise—"For thine is the kingdom, and the power, and the glory, for ever. Amen." (Matt. 6:9, 13).

PRAYER'S FINAL MOMENTS

As we come to these final moments of prayer, the soul pauses to contemplate the awesome wonder of God's being. We vocally magnify the nature of God. To magnify the Lord's name with praise is to put a spiritual magnifying glass to all that God is and declare these discoveries aloud.

The Greek word for magnify in Luke 1:46, *megaluno*, means "to make great." Nothing could provide so meaningful a conclusion to prayer as a statement of the greatness of God. With the psalmist we declare, "Great is the Lord, and greatly to be praised" (Ps. 48:1).

As prayer concludes we praise God because it has been His greatness that has made our devotional hour possible. When we began praying we recognized God's glory in all of its splendor and beauty. Now, we restate our case for worship. In these final moments we add faith to our praise. We actually praise God for future answers to prayer. With the psalmist we declare, "I will praise thee for ever, *because thou hast done it*" (Ps. 52:9; italics added).

LIFE'S HIGHEST JOY

Because every day must be lived in a spirit of praise, the specific practice of praise just before concluding prayer is essential. It prepares us for our highest function in life—to minister unto the Lord continuously.

Praise *in the closet* also prepares us to conquer our foes outside the closet. This truth is well supported by Paul Billheimer's testimony: "It [Praise] is the *summum bonum*, the greatest good, the highest joy, the most exquisite delight, the supreme rapture, and the most ravishing transport of the human spirit. Just as antagonism, hostility, and cursing against God exercises and strengthens all that is most abominable, diabolical, and base in the human spirit, so worship and praise of the infinitely loving, lovely God exercises, reinforces, and strengthens all that is most sublime, transcendent, and divine in the inner being. Thus as one worships and praises God, he is continually transformed step by step, from glory to glory into the image of the infinitely happy God."

Billheimer concludes, "Praise is the most useful occupation and activity in enabling God to realize the supreme goal of the universe, that of 'bringing many sons into glory.' "[1]

The bringing of lost souls to glory is the ultimate focal point for all prayer and praise. We *pray*, "Thy Kingdom come," and we *praise*, "For thine is the kingdom." Although much can be said about prayer, bringing glory to God is at the center of it. Professor Hallesby wrote, "The prayer life has its own laws, as all the rest of life has. The fundamental law in prayer is this: prayer is given and ordained for the purpose of glorifying God."[2]

When Jesus told His disciples, "Ye shall ask what ye will, and it shall be done unto you," He added, "Herein is my Father glorified" (John 15:7, 8). God must be glorified through our praying, and praise enables the prayer warrior to keep this thought continually in focus.

THE ATTITUDE OF PRAYER

Perhaps the greatest secret to learn about prayer is how to maintain a devotional attitude after the devotional hour concludes. We must learn to take the spirit of praise with us from the prayer closet. No amount of prayer holds value if the prayer warrior remains unchanged. Said Andrew Murray, "Let us be careful to consider not only the length of the time we spend with God in prayer, but the power with which our prayer takes possession of our whole life."

The dedicated missionary concluded, "Learn this great lesson, my prayer must rule my whole life. What I request from prayer is not decided in five or ten minutes. I must learn to say: 'I have prayed with my whole heart.' What I desire from God must really fill my heart the whole day; then the way is open for a certain answer."[3]

Seize God's power during these closing moments of worship. Let an attitude of prayer flood your being as you prepare for your day. Always remember, God has been your power during prayer and will be your power throughout the day. Someone wisely suggested, "Spiritual power is not the power of prayer, but is the power of God realized in action through a man in the attitude of prayer."[4]

A STRONG AMEN

Jesus taught us to conclude our praying with the expression, "Amen" (Matt. 6:13). It means "so be it" or "it is done." A student of Greek told the author that *amen* could actually be translated "God, our King, is trustworthy." To say "amen" in prayer is to express confidence that God has heard our petitions.

Martin Luther was known for his bold, almost brash petitioning of God. Yet Luther saw many dramatic answers to prayer. A friend once said of the reformation leader, "What a spirit, what a confidence was in his very expressions. With such a reverence he sued as one begging God, and yet with such hope and assurance, as if he spoke with a loving father or friend."[5]

It was Martin Luther who said of prayer's conclusion, "Mark this! Make your amen *strong*, never doubting that God is surely listening to you. This is what amen means: That I know with certainty that this prayer has been heard by God."

We, too, should end our praying with a strong expression of confidence. Paraphrase your "amen" with a testimony of faith. Say, "God, I know you can be trusted to bring these petitions into being. I confess my confidence in your promises. I praise you because it is done!"

THE GIFT OF PRAISE

Thus, our sixty minutes with God has ended. We have not finished our praying with a list of personal petitions but with a spirit of grateful praise. When we leave the closet, we are not asking, but giving. Prayer has concluded with an offering of our lips. With the psalmist we have declared, "Accept, I beseech thee, the freewill offerings of my mouth" (Ps. 119:108).

Into a busy world we carry these words of divine magnification. Our goal beyond the closet is to magnify God's name in all we do. Every action will be sprinkled with silent worship. His praise shall be the very object of our conversation. The greatness of God shall dominate all thought and conduct. We leave the closet declaring with the poet:

> Speak, lips of mine!
> And tell abroad
> The praises of my God.
> Speak, stammering
> tongue!
> In gladdest tone
> Make His high praises
> known.
>
> —H. Bonar

Lord, teach me to magnify you!

PRAISE
THE TWELFTH STEP IN WORLD-CHANGING PRAYER

1. End your prayer with specific praise concerning God's greatness. Focus your praise on His omnipotence (power), His omniscience (knowledge), and His omnipresence (presence).

2. With the psalmist let us "praise God because He has done it." Look back at the devotional hour and praise God for hearing each of your requests.

3. Let your spirit "rejoice" for a few moments at the close of prayer. Repeat the universal word for praise, Hallelujah!

4. As Martin Luther suggested, when your devotional hour concludes make your "amen" strong. Confess with authority that you believe God is trustworthy.

CONCLUSION

THE DESTINY OF NATIONS

Now that we have a practical plan for prayer, we are faced with the matter of commitment. Am I willing to commit myself to give the Lord sixty minutes daily for prayer and Bible study?

This personal commitment is of the utmost importance. Accomplishment always begins with a commitment of the will. To reach the peak of a mountain, a climber must first commit himself in the foothills. Once a commitment is made, follow-through and persistence are essential.

Concerning commitment in prayer, Professor Hallesby preached, "Certain requirements must be met if the art of prayer is to be acquired. In the main there are two: practice and perseverance. Without practice no Christian will become a real man or woman of prayer. And practice cannot be attained without perseverance."[1]

A faithful persistence is at the heart of a meaningful devotional habit. Andrew Murray, who said much concerning prayer's importance, also spoke about this quality in prayer. Discussing faithfulness, Murray said, "The Lord teaches us to know that the blessing through which we have so earnestly prayed can be preserved and increased in no other way than through intimate fellowship with Christ in the inner chamber, every day practiced and cultivated."[2]

This noted nineteenth-century missionary concluded, "Begin at the beginning. Be faithful in the inner chamber. Thank Him that you can reckon on Him to meet you there. Although everything appears cold, and dark, and restrained, bow in silence before the loving Lord Jesus, who so longs after you."[3]

PURPOSEFUL REGULARITY

Consistency is defined as "purposeful regularity." How do we develop purposeful regularity in the devotional habit?

First, *find the very best time for personal prayer*. Once you determine to develop a daily prayer habit, careful consideration should be given to *when* you pray. To discover your most effective time for prayer it may be necessary to do some experimenting.

Be careful not to rule out early morning prayer if you have never tried it. Set a goal of rising sixty to ninety minutes earlier than normal for at least several days of experimentation. You may be surprised to discover it is possible to function on less than your usual duration of sleep.

Seek also to set a *specific* time for prayer. Heed the warning, "Those who have no set time for prayer, do not pray."[4]

Recently the author conducted a survey of twenty thousand prayer warriors who had pledged to pray sixty minutes daily. One question was directed specifically at those having difficulty keeping their commitment. Of those experiencing problems, the majority testified they set a goal to spend one hour daily with the Lord but never set a *specific* time to spend that hour.

Second, *declare your commitment verbally each day*. This is especially beneficial for the first several weeks of maintaining a daily prayer habit. State your commitment *vocally* upon arising each morning. Whether it is vocal or mental, it is of value to declare, "The most important appointment I have today is my appointment with Jesus in prayer." Other appointments or responsibilities may seem essential for the day, but nothing will approach the importance of intimate fellowship with the Lord.

Third, *fight all interruptions fiercely*. Paul spoke of fighting a "good fight" (I Tim. 6:12). To believers at Ephesus he wrote, "Be ye angry . . . Neither give place to the devil" (Eph. 4:26, 27).

We must become angry at the satanic interruptions that seek to rob our day of prayer. Consistent, daily prayer often demands an all-out spiritual battle. Husbands and wives can assist one another in this regard. When I am in prayer my wife kindly tells visitors or callers that I am unable to be disturbed at that particular time. Such assistance proves of immeasurable help in conquering these interruptions.

Fourth, *develop a practical prayer plan*. Seek to establish prayer goals that provide incentives for entering the prayer closet. Using suggestions provided in previous chapters, develop a personal plan for prayer. Don't hesitate to vary the plan from day to day. Always invite the Holy Spirit to help you develop your program of prayer.

Finally, *recognize the overwhelming importance of your daily hour with God*. Until we recognize the full worth of our prayers, we will never develop a consistent habit of prayer. When I returned from an itinerary to the People's Republic of China, I carried as a reminder of my visit a copy of the small red book *Quotations from Mao Tse-tung*. Once home, I felt a deep conviction to hold this book daily in prayer, rebuking its power over the masses of China. I prayed that Mao's influence would deteriorate throughout Communist China.

Suddenly, newspapers and magazines seemed filled with articles discussing this very thing. As many as five unrelated articles reporting such changes appeared in one week. Although months have passed since the trip, similar articles still appear.

Some might believe these events were a mere coincidence. This author is convinced prayer made the difference. Indeed, only as we become convinced that "believing" prayer truly changes things will we give ourselves to the daily exercise of prayer.

RESULTS OF FAITHFULNESS

To be faithful in prayer is to share with God in

His plan to change the world. Throughout every generation it has been the praying saint who has altered the course of history. Evangelist D. L. Moody reminded us, "Luther and his companions were men of such mighty pleading with God, that they broke the spell of ages, and laid nations subdued at the foot of the Cross. John Knox grasped all Scotland in his strong arms of faith and his prayers terrified tyrants. Whitefield, after much bold, faithful closet pleading, went to the devil's playground and took more than a thousand souls out of the paws of the lion in one day."

With special anointing the evangelist added, "See a praying Wesley turn more than ten thousand souls to the Lord! Look at the praying Finney, whose prayers, faith, sermons and writings, have shaken this whole country and sent a wave of blessing through the churches on both sides of the sea."[5]

What happens when I am faithful to the closet of prayer? Not only do I reach out to help those who serve in the Lord's harvest around the world, but the impact of my personal prayer increases the very potential of my day. I soon find myself testifying with Dr. Payson, "Since I began to beg God's blessing on my studies, I have done more in one week than in a whole year before."[6]

Consider the influence of that eighteenth-century saint, David Brainerd. From a casual observation it would appear little was accomplished with his life. After all, Brainerd died at only twenty-nine years of age, having served only four years as an ordained minister. What could a struggling backwoods missionary possibly accomplish in just four years? Biographers tell us only forty or fifty persons were actually converted to Christ as the result of Brainerd's entire ministry.

Yet, something about Brainerd's devotional intensity affected generations of preachers. They were touched by his many days and nights of prayer in the frozen winter forests of northeastern America.

William Carey read Brainerd's journal and a divine flame ignited that reached across continents to touch the unevangelized of India. Edward Payson, John Wesley, Robert McCheyne, Andrew Murray, and Jonathan Edwards were but a few transformed by a mere contact with the written testimony of the young missionary.

Although he was almost twice the age of Brainerd, Jonathan Edwards—in whose home David Brainerd died—said after Brainerd's early death from tuberculosis, "I praise God that in His providence Brainerd should die in my house so that I might hear his prayers, so that I might witness his consecration, and be inspired by his example."[7]

THE DESTINY OF NATIONS

Beloved, it is not age, experience, talent, or material wealth that makes the difference in the destiny of men and nations. Prayer alone will change the world.

It is true that God may use age, experience, talent, and material wealth to help carry forth His purposes, but only when each is properly backed by prayer. Without prayer, every effort is wasted, for it leaves God out of the picture. Wise is the statement that there is much we can do *after* we have prayed but nothing we can do *until* we have prayed.

Thus, all of our questions are reduced to one: Will I say yes to the supreme plea of Jesus to watch with Him one hour? To say yes *today*, and every day, not only releases power into a neglected world, but it aligns me with the very ministry Jesus carries on *today*. Scripture says, "He ever liveth to make intercession" (Heb. 7:25).

Nothing I can do will please Christ more than my joining *with Him* in daily prayer. And when I do, something happens in the world that could not happen through any other means. My hour with Jesus, though brief in comparison to the ages of recorded time, actually makes a difference in the events that constitute these ages.

So, once again let our hearts stand silent as Jesus softly asks, "What, could ye not watch with me one hour?" It is a question each must answer, and on that answer hangs the destiny of nations. . .

Lord, teach me to recognize the worth of my prayers!

APPENDIX

SCRIPTURAL INTERCESSION

We know it is a good thing to pray for others, especially the millions living in unevangelized nations. But how can we be assured that our praying is truly scriptural?

Scriptural prayer for world evangelism basically centers in four areas. We might label these areas the "four claims" for world-changing prayer.

First, *claim workers for the harvest*. Daily in prayer the author holds in his hands a special world prayer map prepared for concerned intercessors by World Literature Crusade.[1] Prior to my "making mention" of the various nations in prayer, I vocally claim each of these four scriptural items. I include the claim for workers first because Jesus included it first. Of all Christ taught in the Gospels, only once do we find Him sharing the ultimate solution to all problems of world evangelism.

Having painted the picture of a vast harvest, Jesus shares His only plan for reaping the harvest:

"Therefore beseech the Lord of the harvest to send out workers into His harvest" (Matt. 9:38; NASB).

Nothing is more important in the worldwide work of God than those workers who shoulder the responsibilities of the harvest. God's plan centers in people. People who know Jesus must share this knowledge with people who do not know Jesus. It is true that only God can give the "increase" (I Cor. 3:6), but it is equally true that God will allow no increase without man's involvement. Augustine expressed it well, "Without God, we cannot, but without us, God will not!"[2]

Second, *claim open doors*. It is also scriptural to claim open doors for those workers who serve in the Lord's harvest. Indeed, the workers we claimed a moment ago will accomplish nothing if they have no field of labor. Even ten thousand qualified workers would accomplish very little in a nation where laws totally prohibit evangelistic activity. Almost half of the earth's population live under just such restrictions. This is why Paul told the Colossians, "Devote yourselves to prayer . . . that God may open up . . . a door for his word" (Col. 4:2, 3; NASB).

To "devote" suggests we give ourselves earnestly to intercession for the ministry. We should pray earnestly for specific leaders of nations who hold in their political hands the power to permit evangelistic outreach and church worship.

Paul told Timothy, "I exhort therefore, that, first of all, supplications, prayers, intercessions, and giving of thanks, be made for all men; For kings, and for all that are in authority" (I Tim. 2:1, 2).

Paul knew that evangelizing every nation is possible only if these leaders permit the peaceful spread of the gospel. Thus, he instructed us to pray for all those in authority.[3]

Third, *claim "fruit" that will remain*. Paul greatly desired that his efforts would not be in vain. "I desire fruit," he declared (Phil. 4:17). Of the Thessalonians Paul also requested, "Pray for us, that the word of the Lord may have free course, *and be glorified*" (II Thess. 3:1; italics added). Paul longed that nothing would hinder the swift accomplishment of those goals God had given him. But more than that, he desired that every spiritual seed planted would take deep root.

Take time during prayer to lift those of Christ's body involved in caring for new converts. In many cultures a convert is rejected by both family and society. Without help the young believer finds it almost impossible to survive spiritually. Our prayers of intercession can actually make the difference.

Fourth, *claim a strong base of support for missionary outreach*. Until I traveled extensively overseas, I overlooked the importance of this claim. True, there is no specific Bible verse that says, "Pray that people will share more finances to help finish the task of world evangelism," but the Bible does stress the importance of sending forth workers. Of course, the sending forth of these workers bears a price tag.

After declaring that all who call upon the name

of the Lord shall be saved, Paul stressed the need for workers to convey this message. Of Roman believers Paul asked, "How then shall they call on him in whom they have not believed? and how shall they believe in him of whom they have not heard? and how shall they hear without a preacher? And how shall they preach, *except they be sent*?" (Rom. 10:14, 15; italics added).

The sending forth of workers, properly equipped with all the necessary tools, can be a very costly matter. Psalm 2:8 speaks of the heathen being reached in the "uttermost parts" of the earth. Having spent many hours meditating on the difficult aspects of world evangelism, and traveling to remote places like Communist China, I am convinced that many Christians do not comprehend the enormous monetary responsibility in reaching these "uttermost parts."

For example, consider the thousands of islands that dot the world's oceans. Each must be visited by messengers of God's love. None can be overlooked. Jesus commissioned us to go into "all the world" (Mark 16:15).

But how costly and involved will this task be? Indonesia provides an excellent example. The fifth most populated country in the world, with 128 million people, Indonesia has a remarkable 13,677 separate islands. After hearing this fact, one prayer warrior declared, "I suppose we should stop praying for God's army and start praying for God's navy."

Consider further that many islands include only a handful of inhabitants. In visiting both the Indonesian and Philippine island chains, World Literature Crusade workers have traveled entire days by boat to share printed gospel messages with only ten or twelve families *on a single island*. But until all are reached, the completion of the Great Commission is only a spiritual dream. To claim a strong base of support for evangelistic endeavor, and to become a part of that base, is to hasten the day of total world evangelization.

HOW TO PRAY FOR THE LOST

Upon returning from the People's Republic of China, God deeply impressed Jack McAlister to challenge prayer warriors to pray daily for a specific number of unevangelized Chinese. Dr. McAlister challenged intercessors to pray for 100 Chinese each day, asking that God would prepare their hearts for the message of salvation.[4] An overall goal was set of mobilizing 300,000 such prayer warriors, each of whom would claim 100 Chinese daily, or 3,000 each month. Three hundred thousand praying in this manner would touch all 900 million Chinese through prayer at least once every thirty days.

Although thousands initially accepted the challenge, and thousands more are joining their ranks monthly, the question quickly arose, "How do I pray for people I have never met, whose names I do not know, and yet pray for them intelligently *with purpose*? The answer was discovered in prayer.

Because Jesus said, "Ask, and it shall be given" (Matt. 7:7), we must first believe that Christ will honor our simple faith whenever we request that He do something to prepare the hearts of lost souls. Whether praying for 100 specific (though unknown) Chinese in a distant land, or an unsaved relative, we must believe something happens when we pray.

Of course, we do know that every person has a will to choose or reject the message of Christ's love. Therefore, we cannot ask God to force unbelievers, such as the 100 specific Chinese, to believe on Him. In the first place, in the case of China and many other unevangelized nations, the vast majority of people have never heard about Jesus, so it is quite impossible for them to believe. It was this thought that led to a simple six-step plan to help Christians intercede for those they have never seen.

We recall from our elementary English classes the six interrogatives that introduce a question. They include who, what, when, why, how, and where. When praying for the lost, especially those you do not know, claim that God will cause these people to ask certain "heart" questions that will direct their thinking toward the things of God. This will prepare their hearts for the planting of gospel seeds.

Although this plan was originally developed to help intercessors focus prayer on groups of unevangelized Chinese, it can be adopted rather easily for the unsaved of any nation, or even for unconverted friends and family members.

WHOM CAN I TRUST?

First, pray that lost souls will ask the question,

"*Whom can I trust?*" Ask God to cause a specific person, or group of people, to begin questioning whom they can really trust in life. This is especially appropriate in repressed nations of the world. Pray that political leaders, such as the leaders of a particular Chinese province, will do certain things that will cause distrust throughout their province. When the people for whom we pray begin feeling this deep distrust they will wonder whom they can trust. Soon they will look for someone to trust beyond themselves. Eventually this search will direct their thinking heavenward!

WHAT IS MY PURPOSE?

Next, pray that lost souls will search for the meaning of life. Claim that each will inwardly ask, "*What is my purpose for living*?" This, too, will cause those for whom we intercede to contemplate the possibility of a Higher Power.

WHEN WILL I REALLY BE FREE?

Then, pray that lost souls will ask, "*When will I really be free*?" This is especially appropriate for those living in communist nations of the world, like China. Strangely, from a materialistic standpoint, the Chinese are far better off today than ever, especially when we compare current standards of living with those of thirty years ago. Thus, it is easy for the Chinese to be complacent and fail to realize how many personal freedoms have disappeared, including the right of Christians to freely worship or share the message of Christ.

Pray that God will plant in the hearts of these people, or other lost souls for whom you intercede, an inner unrest, together with a longing to know the "Truth" that will someday set them free.

WHY DO PEOPLE HATE RELIGION?

The fourth prayer interrogative concerns the question, "*Why do people hate religion*?" Although this request, like the others, is especially appropriate when praying for people of communist nations, it can easily be adopted when praying for all who are without Christ. Pray that lost souls will question why people find it necessary to fight the concept of God, especially if they don't believe in God anyway.

Ultimately, this question will lead them on a deep "heart quest" that will create serious unresolved questions within them. Before long their desire to know if there is a God will increase with great intensity.

HOW CAN I COPE?

Next, pray that lost souls will ask, "*How can I cope with my problems*?" Pray that they will feel increasingly hopeless about personal problems, realizing that outside help must be found. This, too, will cause them to look for a Power beyond themselves.

WHERE WILL I GO WHEN I DIE?

Finally, ask that lost souls will inwardly question, "*Where will I go when I die*?" This question may be asked by anyone. Even little children ask questions about death, especially when seeing a funeral procession or hearing that a relative has died. When interceding for lost souls, especially those we know very little about, we should pray that an urgency will fill their hearts concerning their eternal destination.

Imagine praying daily for a certain group of Chinese to inwardly ask the question, "Where will I go when I die?" Further imagine that those for whom you pray become obsessed with this question and even find themselves waking during the night and pondering these thoughts.

Then one day several of these Chinese receive a "Gospel of John" and begin to read its message. Imagine their delight when they discover the promise, "For God so loved the world, that he gave his only begotten Son, that whosoever believeth in him should not perish, but have everlasting life" (John 3:16).

This, beloved, is the power of specific, intercessory prayer when focused with compassion, with the aid of the Holy Spirit, on lost souls around the world.

NOTES

INTRODUCTION

1. E. M. Bounds, *The Necessity of Prayer*, quoted in *A Treasury of Prayer*, compiled by Leonard Ravenhill (Minneapolis: Bethany Fellowship, 1961), p. 30.

2. Charles H. Spurgeon, *Twelve Sermons on Prayer* (Grand Rapids: Baker Book House, 1971), p. 31.

3. Ibid., pp. 36–70.

4. Helen Smith Shoemaker, *The Secret of Effective Prayer* (Waco, TX: Word Books, 1976), p. 15.

5. J. C. Ryle, *A Call to Prayer* (Grand Rapids: Baker Book House, 1976), pp. 14–15.

6. David A. Hubbard, *The Problem with Prayer Is* (Wheaton, IL: Tyndale House Publishers, 1972), p. 51.

7. Bounds, *The Necessity of Prayer*, p. 184.

8. O. Hallesby, *Prayer* (Minneapolis: Augsburg Publishing House, 1959), p. 89.

9. Ibid., p. 88.

10. J. Oswald Sanders, *Prayer Power Unlimited* (Chicago: Moody Press, 1977), p. 108.

11. Harold Lindsell, *When You Pray* (Grand Rapids: Baker Book House, 1969), pp. 25–26.

12. R. Humbard, *Praying with Power* (Grand Rapids: New Hope Press, 1975), p. 13.

13. Ryle, *A Call to Prayer*, pp. 29–30.

CHAPTER 1

1. Brother Lawrence, *The Practice of the Presence of God* (Old Tappan, NJ: Revell, 1959), p. 25.

2. Harold Lindsell, *When You Pray* (Grand Rapids: Baker Book House, 1975), pp. 30–33.

3. Paul E. Billheimer, *Destined for the Throne* (Fort Washington, PA: Christian Literature Crusade, 1975), p. 118.

4. D. L. Moody, *Prevailing Prayer* (Chicago: Moody Press, n.d.), pp. 55–56.

5. Billheimer, *Destined for the Throne*, p. 120.

CHAPTER 2

1. E. M. Bounds, *The Weapon of Prayer* (Grand Rapids: Baker Book House, 1975), p. 156.

2. Bridgid E. Herman, *Creative Prayer* (New York: Harper and Row, n.d.), p. 31.

3. Edwin and Lillian Harvey, *Kneeling We Triumph* (Chicago: Moody Press, 1974), p. 66.

4. Ibid.

5. John Bisagno, *The Power of Positive Praying* (Grand Rapids: Zondervan, 1965), pp. 70–72.

6. O. Hallesby, *Prayer* (Minneapolis: Augsburg Publishing House, 1959), p. 146.

7. Ibid., p. 147.

8. Norman Pittenger, *Praying Today* (Grand Rapids: Wm. B. Eerdmans, 1974), p. 35.

9. Harold Lindsell, *When You Pray* (Grand Rapids: Baker Book House, 1975), p. 31.

10. Donald E. Demaray, *Alive to God Through Prayer* (Grand Rapids: Baker Book House, 1965), pp. 126–127.

11. Ralph Herring, *The Cycle of Prayer* (Wheaton, IL: Tyndale House Publishers, 1974), p. 16.

12. Herman, *Creative Prayer*, p. 40.

13. Harvey, *Kneeling We Triumph*, p. 73.

14. D. L. Moody, *Prevailing Prayer* (Chicago: Moody Press, n.d.), p. 18.

15. Andrew Murray, *The Prayer Life* (Chicago: Moody Press, n.d.), p. 43.

16. Herman, *Creative Prayer*, p. 33.

CHAPTER 3

1. Andrew Murray, *The Prayer Life* (Chicago: Moody Press, n.d.), p. 117.

2. D. L. Moody, *Prevailing Prayer* (Chicago: Moody Press, n.d.), pp. 36–37.

3. William R. Parker and Elaine St. Johns, *Prayer Can Change Your Life* (Old Tappan, NJ: Revell, 1975), p. 209.

4. E. M. Blaiklock, *The Positive Power of Prayer* (Glendale, CA: Regal, 1974), p. 43.

5. Harold Lindsell, *When You Pray* (Grand Rapids: Baker Book House, 1975), pp. 37, 42.

6. Parker and St. Johns, *Prayer Can Change Your Life*, p. 220.

7. John Allan Lavender, *Why Prayers Are Unanswered* (Valley Forge, PA: Judson Press, 1967), p. 18.

8. Moody, *Prevailing Prayer*, pp. 31–32.

9. Virginia Whitman, *The Excitement of Answered Prayer* (Grand Rapids: Baker Book House, 1978), p. 107.

10. Helen Smith Shoemaker, *The Secret of Effective Prayer* (Waco, TX: Word Books, 1967), p. 64.

11. David A. Hubbard, *The Problem with Prayer Is* (Wheaton, IL: Tyndale House Publishers, 1972), p. 74.

CHAPTER 4

1. Leonard Ravenhill, *Why Revival Tarries* (Minneapolis: Bethany Fellowship, 1959), p. 59.

2. E. M. Bounds, *The Necessity of Prayer* (Grand Rapids: Baker Book House, 1976), p. 10.

3. E. W. Kenyon, *In His Presence* (Lynnwood, WA: Gospel Publishing Society, 1969), p. 32.

4. Andrew Murray, *The Prayer Life* (Chicago: Moody Press, n.d.), p. 107.

5. Lehman Strauss, *Sense and Nonsense About Prayer* (Chicago: Moody Press, 1974), pp. 65–66.

6. G. Campbell Morgan, *The Practice of Prayer* (Grand Rapids: Baker Book House, 1971), p. 95.

7. George Mueller, *An Autobiography of George Mueller* (London: J. Nisbet, 1906), p. 150.

8. E. M. Bounds, *The Possibilities of Prayer* (Minneapolis: Bethany Fellowship, 1978).

9. Jack R. Taylor, *Prayer: Life's Limitless Reach* (Nashville: Broadman Press, 1977), p. 109.

10. A special brochure entitled "Word-Enriched Prayer" is available upon request from World Literature Crusade, P.O. Box 1313, Studio City, CA 91604. It provides an actual illustration concerning how to pray using this unique method.

11. J. Oswald Sanders, *Prayer Power Unlimited* (Chicago: Moody Press, 1977), p. 9.

CHAPTER 5

1. Jack R. Taylor, *Prayer: Life's Limitless Reach* (Nashville: Broadman Press, 1977), p. 111.

2. Curtis C. Mitchell, *Praying Jesus' Way* (Old Tappan, NJ: Revell, 1977), pp. 79-80.

3. Watchman Nee, *The Prayer Ministry of the Church* (New York: Christian Fellowship Publishers, 1973), p. 121.

4. Christians interested in monthly "prayer fuel" that will aid them in "watching" the needs of world evangelism may write to World Literature Crusade, P.O. Box 1313, Studio City, California 91604.

5. J. C. Ryle, *A Call to Prayer* (Grand Rapids: Baker Book House, 1976), p. 59.

6. Ibid., p. 60.

7. Lehman Strauss, *Sense and Nonsense About Prayer* (Chicago: Moody Press, 1974), p. 31.

8. Donald E. Demaray, *Alive to God Through Prayer* (Grand Rapids: Baker Book House, 1965), p. 81.

9. Taylor, *Prayer: Life's Limitless Reach*, p. 75.

10. O. Hallesby, *Prayer* (Minneapolis: Augsburg Publishing House, 1959), pp. 169–170.

11. Anne J. Townsend, *Prayer Without Pretending* (Chicago: Moody Press, 1973), p. 95.

12. Andrew Murray, *The Prayer Life* (Chicago: Moody Press, n.d.), pp. 64–65.

CHAPTER 6

1. Paul E. Billheimer, *Destined for the Throne* (Fort Washington, PA: Christian Literature Crusade, 1975), p. 19.

2. William L. Krutza, *How Much Prayer Should a Hamburger Get?* (Grand Rapids: Baker Book House, 1975), p. 21.

3. Billheimer, *Destined for the Throne*, p. 105.

4. E. M. Bounds, *The Weapon of Prayer* (Grand Rapids: Baker Book House, 1975), p. 58.

5. Some readers may wonder why two common prayer terms—*travail* and *supplication*—are not listed in our discussion as specific elements of the devotional habit. *Travail* is an intense form of intercession, whereas *supplication* is an in-

tense form of petition. Thus, to plead with great intensity for a personal need is a type of petition called *supplication*. To plead with great intensity for the needs of another is a type of intercessory prayer called *travail*. The author's earlier book on prayer, *No Easy Road: Inspirational Thoughts on Prayer* (Grand Rapids: Baker Book House, 1971), presents a look at both supplication and travail in relationship to prayer.

6. Edwin and Lillian Harvey, *Kneeling We Triumph* (Chicago: Moody Press, 1974), p. 40.

7. Ibid., p. 98.

8. Anne J. Townsend, *Prayer Without Pretending* (Chicago: Moody Press, 1973), p. 82.

9. J. C. Ryle, *A Call to Prayer* (Grand Rapids: Baker Book House, 1976), p. 73.

10. Bounds, *The Weapon of Prayer*, p. 70.

11. Jack R. Taylor, *Prayer: Life's Limitless Reach* (Nashville: Broadman Press, 1977), p. 75.

12. The apostle Paul also referred to "making mention" of fellow workers in prayer in Eph. 1:16; Phil. 1:3, 4; and I Thess. 1:2.

13. R. E. Speer, *Paul, The All-Round Man* (New York: Revell, 1909), p. 92.

14. O. Hallesby, *Prayer* (Minneapolis: Augsburg Publishing House, 1959), pp. 164–165.

CHAPTER 7

1. Helen Smith Shoemaker, *The Secret of Effective Prayer* (Waco, TX: Word Books, 1967), p. 51.

2. Charles H. Spurgeon, *Twelve Sermons on Prayer* (Grand Rapids: Baker Book House, 1971), p. 99.

3. E. M. Bounds, *The Weapon of Prayer* (Grand Rapids: Baker Book House, 1975), p. 106.

4. E. M. Blaiklock, *The Positive Power of Prayer* (Glendale, CA: Regal, 1974), pp. 35–37.

5. Spurgeon, *Twelve Sermons on Prayer*, p. 38.

6. Andrew Murray, *The Prayer Life* (Chicago: Moody Press, n.d.), p. 95.

7. D. L. Moody, *Prevailing Prayer* (Chicago: Moody Press, n.d.), p. 18.

8. Murray, *The Prayer Life*, p. 96.

CHAPTER 8

1. O. Hallesby, *Prayer* (Minneapolis: Augsburg Publishing House, 1959), p. 141.

CHAPTER 9

1. Donald E. Demaray, *Alive to God Through Prayer* (Grand Rapids: Baker Book House, 1965), p. 27.

2. A map of all 210 countries with indexed locations is available upon request from World Literature Crusade, P.O. Box 1313, Studio City, CA 91604.

CHAPTER 10

1. Bridgid E. Herman, *Creative Prayer* (New York: Harper and Row, n.d.), pp. 48–49.

2. E. M. Blaiklock, *The Positive Power of Prayer* (Glendale, CA: Regal, 1974), pp. 38–39.

3. Herman, *Creative Prayer*, p. 55.

4. Ibid., pp. 60–66.

5. Ibid., p. 47.

6. Ibid., p. 53.

7. Brother Lawrence, *The Practice of the Presence of God* (Old Tappan, NJ: Revell, 1958), pp. 11–12.

CHAPTER 11

1. Bridgid E. Herman, *Creative Prayer* (New York: Harper and Row, n.d.), p. 25.

2. Rosalind Rinker, *Prayer: Conversing with God* (Grand Rapids: Zondervan, 1959), pp. 17–18.

3. Hope MacDonald, *Discovering How to Pray* (Grand Rapids: Zondervan, 1976), pp. 53–54.

4. Edwin and Lillian Harvey, *Kneeling We Triumph* (Chicago: Moody Press, 1974), p. 81.

5. Ibid., p. 78.

6. David A. Hubbard, *The Problem with Prayer Is* (Wheaton, IL: Tyndale House Publishers, 1972), p. 51.

7. Donald E. Demaray, *Alive to God Through Prayer* (Grand Rapids: Baker Book House, 1965), p. 41.

8. John Anthony Hanne, *Prayer or Pretense* (Grand Rapids: Zondervan, 1974), pp. 22–23.

9. Herman, *Creative Prayer*, p. 43.
10. Harvey, *Kneeling We Triumph*, p. 81.
11. Herman, *Creative Prayer*, p. 43.

CHAPTER 12

1. Paul E. Billheimer, *Destined for the Throne* (Fort Washington, PA: Christian Literature Crusade, 1975), p. 117.
2. O. Hallesby, *Prayer* (Minneapolis: Augsburg Publishing House, 1959), p. 126.
3. Andrew Murray, *The Prayer Life* (Chicago: Moody Press, n.d.), p. 118.
4. John Anthony Hanne, *Prayer or Pretense* (Grand Rapids: Zondervan, 1974), p. 48.
5. J. C. Ryle, *A Call to Prayer* (Grand Rapids: Baker Book House, 1976), p. 68.

CONCLUSION

1. O. Hallesby, *Prayer* (Minneapolis: Augsburg Publishing House, 1959), p. 40.
2. Andrew Murray, *The Prayer Life* (Chicago: Moody Press, n.d.), p. 134.
3. Ibid., p. 147.
4. Watchman Nee, *The Prayer Ministry of the Church* (New York: Christian Fellowship Publishers, 1973), p. 114.
5. D. L. Moody, *Prevailing Prayer* (Chicago: Moody Press, n.d.), p. 16.
6. Ibid., p. 14.
7. *The Life of Reverend David Brainerd*, consisting of David Brainerd's memoirs and personal journal, has been recently reprinted by Baker Book House, Grand Rapids, Michigan, after being out of print for almost two decades.

APPENDIX

1. A map of the world, listing all 210 countries and showing their locations, is available upon request from World Literature Crusade, P.O. Box 1313, Studio City, CA 91604.

2. Norman Pittenger, *Praying Today* (Grand Rapids: Wm. B. Eerdmans, 1974), p. 152.

3. To further aid the intercessor in meaningful prayer, World Literature Crusade makes available a list of all heads of state from every country on earth. For information write the World Literature Crusade office.

4. A complete explanation of the plan for claiming all of China for Jesus, called "The Must Bring Plan," based on John 10:16, is available upon request from World Literature Crusade.

BIBLIOGRAPHY

Allen, Charles L. *All Things Are Possible Through Prayer*. Old Tappan, NJ: Revell, 1958.

Billheimer, Paul E. *Destined for the Throne*. Fort Washington, PA: Christian Literature Crusade, 1975.

Bisagno, John. *The Power of Positive Praying*. Grand Rapids: Zondervan, 1965.

Blaiklock, E. M. *The Positive Power of Prayer*. Glendale, CA: Regal, 1974.

Bounds, E. M. *The Essentials of Prayer*. Minneapolis: Bethany Fellowship, 1976.

———. *The Necessity of Prayer*. Grand Rapids: Baker Book House, 1976.

———. *The Possibilities of Prayer*. Minneapolis: Bethany Fellowship, 1978.

———. *Prayer and Praying Men*. Grand Rapids: Baker Book House, 1977.

———. *Purpose in Prayer*. Grand Rapids: Baker Book House, 1978.

———. *The Reality of Prayer*. Grand Rapids: Baker Book House, 1978.

———. *The Weapon of Prayer*. Grand Rapids: Baker Book House, 1975.

Bunyan, John. *Prayer*. London: Banner of Truth Trust, 1965.

Chadwick, Samuel. *The Path of Prayer*. Fort Washington, PA: Christian Literature Crusade, 1963.

Christenson, Evelyn, and Blake, Viola. *What Happens When Women Pray*. Wheaton, IL: Victor Books, 1976.

Demaray, Donald E. *Alive to God Through Prayer*. Grand Rapids: Baker Book House, 1965.

Eastman, Dick. *No Easy Road*. Grand Rapids: Baker Book House, 1971.

Edwards, Jonathan. *The Life of Reverend David Brainerd*. Grand Rapids: Baker Book House, 1978.

Finney, Charles G. *Prevailing Prayer*. Grand Rapids: Kregel, 1965.

Gesswein, Armin R. *Seven Wonders of Prayer*. Grand Rapids: Zondervan, 1957.

Goforth, Rosalind. *How I Know God Answers Prayer*. Chicago: Moody Press, n.d.

Gordon, Samuel D. *Quiet Talks on Prayer*. New York: Grosset and Dunlap, 1904.

Grubb, Norman P. *Rees Howells: Intercessor*. Fort Washington, PA: Christian Literature Crusade, 1962.

Hallesby, O. *Prayer*. Minneapolis: Augsburg Publishing House, 1959.

Hanne, John Anthony. *Prayer or Pretense*? Grand Rapids: Zondervan, 1974.

Harvey, Edwin and Lillian. *Kneeling We Triumph*. Chicago: Moody Press, 1974.

Hasler, Richard. *Journey with David Brainerd*. Downers Grove, IL: Inter-Varsity Press, 1976.

Hayford, Jack W. *Prayer Is Invading the Impossible*. Plainfield, NJ: Logos International, 1977.

Herman, Bridgid E. *Creative Prayer*. Cincinnati: Forward Movement Publications, n.d.

Herring, Ralph. *The Cycle of Prayer*. Wheaton, IL: Tyndale House Publishers, 1974.

Hubbard, David A. *The Problem with Prayer Is*. Wheaton, IL: Tyndale House Publishers, 1972.

Huegel, F. J. *The Ministry of Intercession*. Minneapolis: Bethany Fellowship, 1967.

———. *Prayer's Deeper Secrets*. Grand Rapids: Zondervan, 1959.

———. *Successful Praying*. Minneapolis: Bethany Fellowship, 1967.

Humbard, Rex. *Praying with Power*. Grand Rapids: New Hope Press, 1975.

Kenyon, E. W. *In His Presence*. Lynnwood, WA: Gospel Publishing Society, 1969.

Kimmel, Jo. *Steps to Prayer Power*. Nashville: Abingdon Press, 1972.

The Kneeling Christian. Grand Rapids: Zondervan, 1945.

Lauback, Frank C. *Prayer, the Mightiest Force in the World*. Old Tappan, NJ: Revell, 1959.

Lavender, John Allan. *Why Prayers Are Unanswered*. Valley Forge, PA: Judson Press, 1967.

Lawrence, Brother. *Practice of the Presence of God*. Old Tappan, NJ: Revell, 1956.

Lawson, Gilchrist. *Deeper Experiences of Famous Christians*. Anderson, IN: Warner Press, 1911.

Lindsell, Harold. *When You Pray*. Grand Rapids: Baker Book House, 1975.

McClure, J. G. *Intercessory Prayer*. Chicago: Moody Press, n.d.

McDonald, Hope. *Discovering How to Pray*. Grand Rapids: Zondervan, 1976.

McGraw, Francis A. *Praying Hyde*. Chicago: Moody Press, n.d.

Moody, D. L. *Prevailing Prayer*. Chicago: Moody Press, n.d.

Morgan, G. Campbell. *The Practice of Prayer*. Grand Rapids: Baker Book House, 1971.

Mueller, George. *Answers to Prayer*. Chicago: Moody Press, n.d.

Murray, Andrew. *The Prayer Life*. Chicago: Moody Press, n.d.

———. *With Christ in the School of Prayer*. Old Tappan, NJ: Revell, 1953.

Parker, William R., and St. Johns, Elaine. *Prayer Can Change Your Life*. Old Tappan, NJ: Revell, 1975.

Payne, Thomas. *Prayer–The Greatest Force on Earth*. Chicago: Moody Press, n.d.

Pittenger, Norman. *Praying Today*. Grand Rapids: Wm. B. Eerdmans, 1974.

Prater, Arnold. *You Can Pray as You Ought*. Nashville: Nelson, 1977.

Ravenhill, Leonard. *Why Revival Tarries*. Minneapolis: Bethany Fellowship, 1959.

Redpath, Alan. *Victorious Praying*. Old Tappan, NJ: Revell, 1957.

Reidhead, Paris. *Beyond Petition*. Minneapolis: Bethany Fellowship, 1974.

Rinker, Rosalind. *Prayer: Conversing with God*. Grand Rapids: Zondervan, 1959.

Ryle, J. C. *A Call to Prayer*. Grand Rapids: Baker Book House, 1976.

Sanders, J. Oswald. *Prayer Power Unlimited*. Minneapolis: World Wide Publications, 1977.

Sheen, Fulton J. *Life of Christ*. Garden City, NY: Image Books, 1977.

Shoemaker, Helen Smith. *The Secret of Effective Prayer*. Waco, TX: Word Books, 1967.

Sims, A. *George Mueller: Man of Faith*. Chicago: Moody Press, n.d.

Spurgeon, Charles H. *Effective Prayer*. London: Evangelical Press, n.d.

______. *Twelve Sermons on Prayer*. Grand Rapids: Baker Book House, 1971.

Stedman, Ray C. *Jesus Teaches on Prayer*. Waco, TX: Word Books, 1976.

Steere, Douglas V. *Dimensions of Prayer*. New York: Harper and Row, 1963.

Strauss, Lehman. *Sense and Nonsense About Prayers*. Chicago: Moody Press, 1976.

Taylor, Jack R. *Prayer: Life's Limitless Reach*. Nashville: Broadman Press, 1977.

Thielicke, Helmut. *Our Heavenly Father*. Grand Rapids: Baker Book House, 1974.

Torrey, R. A. *The Power of Prayer*. Grand Rapids: Zondervan, 1974.

Townsend, Anne J. *Prayer Without Pretending*. Chicago: Moody Press, 1976.

Tozer, A. W. *The Knowledge of the Holy*. New York: Harper and Row, 1975.

Wallis, Arthur. *Jesus Prayed*. Fort Washington, PA: Christian Literature Crusade, 1966.

Whyte, Alexander. *Lord, Teach Us to Pray*. Grand Rapids: Baker Book House, 1976.

Love on Its Knees

Making a Difference by Praying for Others

Foreword by Larry Lea

To
Jim and Joy Dawson

Jim—a unique man of God whose gentle spirit and profound administrative gifts have made possible the amplification of Joy's apostolic gifts to Christ's Body . . .

and

Joy—whom God has used mightily to impact leaders like myself in the holy and sacred art of intercessory prayer.

Contents

Foreword

Only rarely do we meet those select few people who seem to incarnate their message. Dick Eastman personifies his message. In my mind, I immediately associate statesmanship in crisis with Winston Churchill, evangelism with Billy Graham. And when I think of prayer for world evangelization, I think of Dick Eastman. His passion to mobilize the Church as a prayer force for the Great Commission seems to emanate from him at every turn. I don't believe I've ever heard anyone minister who can get down into my spirit and pull at me like Dick Eastman.

It has been more than a decade now since I answered God's call on my life to seek Him in prayer. I could not conceive then of all that God would do. It is now my high privilege to assist Dick and others in calling the Body of Christ to prayer, the highest call of all. Along the way, the Lord has graced me with mentors. Dick Eastman and his Change the World School of Prayer have been a tremendous source of encouragement to me and thousands of others.

Now Dick has distilled his seasoned wisdom and offers it to you in this book. All of Dick's books are excellent but *Love On Its Knees* is perhaps his best. In these pages you will see the warm portrait of a man and his family who have made a costly commitment to prayer. You will feel the heartthrob of a man agonizing before God for his generation. You may well be challenged as never before. Most importantly, you will be given concrete steps of action to take to change the world for Jesus Christ.

As president of Every Home for Christ/World Literature Crusade, Dick seems postured as no one else to awaken the Church to the inseparable link between prevailing prayer and closure on the Great Commission. Dick is uniquely graced to cut through sectarian and denominational barriers to summon the entire Church to its most noble callings. His passion for world missions is unexcelled. His integrity is unimpeachable. And, in an age when cynicism rages out of control, his heart is unsoiled.

God has a purpose for your life. He also has a purpose for this planet. When you allow Him to fit your life into His ultimate design for humanity, then you are truly fulfilled. You will profit enormously from absorbing this book and its challenge to you. My prayer for you is that not only the didactic truths, but the heart of the man who wrote them, will by God's grace be infused into you.

Larry Lea, Senior Pastor
Church on the Rock
Rockwall, Texas

Acknowledgments

The heartbeat of intercession is servanthood. It is thus fitting to acknowledge those choice servants who have stood with me behind the scenes to help make *Love On Its Knees* a reality.

First, I joyously thank each of our dedicated intercessors who come regularly to our intercessory prayer room at every home for Christ International. Their prayer covering makes possible a continuing harvest that already has seen more than 15,500,000 decision cards come to our more than 50 global offices in the past 35 years.

To Tami Baldwin and John Sherrill I offer special appreciation. Tami's dedication as a servant is unusually exemplary. A fellow member of my home church, Tami gave countless hours, while maintaining her already rigorous work schedule, to type and retype the numerous revisions of *Love On Its Knees,* insisting she receive no remuneration.

John Sherrill, likewise, deserves special acknowledgment. One of this generation's truly gifted Christian writers, John Sherrill has set his mark on most of the pages of this manuscript. His editorial skills have helped cut through the verbiage and bring out the true heart of the message—that the fate of the world is in the hands of praying saints.

Dick Eastman
Canoga Park, California

one
Intercession
A Way of Life

Several years ago, in May 1986, I was preparing to take School of Prayer training to Poland at the invitation of a dynamic young pastor from Pittsburgh, Mark Geppert. Six weeks prior to my departure for Eastern Europe, I met with Mark to finalize our schedule.

"There's been a change in my itinerary," Mark said. "I'll meet you in Warsaw as planned, but first I'll be going to the Soviet Union for a month."

"The Soviet Union?" I asked, puzzled. "What will you be doing there?"

"I'm going to pray," Mark responded. "God spoke to me a few days ago and told me I was to go to Russia just to pray. He told me exactly where to go and what to pray about. I'm to pray that God will shake all of Russia. I'll ask Him to use current events—whatever they are—to shake what can be shaken, so doors will open to the Gospel and believers will have a new freedom to worship."

Thrilled that someone would go anywhere "just to pray," I asked Mark to be sure to send me a copy of his itinerary so our ministry could be praying with him before I joined him in Warsaw. The itinerary arrived and I thought little of the specifics until a few days before my departure. Suddenly, Mark's presence in the Soviet Union praying for God to shake that nation held unusual significance. Just before my departure at the end of April 1986, headlines shouted the story of a shocking incident that occurred there at a nuclear power plant in a small city named *Chernobyl.* Chernobyl, the papers said, was just a short distance from the sprawling Soviet city of Kiev. Wasn't Kiev on Mark's itinerary? In fact, if memory served me, wasn't Kiev the final place God told him to visit?

I immediately got out the letter Mark sent me listing the places God told him to visit. My recollection had been accurate. Mark's mission was to end that very weekend in Kiev with a train trip to Poland that would take him right through the area of disaster. I had been on a train trip with Mark before, in China. To Mark a train is just a long prayer meeting on tracks, moving from one place of prayer to another.

Checking the itinerary more carefully, I noted that Mark had planned to leave Kiev late on the evening of April 25, 1986, and would be passing close to Chernobyl early the next morning. That happened to be the exact time of the explosion of Chernobyl's nuclear power plant.

Only later would analysts see that Chernobyl played a major role in the events of *glasnost*, the Russian word for openness. Under normal circumstances the Soviets would have kept secret the news of such a disaster. But this was not possible with Chernobyl. In a matter of hours after the nuclear accident, scientists spotted a sudden elevation of radiation in Sweden. The source could be traced with absolute accuracy to the Soviet Ukraine.

So in the case of Chernobyl, *glasnost* was forced onto the Soviets. Being secretive was not an option. Suddenly, whether they wanted to or not, they were forced to be open.

I couldn't wait to see Mark in Warsaw. Had he kept his itinerary? If so, how had God asked him to pray?

We had hardly checked into our hotel in Warsaw before I was asking my questions. Mark indeed had kept his schedule, exactly as the Lord directed. It included four days of prayer in Kiev, ending on Friday, April 25. That day was to be the culmination of his mission of intercession. And now I was more anxious than ever to hear how God directed Mark to pray.

"Well," said Mark, settling back in his chair in our hotel room, "I went to the square in the center of Kiev and sat down under a huge statue of Lenin. Every fifteen minutes I changed the focus of my intercession for believers in Russia. I could tell when a fifteen-minute period passed because there was a gigantic clock in the square that let out a bong each quarter hour."

I asked Mark if he felt anything unusual during this prayer. "Only at the end," Mark responded. "It was on the last day, the day I made my final prayer visit to the city square. Just before noon I was suddenly convinced God had heard and that even then something was happening. Something that would shake the Soviet Union. Something God would *use* to bring more freedom."

With excitement Mark continued, "I began to lift my voice in praise, sitting there underneath the statue of the founder of Communism in Russia. But at the same time I needed a confirmation that God had heard me, so I cried out to Him: 'O God, give me a sign, even a little sign.' I waited, wondering what might happen next. And just then in the distance the hands of the huge clock moved into the twelve o'clock position."

Mark laughed as he continued, "And you know what, Brother Dick? It didn't gong. Every hour, for each of the four days I had been praying, the clock had chimed on the hour. So I waited for twelve chimes, but they never came. It was as if God was saying an old pattern was over. The very next day I began hearing about Chernobyl."

Weeks later, after reading volumes on the significance of Chernobyl, I came across fascinating information detailing events surrounding the disaster. Scientists pinpointed the first major mistake as happening twelve hours before the actual meltdown. This would have been within minutes of Mark's declaration of praise, when he knew in his spirit that events were occurring that the Lord would turn into a blessing.

Later still I heard a television commentator discussing the long-term impact of the Chernobyl disaster. "Chernobyl," he said, "means *wormwood* in the Russian language. Wouldn't it be interesting if a decade from today we were to discover that the despotic Soviet system had disappeared from the scene, replaced by a more open society, and that this change came about as the result of a simple mistake at a nuclear facility in a small Ukrainian community called . . . Chernobyl?"

It would seem that *glasnost* may be taking hold more rapidly than anyone was prepared for, opening doors where the Gospel had previously been hindered. Just two years after Chernobyl, new laws were being readied that amounted to an extraordinary retreat from power on the part of Soviet authorities. None other than Soviet Deputy Justice Minister Mikhail P. Vyshinsky said, "A revolution is taking place here. Not everyone realizes this, but that is what it is—a revolution."

And then came the big news.

At the historic General Conference of all party leaders, the first in 47 years, Soviet leader Mikhail Gorbachev made a series of statements concerning coming changes. Among them was a call for new tolerance toward the religious faiths in the Soviet Union—although, to be sure, Communism is still atheistic at its roots, and when dealing with the purported changes this should always be kept in mind.

Intercessors like Mark are rarely surprised when answers come. In fact, I'm convinced that when we stand before God with the record of spiritual successes and failures, we will learn that intercessory prayer had more to do with bringing about positive changes in our world than any other single spiritual activity.

Intercessors, in short, hold the key to releasing God's best for the world. And for the rest of this book, we will be looking at some principles of effective intercession.

These are principles that come out of thousands of hours spent in prayer over the years in a small chapel my wife, Dee, and I built in our backyard. It's just a small tool shed that we've transformed into a unique place of prayer, complete with wood paneling and extra thick carpeting. On the walls are maps and other reminders that help us pray for a lost world.

There we pray every day (well, every day when we are home) for our two daughters, Dena and Ginger; for our work, church, nation; for other nations; for our economy; for individuals in need; for ministries in need. On and on the list could go. Later we will be talking about the *discipline* of intercession. Otherwise, even prayer can become scattered and lacking in power.

The principles we will be looking at also come out of the Change the World School of Prayer, a multi-hour power training course that resulted from my call to prayer ministry almost seventeen years ago.

These two experiences—my own personal intercessory prayer life and our School of Prayer—have brought to my attention the guidelines I will be sharing in the balance of this book.

We Are the Products of Intercession

I am the product of intercession, as are all of us who know Christ as our personal Savior.

First, we are born-again followers of Jesus because our eternal Intercessor, Christ Himself, sacrificed His life on a cross as a "go-between"—or intercessor—nearly twenty centuries ago. Then, we are born-again believers because other intercessors, some not even known to us, have touched our lives over the years, breaking the demonic darkness about us that might otherwise have kept us from a full knowledge of Christ.

The primary intercessor in my life was my mother. While I was a rebellious youth involved in serious stealing and burglary by age fourteen, my mother stood against the darkness enslaving me, praying that the light of Jesus Christ would shine into my heart.

I remember in particular the day my mother's prayers seemed to catch up with me. Mike, my young partner in crime, was on the phone, asking me to go with him to our large local swimming pool.

We had developed a scheme, Mike and I, which we

carried out in the vast area where swimmers placed their towels, along with beachbags and even purses and wallets. When swimmers went into the water, we would walk casually by, select a neglected beach towel and purse or wallet, and lay our blanket on top of it. After tossing a beach ball back and forth for a few minutes, we would pick up our blanket—with the purse or wallet now underneath it—and amble innocently off.

On this particular Sunday, however, when Mike called, something came over me. I not only told him no; I told him I would never do anything like that again. I couldn't explain why. I could only tell him my life was changing.

Mike decided to go alone that day; and unknown to him a man sitting on a hillside near the pool would observe what he was doing and alert the police. Mike was arrested and taken to jail.

That night, as it was a Sunday, I went to church. God had begun to answer my mother's prayers.

Indeed, I am convinced that when we stand before God in preparation for our eternal rulership with Christ, we will discover that *every* soul ever brought to a knowledge of Christ was in some way related to intercessory prayer.

Not only is our salvation related to the power of intercession, but all that God does in and through His people is continually affected by it. Indeed, as we develop the ministry of intercession, God wants to bring to birth through us greater things than we've seen thus far.

What exactly *is* the ministry of intercession?

To Pay the Price

I am a word buff. I can easily get lost for an hour in a dictionary or concordance. Especially appealing to me are the ancient roots of a word, and I enjoy tracing how the words we use every day first came into being.

This fascination is more than just a hobby, because I find that studying the history of a word helps me to understand the concepts represented by that particular term. That's why I often take time when I'm writing about prayer to share the story of some of these words. It helps me—and, I hope, the reader—to grasp the heart of these concepts.

Intercession, for example, is derived from the two Latin words *inter* and *cedere: inter* meaning "between," "among," "involved," "intervention"; and *cedere* meaning "to go," "to yield," "to move," or "to pay the price of."

Let's look at these derivations in the order noted above.

First, the roots suggest that intercession means "to go between," as when stepping between someone and his enemy in battle. Second, these terms describe one who "yields himself" among those who are weak and need assistance.

Third, intercession is a "moving in the direction of involvement" regarding the needs and hurts of others, not unlike the generosity shown by the Good Samaritan who, as the Scripture says, "when he saw [the beaten man by the road], he had compassion on him, and went to him and bandaged his wounds . . ." (Luke 10:33–34).

Finally, intercession means "to pay the price of intervention." Christ Himself provides the most worthy example of this definition. He went to the cross to pay the price of intervention for our sins. In this regard, Christ is the supreme example of all definitions pertaining to the theme of intercession. Because He is the personification of perfection, Christ is truly the perfect "go-between."

Perhaps most essential to a well-balanced understanding of intercession is a recognition that intercession is far more a way of life than it is a type of prayer. True, intercession *is* a specific aspect of prayer, but it is much more than that. It is a style of life. Christ didn't simply engage in the ministry of intercession, for example, while He prayed for others. His very lifestyle was characterized by a *spirit* of intercession. Christ was a loving giver and His greatest gift was Himself. The Bible says He "gave His life a ransom for many" (Mark 10:45). And just as Christ's greatest gift to a lost world is Himself, our greatest gift to a lost world is our intercession. Through that intercession the world will come to know their Christ.

Foundations of Intercession

An intercessor is a man or woman—or child—who fights on behalf of others. As such, intercession is the activity that identifies us most with Christ. To be an intercessor is to be like Jesus because that is what Jesus is like. He ever lives to intercede (Hebrews 7:25; Romans 8:34)!

But where exactly do we begin our quest to become intercessors like Jesus? Four simple foundational insights assist us as we begin our journey.

First, *we must understand our "privilege" as intercessors.* Christ is ever at God's right hand, and from this position He intercedes for the saints continuously. To be at God's right hand is spoken of in the Bible as being a great privilege and pleasure: ". . . At Your right hand are pleasures forevermore" (Psalm 16:11). So when we engage in intercessory prayer, it is our privilege and pleasure to join with Christ at God's right hand in this exciting task. What could be more exciting than to be in the throne room at the heart of world-changing activity? There we are surrounded by angelic beings engaged in tireless worship as we join Jesus in destroying the works of Satan!

Truly, the work of an intercessor is a privilege at the highest level. It is to be a partner with Christ in His supreme ministry of reconciling all of humanity to God the Father.

Second, *we must understand our "position" as intercessors.* Position here, of course, doesn't concern one's physical posture as an intercessor—i.e., whether kneeling, sitting, standing, or praying prostrate—but rather to the spiritual position of being "seated" with Christ in "heavenly places." As Paul says in his letter to the Ephesian believers, God "raised us up together, and made us sit together in the heavenly places in Christ Jesus" (Ephesians 2:6).

Several interesting thoughts emerge as we consider how Christ brings us into this position.

To begin with, He *energizes* us when we are "dead." Paul says, "But God, who is rich in mercy . . . even when we were dead in trespasses, made us alive together with Christ . . ." (Ephesians 2:4–5). The Authorized Version employs the expression *He quickened us.* To "quicken" or "make alive" means to energize. It is to renew and revitalize.

Beyond this, Christ *elevates* the intercessor. Paul explains that we are "raised . . . up together." Such elevation is important in the believer's walk as it speaks of our being spiritually transported to a higher sphere of divine activity, the invisible, heavenly arena. As people who fight battles on behalf of others, we function from this elevated place, with Christ, in the heavenlies.

Finally, we are *enthroned* with Christ in intercession. We are permitted to "sit together" with Jesus beside the Father's throne, which suggests we are not merely observers of spiritual warfare but partners, involved in the administration of His divine authority.

This concept of enthroned intercessors administering spiritual authority is unusually significant. It gives us a fresh understanding of Christ's instructions to speak directly to mountains, commanding them to move (see Mark 11:22–24). When we are enthroned as intercessors we are not just asking God to do things; we are actually empowered with His authority, partners with Him as He declares His will. Bold intercessors know that God's promises empower them to operate on His behalf to command spiritual mountains to move. And it is at this level that we must understand the authority of intercessors. We are not beggars expressing personal desires but "throne room commanders," receiving orders from our Supreme Commander, Jesus, who has permitted us to use His authority in ordering strongholds to fall.

Our third foundational insight: *we must understand our "promise" as intercessors*. It is an absolute certainty that our primary objective in prayer shall be realized. That objective is to see His Kingdom fully established on earth and it is an objective established in God's Word. Isaiah plainly preached, ". . . The earth shall be full of the knowledge of the Lord as the waters cover the sea" (Isaiah 11:9).

John's Revelation describes that momentous event of Christ's Kingdom coming in its fullness as heralded by an angel who sounds with a trumpet while great shouts in heaven declare: "The kingdoms of this world have become the kingdoms of our Lord and of His Christ, and He shall reign forever and ever!" (Revelation 11:15).

One cannot escape the significance that neither this angel nor the six who precede him are permitted to sound their trumpets until first "another angel" holding a golden censer (Revelation 8:3) comes before the altar facing God's throne and with "much incense" (symbolic of worship) offers this sacrifice "with the prayers of all the saints."

John continues the description of his vision, declaring that "the smoke of the incense, with the prayers of the saints, ascended before God from the angel's hand" (Revelation 8:4).

Only then, after the prayers of all the saints are combined at the altar with the praises of God's people (symbolized by the incense), are the seven angels permitted by the Lord to begin sounding their trumpets.

Surely it is significant that all the activities that unfold are the result of the initial release of prayer mingled with "much" worship at the very throne of God (Revelation 8:1–6).

All of this serves to remind us that as intercessors we are operating under promises from God that our prayers do make a difference. Mission researchers say that some 17,000 ethnic groups are yet to be reached with the Gospel. Intercessors know their prayers will ultimately break the chains that keep these groups and people from the knowledge of Christ's love.

Finally, *we must understand our power as intercessors.* Christ called His disciples together and declared to them: "Behold, I give you the authority to trample on serpents and scorpions, and over all the power of the enemy, and nothing shall by any means hurt you" (Luke 10:19). Here we discover a dynamic promise of power most believers rarely exercise. Our Lord is saying that those who move in the direction of involvement and are willing to pay the price of intervention will have all the power necessary to confront demonic forces in their citadels.

Come with me for a closer look at this glorious ministry of compassionate warfare.

two
Compassion in Action
The Functions of Intercession

Centuries ago, during one of the darkest ages in Church history, one of a few bright lights shining was a young man named Francesco de Pietro Bernardone. Francesco was destined to become one of history's most remarkable spiritual warriors, a man who would have cities, parks, hospitals, churches, and seminaries named in his honor.

Francesco was born into wealth, the son of an Italian merchant. He seemed headed for a life of abundance in the footsteps of his father.

But all that was to change one sunny afternoon as young Francesco was riding his pony on the outskirts of the city where his father had earned his fortune. Rounding the bend along the dusty path, the pony suddenly balked, then lurched backwards. Blocking the path was a frightful sight, a leper, his limbs half eaten away, pleading for someone to help him in his final hours of suffering.

Francesco stared but a moment and then had to look away. His stomach churning, he gripped the reins tightly, ready to turn his horse back toward home.

But at that moment a strange thing happened. Francesco's eyes were suddenly opened to eternal realities. God's presence filled the youth's heart and he turned again to look at the leper. This time he did not see the infirm man; he saw himself in the man. He saw himself as God saw him, spiritually depraved. And Francesco knew that what God was seeing was a condition far worse than the dying man's leprosy.

Instantly Francesco leaped from his pony and fell to his knees beside the suffering man. He put one arm tightly around the contagious leper, while loosening a bag of gold tied to his belt with his hand yet free. Thrusting the bag into the leper's half-eaten hands, the youth bent further and gently kissed the man.

Francesco de Pietro Bernardone's life would never be the same. He surrendered to his Savior that afternoon, encountering a supernatural baptism of compassion. And this "baptism" occurred just outside the Italian city of Assisi, a city whose name would be known throughout the world for centuries to come when people spoke reverently of St. Francis of Assisi.

Channels of Compassion

Intercessory prayer begins with this same supernatural compassion; and such extraordinary caring is a gift that can come only from God. He gives it to any and all believers who will make themselves available. Because only God can give this empathy, however, we must draw near to Him to receive it. Paul told believers to "walk in love," or, as a paraphrase reads, "Be full of love" (Ephesians 5:2, TLB). Because God is love, to walk in love or "be full of love" is to be filled with God. This necessitates our spending much time in His presence to be consumed with Him.

So, compassion is at the heart of intercession. *Compassion* is derived from the two Latin words *com* and *pati, com* meaning "with" or "together" and *pati* meaning "to suffer" or "to hurt." Combined, these expressions describe one who *"suffers with"* someone in need or *"hurts together"* with those experiencing pain.

Compassion is more than mere pity. It is love in its dynamic phase, love released through action. It is a life of involvement in the struggles of others. Christ gave us the fullest expression of active compassion when He went to the cross to remove the suffering brought on humankind through sin. Jesus was not an intercessor just when He prayed, as we have already seen; He lived the life of intercession. Jesus *is* compassion. When He prayed, it was compassion praying. *To see Christ in prayer is to see Love on its knees.*

How a person lives will determine how that person prays. As Andrew Murray wrote, "It is as men live that they pray. It is the life that prays."

The fashioning of an intercessor, then, begins not so much with a burden to pray as with a burden to love—a burden that leads the intercessor ultimately to intense sessions of compassionate prayer that flow out of seven functions of intercession.

A Call to Serve

First, *intercession is serving*. It is *making oneself available.* Consider the example of Jesus, our chief Intercessor. He said, "And whoever of you desires to be first shall be slave of all. For even the Son of Man did not come to be served, but to serve, and to give His life a ransom for many" (Mark 10:44–45).

Servanthood is at the very heart of intercession. No one prays effectively for others who does not have the servant spirit of Christ. The Greek word for "serve" in Mark 10:45 is *doulos,* which means "in bondage by choice." It means to subject oneself voluntarily to the ministry of caring.

It still amazes me, looking back on the growth of our two daughters through their infant to adolescent years, that we never had to hire a babysitter. This was in spite of the fact that Dee and I made numerous missionary journeys. Such freedom was given us because a pleasant young schoolteacher, Barbara Blake, spending a prolonged season in prayer for the Eastman family, heard God say, *I'm calling you to service in the Eastman household.* Barb had left her teaching job six months earlier to join our prayer center where college-age youths and other young single adults helped us maintain a 24-hour prayer vigil.

Shortly after, Dee and I received a call from Barb who made a stunning offer, one we were positive would last only a few weeks. Barb told us that no matter how much time was involved, nor how much notice we were able to give her, she would care for our girls while we traveled until they were old enough to care for themselves.

We decided to test the waters, so I called on Barb the evening following her offer. At first Barb simply watched the girls for a few hours while Dee and I spent some much-needed quiet moments together. That weekend there was a ministry engagement so I called Barb again. She didn't just agree to help; she agreed with unusual delight. And when we returned home Barb made us promise we would call her again no matter how short the notice. As time went on, if we didn't go anywhere for a week or two it was not unusual for Barb to call asking if we had any plans so she could guard her schedule.

Perhaps most remarkable was Barb's decision to move 350 miles south from Sacramento, California, to Los Angeles when Dee and I received the call to develop a worldwide prayer ministry through World Literature Crusade. It was Barb's idea completely, and it required finding a new job and apartment. She simply expressed her quiet view that she had made a promise and to the best of her ability wanted to keep it.

But the story doesn't end with the girls reaching their high school and college-age years. Barb still calls and still comes. She watches over our house, cat, and dog whenever the family is away. I just hope I get to stand near Barb when the "servanthood" awards are distributed around God's throne (2 Timothy 4:8)!

A Call to Fight

Second, *intercession is fighting.* It is *engaging in battle.* At first glance this seems a departure from the serving function. A spirit of fighting, however, clearly characterizes intense intercession. It is a picture portrayed best by Christ in His Gethsemane "warfare" experience (Luke 22:39–44). Because Luke is a physician, it's especially noteworthy to study the intensity of his description: "And being in agony, He prayed more earnestly. And His sweat became like great drops of blood falling down to the ground" (Luke 22:44).

The word *agony* used here by Luke comes from the Greek word *agonia.* It refers to a "place of contest" or a battlefield. Its roots are in the Greek word *agon,* which pictures a place of assembly where the Greeks celebrated their most solemn games. Unlike our modern Olympic games, however, it was not uncommon for people to fight to the death in a contest. The winner was the one who came out alive.

Praise God—Jesus came out of Gethsemane alive, victorious in a warfare so intense it could have killed Him before He ever made it to the cross. And even His death on the cross, where Christ became the living personification of intercession, was not a defeat as Satan must have believed, but a victory sealed by the miracle of the resurrection. Again, Christ emerged alive!

Paul uses this fighting theme when he requests the prayers of Roman believers: "Now I beg you, brethren, through the Lord Jesus Christ, and through the love of the Spirit, that you strive together with me in your prayers to God for me" (Romans 15:30). Here, the Greek word for "strive" is *sunagonizomai,* where the root *agonia* appears again, which is the same word translated "agony" in Luke's description of Christ's warfare in Gethsemane. Paul is saying, "While you are praying, engage in warfare against those forces that would limit my effectiveness in spreading the Gospel."

When we intercede for others we are engaging in battle on their behalf. And most interestingly, sometimes the victory we win in prayer on behalf of others actually has a way of returning to us as a blessing!

For years I have had the habit of listing in my prayer diary the names of ministers I've met. Of course, this prayer list has grown over the years, forcing an ever more prayerful selectivity in which names to add. The primary criteria were that I actually meet the person and that the Holy Spirit prompt me to add the name.

So when a Bible college student approached me at a conference asking me to add to my prayer list a friend of his who had just left for Saudi Arabia, I knew it was highly unlikely that such a thing could happen. For one thing, the friend was serving in a secular job and my policy was to put ministers only on the list. And I hadn't met the friend or his wife face-to-face. Before I could even mention my reservation the student said, "His name is George Puia, and his wife is Lynn." He spelled the name quickly and explained that although George had a secular job, his desire was to help start small prayer groups, as well as witness to Muslims as the opportunity afforded itself.

Making a mental note of the name, I added with all honesty, "My brother, I have to tell you that I can only do this if the Holy Spirit prompts me."

The student agreed that this was right. As he walked away I honestly dismissed the matter from my mind, in part because it just didn't seem that the couple fit the criteria of the list.

But two days later a strange thing happened. As I began praying for men and women on that day's prayer list, the names of George and Lynn Puia came to mind. A gentle impression came within: *I want you to add them to your list.*

Two or three years passed as I continued to pray for George and Lynn Puia. Always I wondered what they looked like, and what kind of secular work George did. Then one day I came to their names on my list and wondered if my prayers were making the slightest difference. *After all,* I thought to myself, *I haven't the foggiest idea who these people are.* It seemed to me that I was hearing in my spirit that the time had come to cease my intercession for them. With hardly a further thought I grabbed a pen and scratched their names off the list.

Several weeks later I was in Chicago, to appear on a Christian television program. Going toward the studio, I rounded a corner and ran headlong into a man hurrying in the opposite direction. I apologized, as did the brother, who looked at me carefully. Then he said, "Hey, I know you! You're Dick Eastman. You've been praying for my wife and me. I'm George Puia."

He took my elbow and ushered me gently toward the studio. "My wife, Lynn, and I just returned from Saudi Arabia, and now I'm serving as executive director for the station here."

To my amazement, the time that George and Lynn returned to the United States was around the day I scratched them from my list. Apparently the Lord wanted me to intercede for the Puias especially while they were in Saudi Arabia.

But the real encouragement to me was when George explained that our book and cassette tapes were a tool he and his wife used for starting prayer groups in that rigid Muslim land. This was interesting, since the penalties can be severe for importing such literature into countries like Saudi Arabia.

But here again, the back-up prayers of people who were interceding for George and Lynn made a practical difference. Once when clearing customs, George had a strange prompting that caused them to step back and let an Arab man behind them go first. Suddenly there was a commotion at the counter. Armed police rushed forward. The Arab man who had moved ahead of George and Lynn had been caught smuggling pornographic videocassettes, an offense that meant immediate arrest.

"Because of the commotion," George said, "the agent just motioned for Lynn and me to take our luggage and go."

A Call to Identify

Third, *intercession is identifying*. A committed intercessor often finds that involvement with others affects the very patterns of life. As Paul reminded the Corinthian believers: "Though I am free from all men, I have made myself a servant to all, that I might win the more; and to the Jews I became as a Jew, that I might win Jews; . . . to the weak I became as weak, that I might win the weak. I have become all things to all men, that I might by all means save some" (1 Corinthians 9:19–20a; 22).

Both a spirit of serving and a spirit of fighting are linked to the spirit of identification. To serve is to submit to and to assist others. To fight on behalf of others is to enter into warfare, deflecting the attacks of Satan. Such ministry clearly requires a spirit of identifying with those in need along with a willingness to adapt one's lifestyle, if necessary, in order to help meet those needs.

What does it mean to identify in intercession? It is to become increasingly sensitive to the needs of others, even to the point of denying oneself whatever is necessary to help alleviate those needs.

Intercessors, for example, learn to listen "between the

lines" wherever they go. Ordinary conversation actually becomes an unwritten prayer list for sensitive intercessors.

Learning to identify with others in prayer was an especially unique lesson God taught me over a decade ago. For days, newspaper and television reports had been filled with details regarding a hostage situation involving 153 Dutch grade school children who were being held by terrorists in Holland. The terrorists threatened to execute the children one at a time if their demands were not met.

From the day the crisis began I petitioned God to protect the children and bring about their safe release. Then a strange thing happened. Several days into the crisis the terrorists' threats intensified. That day in my backyard prayer chapel, early in the morning, an amazing thing happened. My mind was filled with a picture. But it was more than just a still picture . . . it seemed alive and I was in the middle of it. I was standing inside the schoolhouse where the 153 Dutch children were being held captive. I could see the boys and girls with my spiritual eyes. But then I saw something startling. Only 151 of the children were Dutch; the other two were our daughters, Dena and Ginger, six and nine years of age respectively.

In the natural I knew this could not be. Both the girls were fewer than a hundred feet away, fast asleep in comfortable beds. But I had forgotten that. I had slipped into the intercessor's role of identification and the Holy Spirit had ushered me into an intensity of prayer I had never before known.

Indignation swept over me and I began to command the terrorists to let the children go. I hit my fist into my palm as I prayed. I pointed my finger with authority, shaking it repeatedly at the terrorists as I demanded they release the children. I wept. I shouted. I trembled. And suddenly I sensed victory. As abruptly as the prayer had begun, it concluded.

Moments later I left my backyard prayer chapel and headed for the office. So real was the sense of victory that not another thought was given to the matter until I sat down to dinner that night with Dee and the girls. The television had been left on in the family room and out of the corner of my eye I could see the screen. I was just bringing a fork full of mashed potatoes to my mouth when the news came on. The announcer, Walter Cronkite, began with the words, "We have good news from Holland!" I froze and turned toward the screen. "We have just received word that a break has come in the hostage crisis in Holland. Three of the 153 children have been released," Cronkite continued. "It could be the beginning of the end of this terrible crisis."

My reaction surprised me. Instead of shouting a note of victory, tears came to my eyes and I returned the uneaten fork full of potatoes to my plate. My family had no idea what I was doing. *Jesus,* I said in my heart, *I didn't ask for three children, I asked for all of them to be released. And that was a prayer born of Your Spirit.*

In that instance a new burst of boldness came over me as I sharply hit the table with my fist, declaring before my startled family, "And I claim the miracle now!"

What happened next will stun me to the day I die. At the exact moment I hit the table the broadcast was interrupted by a news bulletin. Walter Cronkite was replaced by a reporter from a local CBS affiliate: "We interrupt this broadcast to bring you an update on the hostage crisis in Holland. The report given by Mr. Cronkite was recorded earlier for West Coast viewing and is incomplete. All 153 children were freed early this morning."

It was a moment of victory I will never forget. Of course, I wasn't the only believer who had prayed, but I knew my prayers had made a difference. I was especially struck by the means God used—the power of identification.

The path to intercession begins with a willingness to identify with the hurts and concerns of others. Jesus, we must remember, came from the glories of eternal beauty to "dwell among" humanity (or "pitch His tent," as the Greek word implies) so that He might pay the price of involvement (see John 1:14).

A Call to Share

Fourth, *intercession is sharing*. It is making possessions available.

In sending forth His disciples Christ issued a series of commands outlining the basics of their ministry. One simple assignment of the overall list included, "Freely you have received, freely give" (Matthew 10:8).

Sadly, many believers have yet to learn the secret of unhindered giving. They give, but not with an unreserved generosity. We note that Christ's command to His disciples went beyond mere giving. He said, "Freely give."

At the heart of meaningful intercession is the willingness to give. And often this willingness flows not out of a climate of prosperity, but conditions of poverty. In describing the churches of Macedonia, Paul says, "Though they have been going through much trouble and hard times, they have mixed their wonderful joy with their deep poverty, and the result has been an overflow of giving to others" (2 Corinthians 8:2, TLB).

Concerning this church Paul adds: "They gave not only what they could afford, but far more; and I can testify that they did it because they wanted to, and not because of nagging on my part. Best of all, they went beyond our highest hopes . . ." (verses 3, 5, TLB).

In the early days of our School of Prayer ministry there was a time when we desperately needed $5,000 to meet bills due that very day. My heart sank as I went to the post office and found only a handful of letters from our supporters. Opening the first one didn't seem to help. It contained 71 cents.

But then I read the testimony that accompanied that gift, written by a mother on behalf of her six-year-old daughter. For several years the mom had supported our ministry, sending a monthly gift that she saved out of her food budget. The previous month she had sent $20, which we had acknowledged with a thank-you note and a request for prayers concerning our payroll. And pray she did. Her prayers were overheard by her six-year-old daughter. The mother's letter told me what happened then.

"Tonight I went back into the room of our six-year-old daughter, Elisa. Elisa really loves Jesus. She asked Him into her heart when she was four. As I put her clothes away, I was startled to hear her voice. 'Mommy,' Elisa said, 'God just told me to give all the money I've saved to Dick Eastman's ministry, the man you prayed for today.' "

According to Elisa's mother, the six-year-old had tears in her eyes as she spoke, partly because the money she had saved, a grand total of 71 cents, had been carefully set aside to purchase a toy that Elisa wanted badly.

"It was a difficult thing for Elisa to give all that she had saved," the six-year-old's mother wrote, "because she really wanted that toy. But she told me she wanted to obey God even more. So, Brother Dick, enclosed is a gift of 71 cents. It's really far more than I've ever sent because even though every gift I share is a sacrifice, I've never sent all I've had."

It almost seemed as if a spirit of generosity was loosed among our supporters. When the rest of that small handful of letters were opened that morning, we had received over $8,500 in gifts—and it all began with Elisa's 71 cents.

A Call to Rule

Fifth, *intercession is ruling.* It is commanding with authority. To the prophet Jeremiah, who might be described more aptly as a "prophetic intercessor," God said: "See, I have this day set you over the nations and over the kingdoms, to root out and to pull down, to destroy and to throw down, to build and to plant" (Jeremiah 1:10).

Jeremiah was not a king or political leader. Yet he was ordained to rule over both "nations" and "kingdoms." It is significant that there are two spheres of authority—nations and kingdoms. *Kingdoms* here refer to spiritual rulers over the invisible arena, whereas *nations* refer to physical leadership over the visible arena.

Jeremiah's role as an intercessor is clearly outlined.

His calling begins with the assignment to "root out." To be an effective intercessor means going to the very source of a problem—its roots. Roots are the hidden supply source of a plant. When dealing with moral decay, roots refer to unseen forces of evil that feed the decay. Thus, Jeremiah was assigned to remove the "roots of decay" polluting their nation through intercession. To "root out" in prayer is to penetrate so deeply into a spiritual circumstance that we are able to deal directly with the primary source of that condition.

Beyond that, Jeremiah is committed to "pull down" obstacles that have been raised up in opposition to God's best for His people.

To pull down means to remove from a fixed position. The very fact that we are "pulling" something down suggests that we are removing an object that has been elevated and is fixed in that high position. Today this could refer to dictators who have been elevated to power and have become entrenched in that high position.

Jeremiah next is instructed to "destroy" these obstacles. *To destroy* means "to subdue or to defeat someone or something utterly." The intercessor is entrusted with awesome power, including the capacity to remove the influences of Satan "utterly."

There is still more. Jeremiah is commanded to "throw down" that which Satan enthrones. *Throw down* is even stronger than *pull down.* To *throw* means "to discard or remove something quickly with great force."

On my first trip to China in 1978 I often saw tables stacked high with Mao Tse-tung's *Little Red Book,* a collection of political sayings bathed in atheism. The devastating Cultural Revolution of the 1960s resulted largely from a strict allegiance to the tenets set forth in this same *Little Red Book.*

I decided to bring a copy home for use in my intercessory prayer time. I placed the small book in my backyard prayer chapel and whenever I started my intercession I was reminded to pray for China's spiritual deliverance. Day after day for over two years I would clutch the small, vinyl-covered red book in my hand, commanding it to be removed as a factor in Chinese society. My prayers were almost violent. I shouted against the influence of this book, often remembering how I had seen youth in the fields of China reading it as if they were sharing in a small group Bible study setting.

Imagine my amazement when next I visited Hong Kong to see a front page news story of Mao Tse-tung's picture being taken down—*thrown* down—throughout China. I read every word of the English language article. One paragraph leaped out with special excitement: "And as far as Mao Tse-tung's *Little Red Book* is concerned, it is as if it has disappeared from the face of the earth."

But Jeremiah's calling is not complete. Two vital responsibilities remain. What began in the negative suddenly becomes positive. Jeremiah now is told "to build" and "to plant." *To build* means to "give form to something according to a definite plan or process," or "to establish and strengthen." Intercessors must not only remove obstacles through their prayers, but they must help put something in place of what has been removed. Thus, the intercessor not only prays that an evil leader be removed; he must also pray that the right leader will be raised up.

Planting likewise is an essential ingredient to effective intercessory prayer. *To plant* means "to put something into a place where it has the capacity to grow." Intercession here rises above praying for a need. "Planting" intercession is involved with doing, with implementing the answers to our very own prayers. In the last chapters of this book we will see how this works out in practice.

A Call to Weep

Sixth, *intercession is weeping*. It is brokenness before God. The psalmist spoke of this aspect of sensitive intercession when he said: "Those who sow in tears shall reap in joy. He who continually goes forth weeping, bearing seed for sowing, shall doubtless come again with rejoicing, bringing his sheaves with him" (Psalm 126:5–6).

Tears that sweep over us are vitally important in victorious intercession. We see tears mentioned frequently in Scripture. There are, for example, tears of sorrow and suffering (2 Kings 20:5) and tears of joy and compassion (Genesis 33:4, John 11:35). There are tears of desperation (Esther 4:1, 3) as well as tears of travail (Isaiah 42:14) and repentance (Joel 2:12–13). Tears are pictured in Scripture as something God keeps in a bottle (Psalm 56:8), indicating that God treasures the tenderhearted.

Tears are water to the spiritual seeds we plant, thus assuring us a bountiful harvest as the result of our brokenness. More than a mere emotional garnish to our prayers, tears *become* prayers. As Charles Spurgeon explained, "Tears are liquid prayer!"

A Call to Die

Finally, *intercession is dying*. It is death to self. To Roman believers Paul wrote, "Likewise, you also, reckon yourselves to be dead indeed to sin, but alive to God in Christ Jesus our Lord" (Romans 6:11). The word translated *reckon* here means "to approach something as if." As intercessors, we are to approach each situation and circumstance as if "dead" to all presuppositions or worldly considerations. Dead means "being without feeling."

Note also the significance of the word *indeed* in the text. *Indeed* means "in reality," "in truth," or "to be sure." That is to say, we are to treat ourselves as actually being dead. Effective intercession requires death to self. And in spiritual terms it is a real, true death—"to be sure!"

three
Intensity in Vision
The Priorities of Intercession

I am told that vultures, descending on a wounded animal, will go instantly to the eyes of their victim. It is as if they know that if any potential for life remains they must remove the vision of the victim.

Satan, like a vulture, understands the value of vision for the intercessor. Paul recognized this value, too, and prayed that the "inward eyes" of believers would be "illumined" (Ephesians 1:18, NEB).

Unfortunately, too many followers of Christ accomplish little because they lack vision. Their focus is usually scattered. A singular vision is needed. As Jack Hayford says, "When you reduce the scope of an activity or life, you increase the force of that activity or life." Water flowing through a pipe with a three-inch circumference, for example, is going to increase sharply in force if the pipe is reduced to one inch.

So it is with the intercessor who clarifies his or her vision. The Bible has much to say regarding this aspect of our instructions on intercession.

Clarity of Vision

Four foundational Scripture passages provide intercessors with a basis for developing clarity of vision.

First, Proverbs 4:23–26 helps me *determine my direction.* We read: ". . . Let your eyes look straight ahead, and your eyelids look right before you. Ponder the path of your feet, and let all your ways be established." Intercessors must know where they're going. Our eyes must focus on those issues closest to the heart of God. Who specifically has God asked me to pray for today? What nations or groups will be touched by my time with God today?

Second, Job helps me *believe in victory!* Crying out in agony, Job declared, "I will never give up so long as I live. I will not change, I will maintain the rightness of my cause" (Job 27:6, NEB).

In the midst of his intense suffering Job held securely to his belief that a sovereign God was working out something far beyond any human capacity to comprehend. True, there were times Job surely must have doubted any possibility of victory. But he refused to give up. He held onto his promises.

As believers, especially believers who intercede, we need to be tenacious. We must become fanatics who say with Job, "I will never give up." Winston Churchill once was accused of fanatacism. "I plead guilty," he said, adding his definition of *fanatic*—someone who cannot change his mind and will not change the subject. Intercessors who have a burden for a lost world, for example, have trouble keeping silent. You cannot change their minds and they will never change the subject. They've been close to the throne room so long that few other issues really matter. They have become fanatics and will not give up.

Thirdly, Philippians 3:13–14 helps me *receive my prize!* Paul speaks of "the prize" that is set before believers as being "the upward call of God." It is my opinion that no upward call is greater than intercession. Paul told the Philippians: "I do not count myself to have apprehended; but one thing I do, forgetting those things which are behind and reaching forward to those things which are ahead, I press toward the goal for the prize of the upward call of God in Christ Jesus" (Philippians 3:13–14).

To receive our prize as intercessors, Paul points to certain qualities of spirit that help us. Humility is a vital requirement. We must say with Paul, "I do not count myself to have apprehended." Singlemindedness is another requirement of effective intercession. "This one thing I do!" Paul says. A sad reality in the Church today is that so many people attempt so many things that they end up accomplishing little. And we must become good forgetters when it comes to failures. We should learn from failures but, as Paul suggests, we need to forget those things that are behind, and reach forward toward those things God has prepared for us.

Finally, 1 Corinthians 9:26 helps me *establish my goal.* Paul said, "I run with a clear goal before me" (NEB). *The*

Living Bible reads, "I run straight to the goal with purpose in every step." To the Ephesians Paul wrote: "Live life, then, with a due sense of responsibility, not as men who do not know the meaning of life but as those who do" (Ephesians 5:16–17, PHILLIPS).

Do we have clear goals? They are essential to effective intercession. Where should we look as we establish these goals? The answer, again, is to be found in our supreme example of intercession, Christ Himself. We must discover which priorities Jesus established and then pursue them with a passion.

The Priorities of the Great Intercessor

While reading the Gospel of John several years ago, I paused to meditate on the intensity of a single phrase from the lips of Jesus: "I must work the works of Him who sent Me . . ." (John 9:4). It was the expression *I must* that caught my eye. Jesus did not say, "I hope to," or, "I intend to try to." Rather, He declared forcefully, "I must."

The word *must* expresses absolute determination to carry out a task. *Must* when used as a verb, for example, suggests insistence or a fixed resolve, as in the statements "I must eat" or "I must sleep." And when used as a noun, *must* pictures an absolute requirement or unavoidable responsibility, such as, "Eating is a must."

I wondered how many times Jesus spoke of His intercessory mission by using the word *must*. With the help of a good concordance I found that there are 83,898 words in the King James text of the Gospels; yet in describing His own purposes, Jesus used the imperative *must* only eight times. These "musts" portray specific priorities in the life of Christ. Taken together, they are invaluable to us as we try to follow His example as intercessors. They include:

One: A Commitment to Suffering

In the traditional order of the Gospels, the first recorded divine absolute of Jesus (in this case expressed in the third person) is found in the description of Mark: "And He (Christ) began to teach them that the Son of Man *must suffer many things,* and be rejected . . ." (Mark 8:31, italics added).

Although referring to Himself in the third person as "the Son of Man," it is significant that Jesus employs the absolute *must.* It is our introduction to His lifestyle as an intercessor. Christ is saying that all who would become intercessors must recognize the relationship between intercession and suffering. Our first priority as intercessors is simple:

To be like Jesus, I must make a commitment to suffering.

Jesus linked suffering with rejection. Committed intercessors are often misunderstood because of their tendency to believe things very deeply and because they often hear from God in matters of serious concern. Their intensity sometimes draws the criticism that they are "off-balance" in their Christian walk, that they are so heavenly minded they are no earthly good.

Intercessors are not exempt from physical suffering. Interestingly, the Bible actually commands us to suffer. Paul told the Corinthian believers, "Don't let schisms exist in the body . . . but when one member suffers, let all members suffer with him" (1 Corinthians 12:25–26). To the Romans, Paul declared, "Weep with those who weep" (Romans 12:15). Even when we ourselves are not hurting, we are to find those who are and hurt with them. Being commanded to suffer is especially appropriate to intercessors.

This does not mean we should inflict ourselves with physical pain, but rather to realize warfare can leave battle scars as we head for ultimate victory. Jesus enjoyed the victory of the resurrection only after the agony of Gethsemane and Calvary.

Two: A Commitment to Duty

From the first recorded words of Christ as a twelve-year-old, though listed second in the traditional biblical order of the Gospels, emerges a truth that provides us with our second priority principle of Christ (see Luke 2:48–49). As a Jewish child of twelve, Jesus was taken to Jerusalem for the ceremony commonly called the Bar-Mitzvah. He was "coming of age," and the Bar-Mitzvah was that occasion acknowledging His moving into puberty. Many family members joined in the festivities. This makes it easier to understand how, when leaving the Temple for the long journey home, the parents of Jesus thought their son was elsewhere in the large company of family members.

Three days passed before Jesus' parents realized the lad was nowhere to be found. Hurrying back, they were amazed to discover that Jesus had remained at the Temple, and was sitting among Hebrew teachers, answering their questions. Luke wrote of this moment: "So when they saw Him, they were amazed; and His mother said to Him, 'Son, why have You done this to us? Look, Your father and I have sought you anxiously.' And He said to them, 'Why is it that you sought Me? Did you not know that *I must be about My Father's business?'* " (Luke 2:48–49, italics added).

So Christ's first recorded words include a divine absolute. This imperative emphasized His *commitment to duty.* And the "Father's business" was the redemption of humanity.

In this we discover a second principle for the intercessor: *To be like Jesus, I must do God's business.*

Christ prefaced His call to His first disciples with the words "Follow Me and I will make you fishers of men" (Mark 1:17). God's business might be discussed in countless ways, but the bottom line cannot be avoided: Jesus came, lived, and died for the redemption of humanity. Saving souls is the Father's "business," and intercessors committed to doing the Father's business will keep world evangelization high on their list of personal prayer priorities.

Three: A Commitment to Mission

Thus, our next divine imperative from the great Intercessor deals with mission. Of His preaching tour in certain desert cities near Capernaum, Luke said: "Now when it was day, He departed and went into a deserted place. And the crowd sought Him and came to Him and tried to keep Him from leaving them; but He said to them, *'I must preach the kingdom of God to the other cities also,* because for this purpose I have been sent' " (Luke 4:42–43, italics added).

Here, Christ emphasizes His commitment to the ultimate mission of His life, that of establishing the Kingdom of God—everywhere.

Jesus had concluded His ministry at Capernaum and was about to move into a desert place when a crowd of people hurried after Him. They had witnessed the impact of His ministry with the many accompanying miracles occurring wherever Jesus went, and they wanted more. Which is like some in the Church today who want to hoard the blessings of God. Consider those growing congregations that build huge edifices to accommodate their remarkable growth, with the intention that later, vast sums of money will be available for missions. But somehow when that day arrives new local projects arise, further delaying the release of such resources.

But note Christ's reaction to those who would hoard the blessings: "I must preach the kingdom of God to other cities also."

Here we discover our third priority principle for intercessors:

To be like Jesus, I must go somewhere with the Gospel.

It is a principle that emphasizes *a commitment to mission.* All believers are commissioned to become involved in the Great Commission. The Church is called to go into all the world. Everybody, everywhere, must be evangelized. And in order for the Church to go *everywhere,* every believer must go *somewhere.*

For many this can best be done on our knees! That's why we refer to this principle as a commitment to *mission,* singular, rather than a commitment to *missions,* plural. All of us have a specific mission in life. No matter what we do in reference to the Great Commission, we should never look at it in a purely general sense. Missionaries do not go into all the world; they go individually into specific parts of the world. Thus, they impact all the world collectively. But only as we accept our individual mission as an intercessor will we make a contribution to evangelizing "all the world."

Four: A Commitment to Endurance

As Jesus continued His ministry throughout the cities and villages near Jerusalem, the hour approached when He was to sacrifice His life on the cross. As He ministered in one of the villages, a group of Pharisees came to Him with the stern warning, "Get out and depart from here, for Herod wants to kill You" (Luke 13:31).

Jesus responded promptly, "Go, tell that fox, 'Behold, I cast out demons and perform cures today and tomorrow, and the third day I shall be perfected.' Nevertheless, *I must journey today, tomorrow, and the day following;* for it cannot be that a prophet should perish outside of Jerusalem" (Luke 13:32–33, italics added).

When Jesus spoke of His being perfected on the third day, He was referring to His encounter on the cross that would take place just three days later. These were to be trying days, days that would include Gethsemane's warfare, His betrayal, and Calvary itself. Any ordinary person, knowing such warfare awaited, would probably have retreated to a place of solitude to rest before the battle. But Jesus had a job to do and He was going to preach His way to the cross. When told to go into hiding for fear of Herod, Jesus responded with the imperative, "I must journey today, tomorrow, and the day following." It was His way of saying, "I must keep persevering until My appointed time arrives!"

At the heart of intercession is a spirit of perseverance—a quality Christ demonstrated in these final ministry encounters. In so doing He was providing us a basis for our fourth priority:

To be like Jesus, I must refuse to quit. Christ was showing us that ultimate victory required *a commitment to endurance.*

Jesus knew He was going to die in three days. And yet He recognized there was yet work for Him to do. Indeed, even on the cross His earthly ministry continued as He reached out in love to the dying thief.

Note especially the word *perfected* in Luke 13:32. From the Greek word *teleioo,* "perfected" means to complete or finish a task or assignment, or to bring something to a desired end. Christ was going to work faithfully in His final days on earth, ever persevering, until He could "perfect" or "complete" His ultimate work on the cross at Jerusalem.

Such is the picture of the true intercessor. Perseverance is the key to their commitment. It is, by definition, the willingness to continue a course of action in spite of the difficulty or opposition. True intercessors, like Jesus, function from a commitment to endurance.

Five: A Commitment to Relationship

One day Christ's ministry brought Him to the thriving city of Jericho where large crowds had gathered to see Him. Word of His miracles drew throngs hoping for a glimpse of this Galilean preacher. One, a Jericho tax collector of short stature, inched his way through the crowd. Zaccheus was fascinated by what he had heard of this miracle-worker and finally decided to climb a tree to see for himself.

Luke explains: "And when Jesus came to the place, He looked up and saw him, and said to him, 'Zaccheus, make haste and come down, for today *I must stay at your house*' " (Luke 19:5, italics added).

Jesus wanted a personal encounter with Zaccheus. He saw the worth of this lone soul, and was willing to invest whatever time was necessary to introduce him to the Gospel of the Kingdom.

Christ cares about people, a quality vital to the lifestyle of an intercessor. To Zaccheus He expressed the concern in His words, "Today I must stay at your house." It seems to be just a passing remark but it contains another priority for would-be intercessors:

To be like Jesus, I must care about people!

Jesus had made *a commitment to relationship*. He wanted to be close to people. Note that He didn't say, "Zaccheus, I'm holding a series of meetings at the Temple this weekend; I hope to see you there." Jesus went straight to the house of Zaccheus. He met him where he lived.

Most people do not find Christ at an evangelistic meeting but because someone relates to them right where they live. And even those who do find Christ while attending a church gathering usually are drawn there by a friend who has taken the time to relate to that person's need.

How much more effective modern-day evangelism would be if we returned to the New Testament pattern of house-to-house ministry. In Christ's encounter with Zaccheus, the tax collector's entire household was affected by Christ's visit. The intercessor who touches just one person with the Gospel where he or she lives may be touching an entire generation with Christ's message of eternal life.

Six: A Commitment to Sacrifice

Intercession and sacrifice are closely related. As stressed earlier, death to self is essential to intercession. Jesus used the divine absolute in referring to His sacrifice on the cross: "And as Moses lifted up the serpent in the wilderness, *even so must the Son of Man be lifted up*, that whoever believes in Him should not perish but have eternal life" (John 3:14–15, italics added). Employing the third person, Christ refers to Himself as "the Son of Man" who "must be lifted up."

Often this verse has been used by preachers to challenge believers to "lift Jesus" so the world might be drawn to Him. Actually Christ made this statement in reference to His being lifted on the cross. He was making a parallel to Moses' day when a plague swept God's people and Moses was instructed to lift up a serpent on a tree. This was a clear look at the future power of the cross to destroy the serpent's plans.

Here Christ provides us yet another priority principle: *To be like Jesus, I must pick up my cross daily*. The cross represents *a commitment to sacrifice,* a quality vital to intercession.

Paul also pictured this principle when he wrote, "But what things were gain to me, these I have counted loss for Christ. But indeed I also count all things loss for the excellence of the knowledge of Christ Jesus my Lord, for whom I have suffered the loss of all things, and count them as rubbish, that I may gain Christ" (Philippians 3:7–8).

The cross is the perfect picture of intercession. Here we see Jesus, who will soon take up His position as eternal Intercessor at God's right hand, hanging between heaven and earth as a go-between or mediator. As intercessors who bear our own crosses of sacrifice, we too stand between hurting humanity and a loving Father, carrying their concerns to God in prayer.

Seven: A Commitment to Opportunity

Try this simple exercise in opportunity awareness. Pause a moment, close your eyes, and quietly quote John 3:16 from memory.

It probably took you no longer than ten seconds to say, "For God so loved the world that He gave His only begotten Son, that whoever believes in Him should not perish but have everlasting life." Sadly, in that same time, an estimated fifteen people will die. That's 5,400 people in the next hour, or more than 130,000 by this time tomorrow—and half of them have no knowledge that Christ died for their sins.

What a tremendous need for intercession these figures present! We should never miss an opportunity to minister. Jesus certainly is our model here. He recognized the value of the moment. He never missed an opportunity to minister. When He encountered a man who had been blind since birth, His disciples were interested in the cause of this infirmity. "Rabbi," they asked, "who sinned, this man, or his parents, that he was born blind?" (John 9:2).

But Christ saw the situation from a different viewpoint. "Neither this man nor his parents sinned," Jesus responded, "but that the works of God should be revealed in him." He then added, *"I must work the works of Him who sent Me while it is day;* the night is coming when no one can work" (John 9:3–4, italics added).

Here we find another priority principle of Christ for the intercessor:

To be like Jesus, I must do something today! It expresses *a commitment to opportunity* and a sense of divine urgency.

An experience involving a dedicated Every Home for Christ field worker in Brazil years ago illustrates. The worker, distributing simple printed Gospel messages, walked up the busy streets of a shopping area, sharing literature and engaging in conversations about Christ whenever possible. One such conversation occurred in a barber shop. The worker was witnessing to a man who was receiving a haircut when the barber himself began to ask questions. In moments the barber came under unusual conviction and asked if he might receive Christ as personal Savior right then. So while a surprised customer sat quietly in the chair watching, the barber received Christ as Savior.

The worker continued visiting shops throughout the district, and as the day drew to a close began to retrace his steps for home. Nearing the same barber shop where earlier he had led the man to Jesus, he noticed a commotion. The entry to the shop was crowded with people. An ambulance waited. The worker couldn't believe his eyes. The very barber he had led to Jesus earlier that day lay dead by his chair. Tears came to the worker's eyes, but they were tears of joy, not of sorrow. He had been at the right place, at the right time, and had seized the opportunity of the moment. And best of all, the barber was in heaven!

Eight: A Commitment to Finishing the Race

Our final intercessory absolute also comes from John's Gospel (see John 10:1–18). Here Jesus portrays Himself as the Good Shepherd who "gives His life for the sheep." He says, "And other sheep I have which are not of this fold; *them also I must bring,* and they will hear My voice; and there will be one flock and one shepherd" (John 10:16, italics added).

Christ was soon to complete His assignment and fulfill His purpose in coming to earth. The cross was only days away. The urgency with which He walked and worked, loved and lived, was now about to culminate in a glorious burst of eternal completion. He would pursue His purpose to the cross—and beyond. His intercession at the Father's right hand, along with our prayer labors on earth in unity with Him, would be a part of His "must bring" plan to touch every tongue and tribe, people and nation (Revelation 5:9).

He would finish what He came to do. And from Christ's longest recorded prayer, in John 17, we find a clarification of this commitment to completion: "I have glorified You on the earth. I have finished the work which You have given Me to do" (John 17:4).

When Jesus said there were other sheep not of this fold that He must bring He was providing us a basis for our final priority principle of Christ:

To be like Jesus, I must finish my assigned task. It is *a commitment to consummation,* consummation being the completion or fulfillment of a plan or goal. What Jesus prayed before the cross, "I have finished the work," was amplified in a word of consummation on the cross: "It is finished!"

Here is the spirit of the intercessor. We will become partners with Christ, our eternal Intercessor, in carrying out the completion of His "other sheep" commitment. We will give, we will go, we will weep, we will work until "every kindred, every tribe, on this terrestrial ball, to Him all majesty ascribe, and crown Him Lord of all!"

four
Ordered Warfare
Establishing Battle Strategies for Intercession

Have you ever felt that Satan has singled you out for special treatment? As if maybe he's breaking in a new demon and needs just the perfect bumbling specimen to practice on and you get the nod! Any follower of Jesus in close touch with God's Word recognizes the reality of unseen satanic forces. They are well-ordered and seek particularly to wreak havoc with our goals of intercession. Surely if Satan has a strategy it would be well for us, as believers, guided by God's Word and Spirit, to cultivate our own strategy.

Order: A Key Tool of the Intercessor

Scripture is very clear about the spiritual importance of setting our prayer lives in order. David, in describing his desire for daily prayer, said, "My voice You shall hear in the morning, O Lord; in the morning I will direct it to You, and I will look up" (Psalm 5:3).

Charles Spurgeon wrote of this passage,

> If we merely read our English version of this text, and want an explanation of these two sentences, we find it in the figure of an archer—"I will direct my prayer unto Thee." In other words, "I will put my prayer upon my bow, I will direct it toward heaven, and then when I have shot up my arrow, I will look up to see where it has gone."
>
> But the Hebrew expression here has a much fuller meaning than "I will direct my prayer." It is the word that is used for the laying in order of the wood and the pieces of the sacrifice upon the altar, and it is used also for the putting of the showbread upon the table. It means just this: "I will arrange my prayer before Thee." I will lay it out upon the altar in the morning just as the priest laid out the morning sacrifices. I will marshal up my prayers. I will put them in order. I will call upon all powers available, and I will pray with all my might, acceptably.

The Hebrew word employed here for "direct" is *arak*. From this word we derive our English word *arrange. Arak* is a word frequently used in the Old Testament and wherever used it speaks of establishing order at some level or degree.

As Spurgeon suggested, a most frequent use of *arak* in Scripture concerns the order that priests brought to their daily sacrifices. Note God's instructions to Moses in establishing Tabernacle worship: "You shall put in it the ark of the Testimony, and partition off the ark with the veil. You shall bring in the table and *arrange* the things that are to be *set in order* on it . . ." (Exodus 40:3–4, italics added). The word used for both *arrange* and *set in order* in this passage is the Hebrew *arak.*

Scripture is saying that wisdom sets things in order before coming to the Lord with our intercessions. Proverbs says that wisdom has "furnished her table" (Proverbs 9:2). In this case *furnished* means "arranged." The Scripture is saying that wisdom sets things in order just as a table is properly arranged for a meal. Isaiah also used *arak* when he said, "*Prepare* the table; set a watchman in the tower . . ." (Isaiah 21:5, italics added). Here *arak* is used to picture an ordered preparation prior to establishing a watchman in the tower.

Notice the spiritual warfare implications in these passages, especially interesting to us as intercessors. Jeremiah, too, employs *arak* in a warfare context when he prophesies, "*Order* the buckler and shield, and draw near to battle!" (Jeremiah 46:3, italics added). Here *arak* is translated "order."

Especially interesting regarding the use of *arak* in a battle setting is the confrontation between Israel and rebellious Benjamin as recorded in Judges 20. Concerning Israel's battle plan against Benjamin, it says they "put themselves in battle array to fight against them . . ." (Judges 20:20). To establish a "battle array" (*arak*) means to develop an ordered strategy prior to entering the conflict.

Note the significance this holds for the intercessor. We must be prepared prior to our going into each battle. When Job said, "See now, I have *prepared* my case, I know that I shall be vindicated," he used the word *arak* (Job 13:18). A primary definition of *arak* in the Hebrew lexicon is to set in order a cause in a court of justice.

In sum, *we need to work out a plan of attack prior to engaging the enemy in warfare prayer*. There is nothing unscriptural about praying with order. To say, "I pray as the Holy Spirit leads me," sounds good but can become a copout for neglecting ordered, intelligent intercession. Indeed, veteran intercessors demonstrate a deep dependence on the Holy Spirit for power and direction in prayer but likewise recognize that the Holy Spirit will give both order and insight to help us pray effectively. Much on the pages to follow is designed to assist intercessors in developing just such biblical order to their praying.

Strategies for Victorious Warfare

Strategy is a plan of action. Three foundational Bible passages guide us to basic strategies for victorious warfare.

First, *as intercessors we should consider Peter's call to vigilance*. Peter wrote, "Be sober; be vigilant; because your adversary the devil walks about like a roaring lion, seeking whom he may devour. Resist him, steadfast in the faith . . ." (1 Peter 5:8–9). *Sober* used here means we are to be self-controlled in light of our enemy's continuing designs to destroy us through myriad temptations. *Vigilant* means watchful, a reminder that we are to be alert. The use of the word *resist* is especially important. It is from the same Greek word translated "stand" in Paul's challenge to the Ephesians: "Stand therefore, having girded your waist with truth . . ." (Ephesians 6:14). *To resist* simply means to take a stand. And it's not merely a passive, defensive stand. It's an offensive stance that seeks to send the devil running.

Second, *as intercessors we should consider James' call to resistance*. He declared, "Therefore submit to God. Resist the devil and he will flee from you. Draw near to God and He will draw near to you" (James 4:7–8). Here the word *resist* is from the Greek *anthistemi,* meaning to stand against or oppose. It is from the same root used in Paul's warfare chapter (Ephesians 6) in which he tells us to "stand against [*histemi*] the wiles of the devil."

Noteworthy in James' challenge is his linking of submission and prayer to victorious warfare. You might call it James' "warfare sandwich." The apostle's "resist the devil and he will flee from you" is sandwiched between *submission* ("submit to God") and *prayer* ("draw near to God"). This latter challenge is especially vital because it speaks of our intimacy with the Father. And the closer we come to God, the further the enemy has to flee. Satan most fears the presence of God.

Third, *as intercessors we should consider Paul's call to preparation.* The apostle began his admonition with the twofold call "Be strong in the Lord" and "Put on the whole armor of God" (Ephesians 6:10–11).

Paul then systematically outlined the nature of our spiritual conflict, the structures of invisible beings in the heavenlies, and the importance of being properly equipped for the coming warfare. It is here that he used the analogy of armor to show us precisely what is needed by believers in order to prepare adequately for Satan's attacks.

Of particular interest concerning our arsenal of spiritual equipment is that each aspect of the armor is an analogy—except one. For example, we cannot actually see our breastplate of righteousness or our shield of faith. They are types or analogies of realities that can be understood only in spiritual terms. Nor can we actually take into our hands a literal helmet of salvation. But this is not the case with the last aspect of our armor, the sword of the Spirit, which is the Word of God. We can take God's Word literally into our hands and employ it as a spiritual weapon. This is what Jesus did in His wilderness warfare when His repeated response to Satan's suggestions was, "It is written" (see Matthew 4:4, 7, 10).

Our "it is written" is the Word of God employed in prayer. The Word, in fact, is actually the only offensive weapon listed in Paul's arsenal of spiritual weaponry. All other aspects of the armor are defensive.

Following Paul's challenge to put on the whole armor of God, including taking up the sword, the apostle declared, "Praying always with all prayer and supplication in the Spirit, being watchful to this end with all perseverance and supplication for all the saints—and for me . . ." (Ephesians 6:18–19).

Here we discover an important truth: *Prayer isn't so much another weapon on our list of weaponry as it is the actual battle itself.* It is the arena of conflict in which we engage our enemy. In concluding his challenge to Ephesian believers regarding spiritual warfare Paul provided us a unique sixfold strategy.

A Call for "Continual" Intercession

Paul introduced his prayer warfare strategy with the challenge to "pray always." In another letter the apostle said, "Pray without ceasing" (1 Thessalonians 5:17).

Paul was not suggesting, of course, that anyone pray twenty-four hours a day, but rather that we continue in a state of readiness to pray as needs arise. The expression *without ceasing* is from the Greek *adialeiptos,* a word commonly used in ancient Greece to describe someone with a hacking cough. The person certainly couldn't plan his coughs throughout the day but coughed whenever necessary. The need occasioned the response.

So it is with seasoned intercessors. Like the cough that comes when the urge arises, prayer is offered for each need encountered.

To pray without ceasing can be used both as a personal and corporate intercessory discipline. Few accounts are more thrilling than the record of the great hundred-year prayer meeting established by Moravian believers in 1727. Persecuted Christians from Bohemia and Moravia sought refuge in 1722 at the estates of Count Nikolaus von Zinzendorf, a devout nobleman living in Saxony (modern Germany). Zinzendorf had named the community Herrnhut, meaning "the watch of the Lord."

Sadly, during the first five years of Herrnhut's existence the community scarcely resembled its name. By the beginning of 1727, Herrnhut, now numbering about three hundred, was racked by dissension. Any hope of revival was out of the question. In desperation, Count Zinzendorf and others covenanted to seek God for one of the most basic focuses of all intercessory prayers, spiritual awakening.

And then on May 12 it happened. An unusual visitation of God swept through Herrnhut. In days, all dissension disappeared, every unbeliever was converted. Of those days, the Count would later say, "The whole place represented a truly visible habitation of God among men."

The entire community was seized by a spirit of intercession. By August 27 twenty-four men and twenty-four women had covenanted to spend one hour each day in intercessory prayer, thus sustaining continuous prayer. Before long, many others made similar commitments. On and on the intercessions went, month after month, year after year, decade after decade. Quoted in *Decision* magazine, historian A. J. Lewis relates: "For over one hundred years, the members of the Moravian church all shared in the 'hourly intercession.' At home and abroad, on land and sea, this prayer watch ascended unceasingly to the Lord."

The Moravians' spirit of intercession took on tangible form as they started sending missionaries abroad. Within the first two years of beginning their intercession for the nations, twenty-two Moravian workers had died. Future Moravian missionaries would refer to that season as "the Great Dying."

But still they persisted, and still they prayed. Within sixty-five years the Moravians dispatched three hundred missionaries throughout the world. Some of their victories, indeed, altered history. Just eleven years after the beginning of the continuing prayer watch, for instance, a young man troubled by deep spiritual doubts and apprehensions wandered into a Moravian prayer meeting in London. Years later he would say of that night that his heart was '"strangely warmed" as he came to a personal knowledge of Jesus Christ. The man's name was John Wesley, and the rest is history.

A Call for "Complete" Intercession

Paul's prayer strategy follows with the phrase *with all prayer*, an expression *The Amplified Bible* translates *with all manner of prayer and entreaty*. We are to include all manner of biblical prayer as a part of our spiritual warfare.

There are many types of biblical prayer that can be categorized. In the mid-'70s the Lord asked me to "watch" with Him one hour each day (see Matthew 26:41), and because He showed me twelve categories of prayer, I realized that devoting just five minutes to each theme would equal one hour.

Naturally this was only a guide, and when sharing this concept with others I've always been cautious not to convey a sense of legalism.

The complete list, which subsequently became the book *The Hour that Changes the World* (Baker Book House, 1978), includes the following:

1. *Praise*—a time of *exaltation!* The psalmist said, "Because Your lovingkindness is better than life, my lips shall praise You" (Psalm 63:3). To praise God is to acknowledge Him for who He is. It is to exalt God with our words. Praise ought to be the entry point for all prayer.

2. *Waiting*—a time of *adoration.* Although closely related to praise, waiting is a time of silently adoring God for who He is. The psalmist said, "I wait for the Lord . . . my soul waits for the Lord more than those who watch for the morning" (Psalm 130:5–6). Whereas praise means to acknowledge God in words for His greatness, waiting is more a time of just loving Him in silence.

3. *Confession*—a time of *examination.* This is a time devoted to personal evaluation of our spiritual status as believers. The psalmist said simply, "I acknowledge my sin . . . I will confess" (Psalm 32:5). Paul told Corinthian believers, "Therefore having these promises, beloved, let us cleanse ourselves from all filthiness of the flesh and spirit, perfecting holiness in the fear of God"(2 Corinthians 7:1). Confession is our part in the cleansing process. Christ's part is the cross.

4. *Scripture praying*—a time of *appropriation.* Balanced prayer needs time in God's Word. We should read the Word and pray the Word. This might be labeled "promise praying." It is to take the Word of God, which generates faith, and appropriate that faith through our praying.

Through Jeremiah God said of His Word, "Is not My word like a fire? And like a hammer that breaks the rock in pieces?" (Jeremiah 23:29).

5. *Watching*—a time of *observation*. Here time is devoted to cultivate a silent alertness regarding issues needing prayer. Soon we will be interceding for others and petitioning God for ourselves. Watching helps us prepare for these focuses. Paul taught believers to "continue in prayer, and *watch in the same* with thanksgiving" (Colossians 4:2, KJV, italics added).

6. *Intercession*—a time of *intervention*. No devotional hour could ever be complete without at least some time being set aside to minister in prayer on behalf of others. Intercession is essentially compassionate warfare. It is to intervene in someone else's battle. Note Paul's appeal for compassionate warriors: "Strive together with me in your prayers to God for me; that I may be delivered from them that do not believe in Judaea" (Romans 15:30–31, KJV).

7. *Petition*—a time of *expectation*. Petition focuses on our personal needs. It might be described as the verbalizing of our desires to the Lord. More than fifty passages in the Psalms, for example, include expressions like *Cleanse me, Help me,* or *Strengthen me.* Jesus emphasized petition when He said to His disciples, "What things soever ye desire when ye pray, believe that ye receive them, and ye shall have them" (Mark 11:24, KJV).

8. *Thanksgiving*—a time of *appreciation*. Another important aspect of ordered prayer is thanksgiving. The psalmist said, "Enter His gates with thanksgiving" (Psalm 100:4). Paul, too, showed this to be an important aspect of prayer when he wrote, "Devote yourselves to prayer, being watchful and *thankful*" (Colossians 4:2, NIV, italics added).

9. *Singing*—a time of *edification.* Singing need not be tied exclusively to corporate worship. This aspect of worship not only exalts the Lord but edifies the believer. The psalmist sang, "My lips shall greatly rejoice when I sing to You" (Psalm 71:23). When Paul told believers to be filled with the Spirit, which brings edification, he added, "Speaking to one another in psalms and hymns and spiritual songs, singing and making melody in your heart to the Lord" (Ephesians 5:19). In several places in Scripture we see the ministry of music linked with effective spiritual warfare (2 Chronicles 20:20–22; Acts 16:25–26).

10. *Meditation*—a time of *investigation.* Another significant aspect of prayer is meditation. This involves a spiritual investigation of God's nature and character as revealed in His Word as well as in creation. The psalmist said, "I meditate on all Your works" (Psalm 143:5). Specifically, meditation is to probe the nature of God, His ways, His acts, and His deeds with careful intensity. When focused on God's Word it is to investigate a passage carefully, searching out all hidden truth. The psalmist also said, "In His law doth [the godly man] meditate day and night" (Psalm 1:2, KJV).

11. *Listening*—a time of *revelation.* Listening, too, is a type of prayer necessary for a balanced warfare strategy. It is a quiet receptivity that allows God to reveal to us what might be called revelation insight concerning the activities of each particular day. Paul spoke of this receptivity when he prayed for the Ephesian believers "that God . . . may give to you the spirit of wisdom and revelation" (Ephesians 1:17).

Listening, of course, is but one of the several silent

aspects of prayer on our list. Because these silent prayer focuses seem similar, it is important to understand how they differ. Waiting, which is our first quiet aspect of prayer, is to *love* God. Meditation, also a silent prayer focus, is to *study* God. Listening, on the other hand, is to *hear* God. Thus, all three of these focuses, though quiet in nature, have uniquely differing functions.

12. *Praise*—a time of *jubilation.* We return to the place where we began in prayer—praise! We do this because Christ taught us to begin and end our prayer with praise (see Matthew 6:9, 13, KJV). But whereas we began with a time of *exaltation* in praise, we now conclude with a time of *jubilation* in praise. Seasoned intercessors recognize the significance of cultivating a spirit of rejoicing in prayer. Take time to rejoice! Be jubilant! And remember, true worshipers never run out of focuses for praise. The psalmist said, ". . . I will hope continually and will praise You yet more and more" (Psalm 71:14).

As you develop the above steps, or any other patterns for intercession, cautiously avoid dead, ritualistic praying, which is prayer without the Holy Spirit. Spiritual alertness will help you stay sensitive to the Holy Spirit's promptings.

If you use the above twelve steps, keep in mind that several may overlap. For example, you might sing the Word in prayer, which combines Scripture praying and singing. If you first meditate on the passage to be sung, you're adding meditation to that prayer. And if all this is focused on a nation, such as the singing of a song from Scripture over a nation, claiming that God's glory will touch that land, you've added yet another aspect of prayer, intercession.

Indeed, it is truly possible to use a plan and yet keep it fresh.

A Call for "Energized" Intercession

Paul's warfare strategy continues with his admonition to pray with "supplication in the Spirit." Supplication represents an intense form of intercession. *Deesis,* the Greek word for *supplication* (Ephesians 6:18), refers to continual, strong, incessant pleading.

James pictured this level of prayer when he wrote, "The effectual, fervent prayer of a righteous man availeth much" (James 5:16, KJV). The Greek word translated "effectual" in this passage is *energeo,* from which we derive our word *energy*. James was speaking of prayer energized by the Holy Spirit. Perhaps this is why Paul referred not merely to supplication in his Ephesian strategy but to supplication "in the Spirit." It is fervent intercession "supernaturalized" by the Holy Spirit.

We also see this level of intensity linked to our Lord. The author of Hebrews tells us Christ "offered up prayers and supplications with strong crying and tears" (Hebrews 5:7, KJV). Here we note that the word *supplications* is plural. Christ's prayer intensity was not a one-time emotional display in Gethsemane the night before Calvary. His intercessions were filled constantly with the energy and intensity of the Holy Spirit.

A Call for "Sensitive" Intercession

After Paul challenged believers to pray with "supplication in the Spirit," he added the injunction, "being watchful." As stated earlier, watching in intercession is to develop a sensitive alertness to the Holy Spirit's promptings. The intercessor must know what to pray for. Paul told Roman believers, "For we do not know what we should pray for as we ought, but the Spirit Himself makes intercession for us . . ." (Romans 8:26).

Earlier in the verse Paul said, "Likewise the Spirit also helps in our weaknesses." The Greek word translated *helps* is one of the longest New Testament Greek words—*sunantilambanomai*. The word means "joint help." It describes the strength and assistance afforded by any two persons who are working together. Another definition is "the mutual bearing of the same load by two people." This suggests that the Holy Spirit does not do all the work for us in prayer but works with us! It is a joint effort. As we depend on God's Spirit in prayer, He will show us how and what to claim in prayer.

A Call for Persistent Intercession

Next, Paul instructed warriors to pray with "all perseverance." This two-word expression, from the Greek *proskartero*, means "to adhere firmly to" or "to be in close pursuit of an object sought." It also means "to be always intent on the goal before you."

The combination of these meanings would suggest a spirit of intercession that never forgets its true purpose. We're not praying just to appear more spiritual. Nor are we praying to gain blessings. Our goal is much greater. *We are reaching out in prayer with the supreme purpose of seeing Christ's Kingdom ultimately established throughout the earth.* And to that end, we must persist. All God's promises must be taken at face value. Like Daniel who persisted for many days because he was intent on his goal (Daniel 10:2, 12–13), intercessors must develop a quality of faithful persistence.

Noah is a perfect example. From the Genesis account of the flood (see Genesis 5–6) we discover that one hundred years passed from the time God warned Noah of a flood until the actual first rains that caused it. Imagine the potential self-doubt coupled with the almost certain ridicule and criticism! Still, Noah persisted in building something no one had ever seen before, an ark, to prepare for something no one had ever experienced before, a flood. And it took a full century. Little wonder Scripture reads, "Noah was a pleasure to the Lord" (Genesis 6:8, TLB).

A Call for "Focused" Intercession

Paul's warfare strategy concludes with a twofold appeal for focused prayer. He pleads, "Pray always with all prayer . . . for all saints and for me." Paul was suggesting both a *general* focus ("for all saints") and a *specific* focus ("for me").

A general focus for prayer might include praying for general categories of needs regarding God's work and those who sustain it. To pray for several countries each day in prayer, for example, asking God to strengthen and bless Christian work and workers in those countries, is a general focus. Fuel for this kind of praying can come from various sources, including newspapers, TV newscasts, even church bulletins or regular missionary magazines. Of course, the more detail this information includes, the more one moves toward a more specific focus, which Paul emphasized by his appeal to pray "for me, that utterance may be given to me, that I may open my mouth boldly to make known the mystery of the Gospel . . ." (Ephesians 6:19).

It is significant that when Paul appealed personally for

prayer, he didn't request material blessings, such as finances or health, but the right words and boldness to proclaim the Gospel. Here again we see prayer's primary priority—glorifying Christ throughout the world and thereby "bringing many sons to glory!" (Hebrews 2:10). Indeed, prayer that scarcely mentions missions is prayer missing the very heartbeat of God. "God," after all, "so loved the world that He gave. . . ."

five

Authoritative Intercession:

Keys to "Fasting" Down Strongholds

Fasting. It might be called prayer that isn't fun!

Describing a particularly intense encounter with this aspect of prayer, Martin Luther said, "My flesh was wont to grumble dreadfully."

Of course, consistency in prayer at any level is difficult. That's because, as a child once wrote, "Satan trembles when he sees the weakest saint on his knees."

But of all the levels of intercession, this one seems to terrify our enemy the most. It saturates our petitions with an authority that comes in no other way.

To combine fasting with intercession is to add special power to our prayer. It is authoritative praying that allows us to "fast" down enemy strongholds.

Authority is defined as power to influence or persuade

from knowledge or experience. It is also the legal or rightful power to command or act in specific situations.

How does fasting relate to intercession? Intercession is the denial of self in prayer so that our praying is focused on others; and fasting is a physical form of humility and self-denial for which Scripture indicates special power. Fasting in conjunction with intercessory prayer is authoritative praying at its highest level.

Fasting, of course, is the practice of deliberately and voluntarily abstaining from usual nourishment, which, when performed in the context of prayer, brings supernatural power to our praying. Fasting is to do without, or to practice self-denial. Its meaning can be expanded to include temporary abstinence from anything in order to give more concentrated attention to spiritual matters. Scripture reveals five distinctive aspects of this difficult-to-understand category of "authoritative praying."

Brokenness in Intercession

First, *fasting is a personal, voluntary humbling of the heart before God that increases spiritual brokenness.*

The psalmist said, "When I wept and humbled myself with fasting, I was jeered at and humiliated" (Psalm 69:10, AMPLIFIED). The New English Bible reads, "I have broken my spirit with fasting."

Humility is at the heart of fasting. Humility is a quality that manifests itself in how one acts in relation to God and others. It is to lower one's estimate of self by elevating one's estimate of others.

And because fasting carries this quality of humility into the tangible, physical realm, it brings about a brokenness before God that can come in no other way. Such brokenness not only honors God but makes the intercessor's heart more pliable to hear from Him. He is thus more useful in carrying out God's Kingdom plans.

Control in Intercession

Second, *fasting is a commitment to self-control that enables a believer to die to self.*

Paul spoke of *temperance* (or self-control) as a fruit of the Spirit (Galatians 5:23). Temperance is the quality of moderation in one's appetite and passions. It is to take control over one's flesh by not allowing anything to grow to the point of excess. In this case it is to put to death that which is impure or excessive.

Note how fasting amplifies this action. The psalmist said, "But as for me, when [my enemies] were sick, my clothing was sackcloth; I afflicted myself with fasting, and I prayed with head bowed on my breast . . ." (Psalm 35:13, AMPLIFIED).

Afflicted is a strong word in the text that might equally be translated *torture.* Surely anyone who has fasted any length of time can readily identify with the use of this expression to describe fasting.

But the *New English Bible* suggests an even stronger translation: "I mortified myself with fasting," which could be paraphrased, "I put myself to death." Fasting truly helps us die to self, and death to self is the key to spiritual vitality and productivity.

In an age in which so many believers (prominent spiritual leaders included) are succumbing to the works of the flesh, surely a fresh call to fasting and prayer is in order.

Could it be that fasting is the key to overcoming Satan's

increased attacks on the moral well-being of even our spiritual leaders?

Paul certainly understood his need to keep his body in subjection. He said to the Corinthians, "I beat my body and make it my slave so that after I have preached to others, I myself will not be disqualified for the prize" (1 Corinthians 9:27, NIV.) Paul wasn't speaking of engaging in some form of penance for his failures but of maintaining self-control when confronting fleshly desires. And certainly this chief apostle knew that fasting and prayer was high on the list of maintaining that authority.

Receptivity in Intercession

Third, *fasting is a worship activity that increases spiritual receptivity by creating a climate for the Holy Spirit to speak.*

Fasting often brings a heightened sensitivity to those making personal or corporate decisions.

The author of Acts described such a circumstance regarding the sending forth of laborers: "As they ministered to the Lord, and fasted, *the Holy Ghost said,* 'Separate me Barnabas and Saul for the work whereunto I have called them.' And when they had fasted and prayed, and laid their hands on them, they sent them away" (Acts 13:2–3, KJV, italics added).

Here we see the combination of a spirit of worship with a spirit of fasting. Another translation reads, "While they were worshiping the Lord and fasting . . ." (NIV).

Not only did the disciples see the worth of fasting as they faced the issues of reaching the lost, but as the result of their fast they were able to receive specific guidance from the Holy Spirit. Indeed, it is possible that had they not fasted, the Holy Spirit might not have spoken.

Ezra, too, recognized the power of fasting in seeking guidance. When the scribe proclaimed a fast prior to leading God's people from their Babylonian captivity (see Ezra 8:21–23), he noted three specific focuses for the fast:

First, Ezra called the people to humble themselves before God and seek of Him a "right way for us." Guidance was clearly the first focus for their fast.

Second, they sought God with fasting regarding the care of their "little ones."

Finally, God's people sought the Lord with fasting for protection of "all their possessions."

In looking at the details of this fast, we immediately note the significance of the first focus. Ezra knew it was possible that enemies would attack them along the way. Already he had told the king they needed no military escort. But suddenly the reality of the situation faced Ezra squarely. Ordinary prayer wasn't enough. A time to fast and pray was essential. Fasting is a key to hearing "the right way"!

Power in Intercession

Fourth, *fasting is concentrated spiritual preparation for Holy Spirit-empowered service that increases the believer's spiritual power.*

Recall the baptism of Jesus as pictured by Luke: "Then Jesus, being filled with the Holy Spirit, returned from the Jordan and was led by the Spirit into the wilderness" (Luke 4:1).

Here we note that Jesus was "led" into this season of fasting by the Holy Spirit. God's Spirit must always be our Guide as we encounter any level of spiritual warfare.

Jesus' fasting lasted forty days, during which time Satan

confronted Him repeatedly. But Christ returned "in the power of the Spirit" to Galilee. Note how this differs from Luke's earlier words that Christ was "filled with the Spirit" before going into the wilderness (see Luke 4:14).

This seems to suggest that whereas Christ was filled with the Spirit before the fast, after the fast, He went forth in the power of God's Spirit, with the Spirit flowing out of Him. Jesus went into the wilderness with internal power, but He emerged with external power.

Something had happened during those forty days of fasting that brought added spiritual power. And significantly, that power was first released during the fast itself to thwart Satan's attempts at leading our Lord into temptation. Thus, Jesus not only defeated Satan with the power of the Word—"It is written"—but with the power of a fast that surely amplified the employment of the Word.

In all this we discover again that Christ is our supreme example of an intercessor. And here we see Him fasting His way to victory. Thus, those who would ask to be like Jesus will sooner or later follow His leading to a life sprinkled with seasons of prayer and fasting.

Ministry in Intercession

Finally, *fasting is a specialized service ministry that increases spiritual usefulness for the totally committed believer.*

One of Scripture's most remarkable women considered fasting her calling. The Bible says, "Now there was one, Anna, a prophetess, the daughter of Phanuel . . . of a great age, and had lived with a husband seven years from her virginity; and this woman was a widow of about eighty-four years, who did not depart from the temple, but served God with fastings and prayers night and day" (Luke 2:36–37).

Interestingly, the Authorized Version's expression "there was *one* Anna" (italics added) has special significance. Of the Bible's 2,989 characters mentioned by name, there indeed is only one Anna. Further, she has a ministry no one else is pictured as possessing. Anna served God by praying and fasting day and night.

Naturally, this is not to say Anna never ate or slept. God never calls anyone to a level of ministry that requires such intensity of effort that ends up destroying the very temple (our bodies) that He has commanded us not to destroy (see 1 Corinthians 3:16–17).

But it is interesting to note that the Scripture refers to Anna's "fastings" and "prayers" in the plural. This suggests that Anna experienced recurring occasions of sustained fasting and prayer. Note also the phrase *night and day*. Anna was sensitive to the Holy Spirit's direction, even if it meant sustained times of prayer at night. Fasting and prayer was Anna's specialized ministry as a committed believer. It is a calling available to any believer who would begin his or her ministry of prayer and fasting with periodic appointments with the Lord, during which self is denied for a portion of a day (or even an entire day or two) as the Lord leads.

Fruitful Fasting

Any who would seek an entry into this exciting ministry of fasting and prayer would do well to follow several simple suggestions:

First, *we should fast sensibly*.

A danger of discussing only those Bible characters or historic Christian leaders who engaged in sustained times of fasting, like seven, twenty-one, and forty days, is that we appear to be picturing prolonged fasts as the norm. The fact is, Scripture often refers to fasts of twenty-four hours or less.

Note, for example, Israel's battle with the rebellious tribe of Benjamin. When Israel saw the circumstances and feared the worst, they "went up and came to the house of God and wept. They sat there before the Lord and fasted that day until evening" (Judges 20:26). David fasted in a similar fashion (2 Samuel 3:35), as did Cornelius, the centurion, who fasted until "the ninth hour," which was mid-afternoon (see Acts 10:30). In all of these cases the fast was twenty-four hours or less.

John Wesley, when establishing the Methodist Church, considered fasting so important that he required all candidates for ordination to fast until 3:00 P.M. on Wednesdays and Fridays. Wesley realized that fasting and prayer for even a portion of a day made a difference.

So one need not begin a personal ministry of fasting and prayer by setting unrealistic goals. Begin simply, perhaps with the denial of one or two meals each week. To fast until 3:00 P.M. would mean to deny oneself breakfast and lunch that day. It may not seem like much to those who speak of fasting twenty-one or forty days, but your stomach will let you know within moments that even the missing of a single meal is a denial that brings the body into subjection.

Second, *we should fast secretly*.

When addressing the subject of fasting in His Sermon on the Mount, Jesus said; "Moreover, when you fast, do not be like the hypocrites, with a sad countenance. For they disfigure their faces that they may appear to men to be fasting. Assuredly, I say to you, they have their reward. But you, when you fast, anoint your head and wash your face, so that you do not appear to men to be fasting . . ." (Matthew 6:16–18).

Christ was not suggesting we never tell anyone we intend to fast. Family members need to know why we are not coming to meals, as do friends who might wonder why we have suddenly stopped usual fellowship. Rather, Jesus was chiding people who tried to appear more "spiritual" than they really were by pretending to fast. The text does not say the hypocrites fasted but that they tried to look as if they were fasting. To fast secretly, then, has more to do with humility than with secrecy.

Third, *we should fast sensitively.*

When Israel fasted prior to its battle with Benjamin, we note they "inquired of the Lord" during their fast (see Judges 20:26–27). One of the most important results of fasting is that it increases our sensitivity to guidance. This sensitivity can be cultivated more richly by including significant seasons in God's Word during a fast.

Fourth, *we should fast systematically.*

When Jesus taught His disciples about fasting, He began with the easy-to-overlook phrase "When you fast" (Matthew 6:16). Notice He did not say, "If you fast." Christ was making it clear that fasting was to be part of their ongoing spiritual development. And for this to happen in a meaningful way, we should consider a systematic approach to times of fasting.

To fast systematically is to set aside time on a regular basis for the purpose of drawing near to God with fasting and prayer. It may involve one day a week, or one day a month, or even a portion of a day. The key is that the fast be on a regular basis.

For several years in our ministry, hundreds of intercessors have helped us sustain a continuous fast for spiritual awakening and world evangelization. Each takes one day a week or month to fast and pray for the Church and her mission to reach a lost world. They don't pray that entire day but they do fast and pray sometime during that day.

Because these intercessors help our ministry break through difficult barriers, we call them "Breakthrough Partners." Many churches are responding to this call and are encouraging entire congregations to participate in their own sustained times of fasting. It can easily be accomplished if just a handful of people take a specific day, or portion of a day, on a systematic basis.

Seven people, for example, each fasting a different day a week, would cover the week. Only 31 persons, each taking an assigned calendar day per month, would also make possible a continuous fast. All it takes is coordination and a little spiritual creativity and discipline. Posting a large, plastic-covered handmade calendar, for example, on which names could be added or removed, helps stir up others to enlist.

Fifth, *we should fast sacrificially.*

Of fasting Andrew Murray said, "Fasting helps to express, to deepen, and to confirm the resolution that we are ready to sacrifice anything, to sacrifice even ourselves, to attain what we seek for the kingdom of God."

For the person who normally skips breakfast, to offer to miss the breakfast meal for a time would hardly be a sacrifice. To sacrifice is to deny oneself something for the sake of another. The hunger pains we feel during a fast serve to remind us that self-denial is indeed taking place. No doubt fasting brings power because it costs us something we can feel.

Sixth, *we should fast specifically.*

When God chided His people for the hypocrisy and

emptiness of their spiritual celebrations, including their fasting, He concluded: "Is this not the fast that I have chosen: to loose the bonds of wickedness, to undo the heavy burdens, to let the oppressed go free, and that you break every yoke?" (Isaiah 58:6).

God must choose the focus of our fast. We recall how the disciples fasted specifically before sending Barnabas and Saul on their missionary journey (Acts 13:2–3). It was a focused fast. Ezra, too, had clear direction as he fasted before leading the people from captivity back to Jerusalem (Ezra 8:21–23).

When moving into a fast, ask the Lord to give you clear direction concerning His purposes for the fast.

Finally, *we should fast supernaturally.*

A special characteristic of fasting is that it requires trust and confidence in God. The very nature of fasting requires dependence on God's supernatural power to see us through.

Note again the corporate fast of those involved in the mission of the early Church. The Scripture says that while they worshiped and fasted, "the Holy Spirit came!" (Acts 13:2–3). Their sacrificial fast brought a supernatural visitation of the Holy Spirit, during which specific directions were given.

The Gift of Wednesdays

Have you ever considered giving a loved one the gift of fasting?

Just before Christmas seven years ago, I asked God to show me what I could give our two daughters, Dena and Ginger, for Christmas. "A gift, Lord, that will touch them for the rest of their lives."

What a strange prayer! It was almost as if it had not come from me at all but from God Himself. What could I possibly give two teenagers that would touch them every day of their lives?

Then I heard a distinct question whispered in my heart: *Are you willing to give your daughters a year of Wednesdays?*

I was baffled. Did God want me to cancel my schedule for every Wednesday during the coming year so I could spend more time with the girls? I knew the idea was impractical. On many Wednesdays I would be out of town in ministry. On others the girls would have school activities.

Then I seemed to hear a further clarifying question. *Could you set aside every Wednesday as a time of fasting for your two daughters?*

I went numb. "O Lord, I could never do that!"

Why? came the gentle response.

"For one thing," my heart answered, "I'd forget."

Not if you mark every Wednesday on your calendar as a fast, the Lord suggested. *During the day when you'd normally be having a meal, you could pray.*

"But there's another reason I couldn't fast like that," I added hastily. "I really, sincerely don't want to, Lord!" And I chuckled.

But I knew God had talked to me. *Come,* He was saying. *Let Me teach you a way of prayer you have never known.*

So I said yes to Christ that day seven years ago. As the weeks passed a new habit was formed, one that continues to this day. I am convinced that our daughters have had a spiritual hedge about them as they encountered the personal problems of youth.

And I am convinced that the greatest single help in building that hedge was the Lord's suggestion that I give our children the gift of Wednesdays.

A Company of Givers

Those who fast follow in the footsteps of a glorious company . . . Moses, the Lawgiver; David, the king; Ezra, the teacher; Elijah, the prophet; Daniel, the prime minister; Nehemiah, the statesman.

Fasting believers keep company with Luther, Calvin, Knox, and John Wesley; they walk with Jonathan Edwards, David Brainerd, Charles Finney, and Hudson Taylor.

But most of all, they walk in the steps of Jesus who denied Himself through fasting, and who continues to give of Himself as our chief Intercessor at God's right hand.

six Praying for the Lost

Monday: Six Interrogatives of Intercession

In evaluating a balanced strategy of intercession, seven distinct categories emerge. Although appropriate any day, they may conveniently be assigned to the seven days of the week for a practical plan of intercession.

The first category, our Monday focus, is lost souls. World evangelization and the Great Commission represent a biblical theme not limited to the New Testament. When the people of Israel brought the Ark of God into the midst of the Tabernacle, for example, David offered a beautiful psalm that included the admonition, "Proclaim the good news of His salvation from day to day. Declare His glory among the nations, His wonders among all peoples" (1 Chronicles 16:23–24).

Before His ascension into heaven, Christ commissioned

His disciples to "go therefore and make disciples of all nations, baptizing them in the name of the Father, and of the Son, and of the Holy Spirit, teaching them to observe all things that I have commanded you . . ." (Matthew 28:19–20).

Sadly, as we meditate today on these passages, nearly half the population of the world waits for word of Christ's love. Needed is an army of committed intercessors who will intercede for the lost so they may have access to the Gospel of Jesus Christ.

The Example of Jesus

But to approach this subject intelligently, we first need to address a question: Are we really given authority to pray for the lost? Consider this paraphrase of Christ's High Priestly Prayer:

> "I am not praying for these alone, but also for the future believers who will come to me because of the testimony of these. My prayer for all of them is that they will be of one heart and mind, just as you and I are, Father—that just as you are in me and I am in you, so they will be in us, and the world will believe you sent me."
>
> (John 17:20, TLB)

Isaiah painted this picture of the coming Messiah: "And He was numbered with the transgressors, and He bore the sin of many, and made intercession for the transgressors" (Isaiah 53:12). *The Living Bible* reads, "He was counted as a sinner, and he bore the sins of many, and he pled with God for sinners."

To plead for sinners is to pray for the lost.

Note also Paul's admonition: "Therefore I exhort first of all that supplications, prayers, intercessions, and giving of thanks be made for all men . . ." (1 Timothy 2:1–2). The call for intercession on behalf of "all men" clearly includes the lost. The passage goes on to declare that God "desires all men to be saved and to come to the knowledge of the truth" (v. 4).

So we have clear biblical authority to pray for the lost. How might we proceed?

Shortly after returning from my first trip to mainland China, I began praying daily for Chinese people to hear about Jesus. But I faced the problem of how to pray for people I did not know who lived in cities whose names I couldn't even pronounce.

Praying for wisdom (James 1:5), I was promptly reminded of a passage in Romans revealing how unregenerate man by nature keeps some of the Law even if he's never heard it (Romans 2:14). Of God's judgment Paul said: "He will punish sin wherever it is found. He will punish the heathen when they sin, even though they never had God's written laws, for down in their hearts they know right from wrong. God's laws are written within them; their own conscience accuses them, or sometimes excuses them" (Romans 2:12–14, TLB).

So there were points of contact with these unknown people, places where the Law was already inscribed on their hearts. Thinking on these words, I asked the Lord to give me a plan of prayer that would make contact with that place in their hearts.

Suddenly, the six interrogatives I learned as a youth in English class came to mind: *who, what, when, why, where,* and *how*. I knew God had given me these interrogatives to help me pray.

Whom Can I Trust?

First, I could intercede for lost souls by praying that they be confronted with questions regarding trust. I might ask that God would plant in the hearts of lost people a skepticism about the lies they hear, whether philosophical, social, or political.

This is especially appropriate when praying for people in oppressed nations of the world like Communist or Muslim nations. We can pray that political leaders will do things that cause distrust throughout their areas. Once people begin feeling distrust, they will wonder whom they really can trust. Soon they will discover it is not possible to trust anybody other than someone who is absolutely perfect. Eventually this search will direct their thoughts toward God.

What Is My Reason for Being?

I might also intercede for unevangelized people by praying that they begin to ask, "What is my purpose for living?" Ask God to plant in their hearts an urgency concerning this question. This will cause a reevaluation of their reason for being and lead them to consider a purpose not found at a human level. This will likewise direct the person's attention heavenward.

When Will I Really Be Free?

When interceding for people where there is relatively little freedom, we can pray that God will use this lack to draw people to Himself.

When praying for lost souls in Muslim nations we might change this question slightly to ask, "Am I really free?"

Muslims do have a deep faith but need to recognize they are not really free from sin. Pray they will feel an emptiness that can be satisfied only by receiving Christ into their lives.

When interceding for the lost in free nations, we might pray that the person will ask, "When will I be free of this emptiness in my heart?"

Why Do People Reject God?

The fourth intercessory question concerns the reality of God. This prayer interrogative relates especially to those who live in atheistic countries. Ask God to cause lost souls to question why their leaders so vehemently reject the existence of God. Asked often enough, this question leads people on a deep heart-quest. They will not only wonder if there is a God; soon they will actively seek after Him.

Some two years after praying these interrogatives, I read about a Soviet fighter pilot who defected to Japan in his MIG jet. I was amazed to read that almost all six of the interrogatives on our list were questions the pilot had been asking for months leading up to his defection. The final question concerned God's existence. For weeks he had been asking, "Why, if our government leaders are so convinced there is no God, must they fight so intensely against the idea of His existence?" His reasoning led him to the conclusion there must be a God, and a short time later he defected.

How Can I Cope with My Problems?

This interrogative of intercession applies to all lost souls for whom we pray. We may ask God to plant a sense of hopelessness in their hearts. Every person faces some problem beyond his abilities. Our prayers of intercession would cause these people to realize their need for deliverance and thus prepare their hearts for the day the Gospel will be given to them.

We realize, of course, that praying these prayer interrogatives does not force salvation upon an individual, but rather prepares his or her heart for the Gospel. Intercession, indeed, is vital for the preparation of all hearts that ultimately receive salvation. Rare is the believer who does not know the person or persons who prayed for his or her salvation.

Where Will I Go When I Die?

Finally, we might ask God to cause unbelievers to ask, "Where will I go when I die?"

The reality of death is understood in every culture. Everyone wonders about death at some point in life. Indeed, in poorer regions of the world the reality of death is ever close. We should pray that God will turn these questions into a quest for an eternal answer, that He will plant a longing to resolve the issue. Imagine the reaction of one for whom we are praying if one evening he asks, "Where will I go when I die?" and the next day he receives a Gospel booklet on eternal life!

Do Something!

The more we study intercession, the more aware we become of the vast scope of this spiritual activity. Any of the patterns presented on these pages could absorb an entire intercessory hour. Veteran intercessors know that the more we are touched with a burden, the more time it takes. It becomes easy to understand how Anna grew into a full-time intercessor (see Luke 2:36). Anna was able to fast and pray day and night because she was touched with the great concerns of those around her.

Applied to our praying, we must be touched with the ultimate burden of God's heart, the total evangelization of the world and the resulting completion of the Bride of Christ. When this happens His Kingdom will come! (See Matthew 24:14; Revelation 11:15.)

seven
Praying for Authorities
Tuesday: Invading Areas of Influence

Paul admonished Timothy to pray for "all who are in authority, that we may lead a quiet and peaceable life in all godliness and reverence" (1 Timothy 2:2).

Interceding for our leaders, Paul suggests, will result in our being able to follow the commands of Christ so that people everywhere will know His love. This conclusion is borne out in Paul's summation that God "desires all men to be saved" (1 Timothy 2:4).

A Primary Focus

It is clear from Scripture that the spiritual health of a nation is related to the spiritual health of its leaders. In Proverbs we read, "With sensible leaders there is stability" (Proverbs 28:2, TLB.)

When taking the reins of leadership from David, Solomon declared, "You know how my father David could not build a house for the name of the Lord his God because of the wars which were fought against him on every side, until the Lord put his foes under the soles of his feet. But now the Lord my God has given me rest on every side; there is neither adversary nor evil occurrence" (1 Kings 5:2–4).

It is almost impossible to fulfill God's *ultimate* plan for a nation if it is constantly embroiled in conflict. This is why we pray for peace. Generally speaking, a climate of peace is the best climate for evangelization. And because the spread of the Gospel is most hindered in repressed nations because of restrictive laws enacted by their leaders, we must make these leaders a primary focus for our prayers.

Praying the "Micah Plan"

In Micah 6:8 we find the basis for what I call the Micah Plan to help us pray for world leaders. Here Micah describes the lifestyle and conduct of a leader: "He has shown you, O man, what is good; and what does the Lord require of you but to do justly, to love mercy, and to walk humbly with your God?" (Micah 6:8). From these words emerge three simple focuses to help us pray for leaders.

First, we must pray that a particular leader will "do justly." This is to pray that he or she will govern *truthfully*, with *a spirit of sincerity*.

When the Bible speaks of doing what is just, it is speaking of one's carrying out his or her functions on a foundation of that which is truthful and right. The word *just* means ethical, equitable, and fair. Thus, we can pray that a leader will be drawn toward that which measures up to these important qualities.

Second, we may pray that a leader will "love mercy." This means he or she will govern *compassionately, with a spirit of generosity.* "To love mercy" is to conduct oneself humanely. Pray that God will cause leaders to be flooded with a spirit of unselfishness mixed with much loving-kindness toward their subjects.

Third, we may pray that the leader will "walk humbly with God." This means he or she will govern *modestly,* with *a spirit of sensitivity.* These qualities are in direct conflict with the roots of original sin, a spirit of pride. As Scripture declares, "Pride goes before destruction, and a haughty spirit before a fall" (Proverbs 16:18). It was a haughty spirit that caused Lucifer to fall. And it is a haughty spirit that causes leaders to fall. Our prayers for leaders, then, should include warfare against all forms of pride and arrogance that might diminish that leader's effectiveness.

Concentrated Warfare

Because the Micah Plan features several *generalized* prayer focuses, it is important that we share a variety of specialized prayer focuses for intercessors who wish to conduct more concentrated warfare for those in authority.

First, we can pray that *unjust leaders* will make mistakes that help advance the Gospel of Jesus Christ. The psalmist prayed concerning unjust accusers: "Make them fail in everything they do. Clothe them with disgrace" (Psalm 109:29, TLB). The King James relates, "Let them cover themselves with their own confusion."

Missionaries have often testified how doors have been

opened for evangelistic activities simply because of mistakes made by leaders. In one Communist nation, for example, the government sought ways to lessen the political impact of the Catholic Church. At that very time Every Home for Christ, over which I serve as president, was seeking permission to take Bibles house-to-house throughout their nation. Thinking that allowing a Protestant group such freedom would undermine the Catholics, the government agreed. The fact was, the Catholics were delighted that tens of thousands of people in their land would receive Bibles.

Second, we can pray that *tyrannical leaders* will fall from power by receiving unsound advice.

When David cried out concerning those who were persecuting him, he declared, "Pronounce them guilty, O God! Let them fall by their own counsels" (Psalm 5:10). *The Living Bible* reads: "O God, hold them responsible. Catch them in their own traps; let them fall beneath the weight of their own transgressions, for they rebel against you."

Is it God's will for evil leaders to fall from power? What we read in God's Word is His will. If we are convinced, according to His Word, that a particular promise applies to a situation, we ought to claim that promise with total authority in that situation. Thus, if we see a tyrannical leader insanely directing a nation away from God, killing multitudes of its people in the process, we have every right to pray like David, "Catch them in their own traps!" We should pray that the snares these tyrannical leaders set for others will turn against them.

Third, we can pray that all *godly leaders* will discover spiritual wisdom to govern their nations.

Not all leaders are godless. Some are genuinely searching for truth, as in this paraphrase from Proverbs: "Where there is moral rot within a nation, its government topples easily; but with honest, sensible leaders there is stability" (Proverbs 28:2, TLB).

Many world leaders may have had the seed of truth planted in their hearts. Usually this will manifest itself in small ways, alerting sensitive intercessors to pray. When such evidence arises, we should pray that these seeds will grow up to produce spiritual wisdom to help these leaders govern righteously.

Fourth, we can pray that *all leaders* will receive a personal message of God's love.

After Isaiah spoke of "beautiful feet" bringing good news (Isaiah 52:7), he said of the Messiah, "So shall He sprinkle many nations. Kings shall shut their mouths at Him; for what had not been told them they shall see, and what they had not heard they shall consider" (Isaiah 52: 15).

We know it is God's will that all people come to a knowledge of salvation. We have the assurance then, that we are praying in God's will when we ask that all leaders will receive knowledge of God's love. For years ministries like Every Home for Christ (formerly World Literature Crusade) have sought various means to communicate the Gospel with leaders at the highest level. Hundreds of specific acknowledgments of either Gospel messages, Bibles, or other Gospel communications have been received from such leaders. Seeds have been planted and the possibility of future fruit exists if we pray.

Fifth, we can pray that *leaders in troubled nations* will grow weary of the continuing bloodshed in their lands.

We recall again David's inability to build the Temple because of wars about him (see I Kings 5:3–4). We should ask God to put on the hearts of leaders in these troubled lands the recognition that they need help from a higher Source.

Sixth, we can pray that *corrupt leaders* will recognize their evil ways and turn to God.

When Manasseh, king of Judah, was bound and carried into Babylon, his affliction caused him to humble himself and turn to the Lord (2 Chronicles 33:11–13). We might pray for corrupt leaders to encounter circumstances that would draw them to the Lord.

Finally, we can pray that *all leaders* will realize that God alone gave them their positions of authority.

Picturing God's sovereignty, Daniel said, "Blessed be the name of God forever and ever, for wisdom and might are His. And He changes the times and the seasons; He removes kings and raises up kings; He gives wisdom to the wise and knowledge to those who have understanding" (Daniel 2:20–21). Because God alone places leaders in their positions, and God alone has the power to remove them, we need to pray that these leaders will recognize this fact and know they must answer to God.

Interceding for Areas of Influence

Not all prominent leaders of a land, of course, come under the category of government. There are at least eight distinct areas of influence in modern society for which we can find authority figures needing prayer. Ask the Holy Spirit to show you which specific area you might include on a regular basis in your times of intercession.

They include:

1. *The political arena.* This area of influence includes elected or appointed officials involved in every aspect of government. Under this category would come presidents, prime ministers, dictators, and all political advisors who might help shape decisions regarding a nation. Also included would be such groups as those involved in Islamic courts (which make key laws), the Soviet Politboro, and such groups as a Communist Party Central Committee. Under any of these categories, naturally, the list of specific political functions could be rather long. As intercessors we should ask the Holy Spirit to lead us to His choice of specific focuses in any of these categories.

2. *The judicial arena.* This focus includes those responsible for interpreting and enforcing the laws that govern a land. We should pray for our judges, courts, and law enforcement agencies. In some countries, military leaders also might come under this category because they also have responsibility for maintaining law and order.

3. *The spiritual arena.* The Bible tells us to pray for *all* who are in authority. This means we need to remember such authority figures as pastors, priests, rabbis, mullahs, ayatollahs, and other religious leaders. If they are not believers, we should contend for their salvation. If they do know Jesus, we should pray for their growth and integrity. Consider the tremendous influence certain evangelical leaders have developed in recent years through the use of television and radio. Little wonder Satan has sought to bring disgrace to this vital area!

4. *The educational arena.* This area of influence includes teachers at every level, from grade school to graduate

school. It is at the earliest level of teaching that children begin to form concepts that will dictate how they will think and live in later years. Parents who believe in the power of prayer ought to maintain a regular prayer list of the teachers instructing their children.

5. *The cultural arena.* This vast area of influence includes such categories as the entertainment industry, the arts, and sports. Entertainers attract the attention of millions of people throughout the world, and ought to be the focus of intelligent, systematic prayer by committed intercessors.

6. *The commercial arena.* Business and the media, which we combine in the commercial category, desperately need concerted intercession. The commercial arena includes influential people in advertising and the media, including television, radio, and newspapers, as well as all who may be involved in leadership positions related to the industrial complex of a nation. Key corporate executives and television news personalities ought to be included on the prayer lists of those intercessors called to concentrate on this arena.

7. *The civic arena.* Although closely related to the first area, there are so many influential leaders serving civic governments that a special category is reserved just for them. True, these leaders occupy political positions, but because they are not in what we generally consider the primary political roles, such as high-level government positions, we often neglect to pray for them. They are essential, however, to the health and morality of the community and are worthy of continuing prayer.

8. *The social arena.* This final category touches all leaders of influence over any kind of group that might not be included under the previous seven. It includes prominent

leaders over social groups, clubs, even fraternities and sororities. Even a family unit, with the head of that household, would come under this classification. Note again Paul's words: "All who are in authority."

As we take up the mantle of intercession "for all in authority," we are hastening the day that Christ's Kingdom will fully come and peace will indeed reign on earth.

eight
Praying for Nations
Wednesday: Confronting Enemy Strongholds

There are some 235 geographical entities we call nations,* and of these an estimated 97 are all but closed to conventional resident missionary activity. More than three billion people live in these 97 so-called "closed" nations. If they are to have access to the Gospel, a miracle of intercession must take place.

The intercession must be both fervent and all-encompassing if we are to see this miracle released in our generation. "God be merciful to us and bless us," says the psalmist, "and cause His face to shine upon us, that Your

* By *nation* I refer to all geographic entities that might be considered distinct countries. Some may be protectorates of larger nations, as Guam is to the United States, but because of their distance or isolation from the protectorate, we call these *nations* or *countries*.

way may be known on earth, Your salvation among all nations" (Psalm 67:1–2). Note the three-word phrase *among all nations*. Our intercession must encompass all the world and result in action on our part.

Consider the paraphrase of verse 2: "Send us around the world with the news of your saving power and your eternal plan for all mankind" (TLB). The psalmist isn't just saying, "Send workers, O God," but, "Send *us*, O God!"

The Redemption Factor

John describes a vision of the throne in which a glorious redemption song is sung. As the Lamb (Christ) takes into His hands a great scroll, four living creatures and twenty-four elders fall before Him in worship. Each has a golden bowl filled with incense and the prayers of the saints (Revelation 5:8). John then describes the redemption factor in God's eternal plan with the song,

> "You are worthy to take the scroll, and to open its seals; for You were slain and have redeemed us to God by Your blood out of every tribe and tongue and people and nation, and have made us kings and priests to our God; and we shall reign on earth."
>
> (Revelation 5:9–10)

Because the Bible tells us redeemed humanity will come from every tribe, tongue, people, and nation, we know that we are interceding in God's will when praying for all four of these categories systematically in our prayers.

Interceding for "Every Tribe"

From the Greek word *phulee* comes our first focus. *Phulee* is most often translated "tribe," such as the tribe of

Reuben or the tribe of Judah. Because a tribe is not a complete nation, we may conclude that it refers to a smaller group within a nation, such as a cultural group. *Culture* means the totality of socially transmitted behavior or patterns, arts, beliefs, and institutions. Such ethnic groups within a nation have clearly defined patterns of behavior or beliefs that differ from the general population of that nation. If we are to intercede for these people to be reached with the Gospel, we will need methods quite unlike those used to reach others.

The job is enormous. There are an estimated 17,000 such groups scattered around the globe without a resident missionary or functioning church or even an evangelical witness.

How might we translate this opportunity into meaningful intercession?

We must pray for frontier evangelism.

Thankfully, various ministries have responded to the need to evangelize the "hidden people" of the earth. The majority of these ethnic groups can be identified, yet no one has taken the time to go to them with the Gospel. Such pioneer ministries as Every Home for Christ and the U.S. Center for World Missions have sought to mobilize Christians to focus prayers on these groups.

Interceding for "Every Tongue"

From the Greek word *glossa* comes our next prayer category. "Tongue" refers to languages and dialects. During the 1980s Wycliffe Bible Translators passed the 1,000 mark in the number of languages now possessing at least some portion of the Scriptures. There are, however, more than 6,000 known languages and dialects still needing the Gospel, which means much work has to be done. Yet the

Bible says converts will come out of every "tribe *and tongue.*"

To translate this promise into effective intercession, *we must pray for translation evangelism.* Such groups as Wycliffe Bible Translators and Lutheran Bible Translators are working faithfully in this field. P. J. Johnstone's significant manual for intercessors, *Operation World* (Send the Light Publications, P.O. Box 28, Waynesboro, GA 30830), provides names of many other ministries involved in translation evangelism, and is a day-by-day guide to praying for the world.

Interceding for "Every People"

From the Greek word *laos* comes our third focus regarding the nations. Employed 143 times in the New Testament text, *laos* simply means "people." It is a reference to human beings and individuals of a particular race. From childhood we recall the chorus:

> *Jesus loves the little children,*
> *All the children of the world.*
> *Red and yellow, black and white,*
> *They are precious in His sight.*
> *Jesus loves the little children of the world.*

There are three major classifications of races in the world: Caucasoid (white), Negroid (black), and Mongoloid (yellow and red). Veteran missionaries know that to reach a nation they must mobilize the people of that nation, the nationals, to do the task of evangelism. The missionaries simply get the nationals started in the right direction.

Translated into a focus for intercession, *we must pray for national evangelism.* We should claim sound Bible training that equips national believers to reach their own people with the Gospel. We also should pray that conventional missionaries will learn to release authority to those who were raised in that culture.

Interceding for "Every Nation"

The word *nation* in our text is from the Greek word *ethnos.* It appears 164 times in the New Testament and is commonly translated *Gentiles.* The term refers generally to all nations of the world other than Israel.

Nations are usually defined by boundaries. Someday we may understand more fully the spiritual significance of the various geographic borders. It has been suggested that they picture in the visible realm the controlling spiritual forces operating from the unseen realm. God does speak of establishing boundaries in Scripture (Psalm 16:6).

How can we intercede for the nations living within these boundaries? *We must pray for systematic evangelism.* The key word here is *systematic.* We need to pray for all aspects of evangelism that seek systematically to impact a nation, including door-to-door literature evangelism, all plans of personal evangelism, and regularly scheduled radio and TV programs.

To help develop intercession with a systematic emphasis, I have developed a World Prayer Map that divides countries into 31 groups, a different one for each day of the month. The heads of state are listed for these nations, and a list of major world evangelism ministries that serve in all the categories mentioned in this chapter. (For a sample map write to me at P.O. Box 7139, Canoga Park, California 91304–7139.)

Confronting Strongholds

Missionaries who visit the "dark places" of the earth (Psalm 74:20) recognize that certain regions are unusual strongholds of Satan. Satan is at work in every nation, yet it seems he has selected some regions to control more blatantly. We see this especially in Communist and Muslim lands.

When praying for a nation, we should try to determine which satanic strongholds exist there, then exercise our God-given spiritual authority to confront these bastions. The day will come, I believe, when God will reveal specific details about these strongholds to sensitive intercessors. These may include pictures of the controlling forces in the unseen realm that influence Satan's activities in that land.

For now, we do know of several general categories of strongholds deserving special attention.

1. *Government strongholds.* Intercessors should pay special attention to the political characteristics of a nation. Laws decreed by evil governments often hinder the spread of the Gospel. Restrictions imposed by Communist governments especially fit this category. In Albania, for example, the Communist government has added to its constitution an article declaring atheism to be Albania's official state religion. Any other religion is considered a threat to the state—and illegal. Executions have occurred as the result of these restrictions.

One recent report from Albania related how a tourist had left a Bible in the Albanian language at a hotel, hoping it would fall into the right hands. Days later when he was leaving the country, an official handed him the same Bible with the words, "You left this at the beginning of your trip. I am returning it to you, but don't ever do this again."

How do we pray about government strongholds in such difficult political climates? Jesus told us to speak directly to the mountains (Mark 11:23). So *we must pray against the spiritual mountain of satanically inspired laws.* These mountains must be dealt with in the power and authority of Jesus' name.

2. *Cultural strongholds.* Every nation possesses behavioral characteristics. Collectively we refer to these as the culture of a people, and in some cases such characteristics restrict the spread of the Gospel. A spirit of nationalism provides an example. People of a nation may say, "Our way of life is superior to yours." This spirit makes it difficult for someone of another culture to bring the Gospel to those so bound.

The behavioral characteristic of xenophobia, manifested by certain Oriental cultures such as the Japanese or Chinese, provides another example. Xenophobia, a fear of outsiders, causes people to reject those who come from another culture bringing the Gospel.

How do we deal with these cultural strongholds in our prayers? *We must pray against satanically inspired attitudes.* We should ask the Holy Spirit to show us what satanic attitudes exist in a particular nation, and then systematically command these strongholds to be removed.

3. *Religious strongholds.* This focus touches the spiritual characteristics of a land. The Islamic religion is a prime example. It is a religious stronghold seriously hindering the spread of the Gospel in many parts of the world. In addition, there are Buddhism, Hinduism, Taoism, Confucianism, Jainism, Sikhism, Zoroastrianism. Sadly, whereas Christianity is said to have grown 47% in the last 50 years,

Buddhism is said to have grown by 63% and Hinduism by 117% during the same period.

In some countries of the world today it is virtually impossible to engage in open evangelism because of the religious restrictions.

How do we pray against such religious strongholds? *We must pray against satanically inspired beliefs* that enslave entire nations or major people groups of a nation. We must become "new sharp threshing instruments" of the kind God promised to raise up in Isaiah's day: "Behold, I will make thee a new sharp threshing instrument having teeth: thou shalt thresh the mountains, and beat them small, and shall make the hills as chaff" (Isaiah 41:15, KJV).

4. *Material strongholds.* A final focus regarding strongholds in nations concerns the materialistic characteristics of a land.

Some nations appear to be free and have experienced prosperity. Yet there is often lukewarmness in the churches of those nations. Soon apathy toward spiritual things moves a people toward humanism, which puts the emphasis on human development and rejects spiritual values. As with other strongholds, this materialistic spirit can greatly hinder the spread of the Gospel, especially in societies considered free. Mission leaders in Europe, for example, report that evangelism is more difficult in materialistic Western Europe than socialistic Eastern Europe. Materialism is so strong, and its corresponding apathy so great, that many refuse even to listen to the Gospel.

How do we contend with so powerful a stronghold in prayer? *We must pray against satanically inspired ideals.* Direct authority needs to be taken in prayer against Satan's ideals. Social, political, or religious movements that move people toward a materialistic or humanistic view of life should become serious matters for intercessory prayer.

These "mountains," like the others discussed, must be dealt with directly. Intercessors are not just quiet pray-ers. They are mountain movers.

nine
Praying for Laborers
Thursday: Co-Workers in the Conflict

The idea flashed through my mind as I prepared for a trip to Communist Eastern Europe. I needed to take along with me instructors' notes for our School of Prayer, so that leaders there could translate and distribute these materials. But I had heard stories of how Westerners going to this particular region were regularly searched and often had all printed materials confiscated.

I remembered Paul's appeal to Roman believers when he pleaded, "Strive together with me in your prayers to God for me, that I may be delivered from these . . . who do not believe . . ." (Romans 15:30). I needed intercessors not only "striving with me" in a general sense while on this mission, but specifically as I crossed borders into these difficult nations.

So I contacted a handful of our most committed intercessors scattered across the country and told them the exact time periods involved. I was careful to ask those responding favorably to cover me in prayer for at least one hour before a crossing time and an hour after to allow for the possibility of an early or late arrival. Because of the difference in time between Europe and the United States, many participants would have to get up in the middle of the night.

Yet many responded and soon I had a page full of intercessors' names who had promised to pray with me. Because I wanted to be able to "agree with them in prayer," I carried the list with me on my trip.

Little did I realize how important these intercessors would become. Several weeks prior to my departure, a young Christian courier from Western Europe, working with a group sponsoring my visit, had the assignment of going to the country to set up my schedule. He carried with him a single sheet of paper, carefully hidden, on which were typed all the details of my visit. It included the date of my arrival, the fact that I would be coming from Warsaw, Poland, and my plans to train leaders about prayer mobilization.

Later I learned that the young brother was detained at the border for some four hours and that the authorities had found and confiscated all the details of my visit. Fortunately for me, my full legal name, as it appears on my passport, was not on the sheet. Rather, they had referred to me only with the abbreviation DK (from Dick). Also the sheet did not show the exact details of my flight—only that I was to arrive from Warsaw on the date in question.

Preparing to depart from Warsaw, I had no idea authorities would be looking for DK, an American, coming from Warsaw that day. Naturally, had I been the only American arriving, they would have known I was that person and that the DK had been a code. Up to that point, in fact, I *had* been a lone American struggling to find anyone with enough English to point me to the correct departure gate.

Suddenly I heard someone speaking in my language with no foreign accent. Then I heard another, and still another. I turned to speak to a middle-aged lady who seemed to be giving instructions to a group. I had taken a flight filled with American tourists. The lady was a travel agent from New Jersey and this was an Eastern European tour her agency scheduled only once every three years. Now instead of one American on the flight, there were thirty!

All the while, I carried that slip of paper listing intercessors who even then had been up in the night praying for me. As the plane taxied down the runway I reached into my pocket, held the list, and prayed, "I agree with these who are praying with me now and claim my total protection."

Upon my arrival I blended in with thirty American tourists, chatting with those about me as we moved through immigration.

Then came the tougher task of clearing customs with my luggage. Before me were five large customs counters. Each was staffed with an agent searching every bag with vigor. Knowing how important it is to get just the right agent, I stopped for a few seconds to pray quietly. I reached into my pocket and touched the slip—agreeing again with those who were praying—and chose an agent.

Now I was waiting for the traveler before me to go

through. Every item in his large suitcase was removed and examined. Then the agent grunted and motioned toward another of the man's bags lying at my feet. Stepping to the side to allow the man room to pick up his bag, I found myself facing the agent. We were less than three feet apart. Without a word, the agent snapped his fingers twice, pointed directly at me, and then pointed toward the exit. I knew he was saying, "You can go," and my spirit leaped toward the door, though my body walked casually as if nothing out of the ordinary was happening.

Later I learned the whole story, when I spoke to several Westerners who also had arrived that week. All had been detained, some for as long as four hours, and many had had Christian literature confiscated by customs agents.

In discussing the role prayer played in these circumstances, some said that they, too, had friends praying back home. But when I asked if they knew for certain that those friends had been praying at the exact time of the confrontation, each responded negatively. Nor did they have a list of the intercessors' names to touch, agreeing in prayer. They could only report that friends had promised to pray while they were away.

I knew God had allowed this experience to prove to me the power of agreement in prayer.

The Sentence of Death

Paul spoke of the significance of those who helped him fight his spiritual battles through prayer. To the Christians at Corinth Paul wrote: "For we do not want you to be ignorant, brethren, of our trouble which came to us in Asia: that we were burdened beyond measure, above strength, so that we despaired even of life. Yes, we had the sentence of death in ourselves, that we should not trust in ourselves but in God . . . you also helping together in prayer for us . . ." (2 Corinthians 1:8–11). *The Living Bible* provides this paraphrase: "We felt we were doomed to die" (v. 9).

Not only are we to pray that the Lord of the harvest will "thrust forth" workers into His harvest (Matthew 9:37–38), but we must cover those who already are laboring in that harvest. Paul saw this need. He often spoke of "making mention" of his fellow workers in prayer (see Romans 1:9). One prayer pattern Paul employed for his co-workers is particularly meaningful. It begins: "For this reason we also, since the day we heard it, do not cease to pray for you . . ." (Colossians 1:9). Paul then lists several objectives he desired of the Lord in prayer. We might term these objectives the tenfold "Colossians claims" for Christian workers.

The first set of five claims relates to *a release of revelation:* God revealing His desired results to the worker. The second set of five claims relates to an *increase of blessings* from the Lord for that worker.

Helpful in employing these claims in prayer is to picture oneself as reaching out with both hands to touch the person for whom you are praying. The five fingers of one hand remind us to pray for the first five qualities, while the five fingers of the other hand remind us to pray for the five additional blessings. These ten claims in two sets of five each are:

Revelation

In our first step of intercession for workers, we should claim *a revelation of God's will* for the worker. This claim concerns *divine direction*. Paul prayed that his fellow workers would be "filled with the knowledge of God's will." In touching a worker on our prayer list, we need to ask God to reveal His desire concerning that worker for that very day.

Second, we should claim *a revelation of God's wisdom* for that worker. This claim concerns *divine perception*. Paul prayed that the worker would be "filled with all wisdom." Here we ask God to reveal to a worker how he or she might apply God's plan for that day. Wisdom is simply common sense. Spiritually speaking, it's spiritual common sense. One preacher defined it as knowing where you're going and knowing how to get there. Wisdom is to apply practically what we know theoretically.

In our third aspect of intercession, we should claim *a revelation of God's understanding* for the worker. This claim concerns *divine comprehension*. All too frequently Christian workers view problems as man sees them, overlooking God's perspective. Paul prayed that his fellow workers would be "filled with spiritual understanding." To *understand* means to perceive or comprehend the nature and significance of a thing.

In touching a worker, we need to pray that as the result of his experience in the Lord, he will know what he is to do in situations that develop that day.

Fourth, we should intercede for *a revelation of God's holiness* in the worker. This claim concerns *divine perfection*. Paul prayed that Colossian believers would "walk worthy" before God. This means the worker would walk in an understanding of God's holiness as it flows through him or her. One translation of the verse reads: "That you may live a life worthy of the Lord and may please him in every way" (NIV). Here we claim that God's holiness will manifest itself both in and through the worker for whom we pray on this specific day.

Our fifth aspect of intercession claims *a revelation of God's pleasure* in that worker. This claim concerns *divine gratification.* Paul prayed that his fellow workers would walk worthy of the Lord "unto all pleasing." It is to pray that a worker's every act that day would bring gratification to the Lord. Paul longed to see his spiritual friends become treasures to the Lord through their conduct and testimony. Surely this is a quality greatly to be desired by all Christian workers!

Increase of Blessings

After claiming revelation in these five areas, we should intercede for an increase of God's blessing for the worker in five additional categories. They include:

In our sixth aspect of intercession we claim *an increase of effectiveness* for the worker. The focus here is on *increased productivity.* Paul prayed that his fellow workers would be "fruitful in every good work." He was claiming that their effectiveness would increase at every level. When we pray for Christian workers on our list, we should ask God to give them lasting fruit as a result of that day's activities.

Seventh, we should claim *an increase of devotional growth* for the worker. Here the focus is on *increased spirituality.* Paul requests that his fellow Christians would increase "in the knowledge of God." It is possible to increase in our knowledge of God only with a strong devotional life. We should thus pray for each worker on our list that he or she would grow in a hunger for God and His Word.

Eighth, we should intercede for *an increase of strength* for the worker. This focus concerns *increased durability.* Paul desires that his fellow workers would be "strengthened with all might according to God's glorious power." Every worker needs a daily renewal of both physical and spiritual strength. In touching a laborer through prayer, we should claim for the worker a baptism of "fresh oil" (Psalm 92:10).

Ninth, we should claim *an increase of patience* for the worker. This claim touches *increased tenacity.* Tenacity is the quality of holding tightly to a task or promise no matter the circumstance. Paul's desire for his fellow soldiers is that they would be strengthened "unto all patience and longsuffering." Patience is the ability to wait under pressure. Longsuffering is the ability to put up with difficult situations for extended periods of time. Longsuffering is a special form of what might be termed extended patience. Pray that God will give workers on your list a quiet confidence in Him that manifests itself in an increased measure of patience.

Finally we come to the wonderful claim of *an increase of joy* for the worker. This intercession concerns *increased delight.* When Paul says that his companions will be "strengthened unto all patience and longsuffering," he adds, "with joyfulness." The word *joyfulness* in this passage comes from the same Greek word translated elsewhere as "exceeding great joy" (Matthew 2:10).

Note the word *with* in this passage, which shows that all of the claims on this list are to be saturated *with* joy. Fruitfulness should be mixed with joy. Spirituality should be bathed in joy. Strength flows from joy—"The joy of the Lord is our strength" (Nehemiah 8:10). Joy, indeed, is a special ingredient that makes everything we do in Jesus delightful.

We should transfer that joy from our hearts to those on our prayer lists every time we lift them in prayer. One of ancient Israel's statutes declared, "You shall rejoice before the Lord your God in all to which you put your hands" (Deuteronomy 12:18). May we remember that admonition when we daily reach out our hands in prayer, with rejoicing, to touch laborers on the front lines of spiritual battle.

ten
Praying for the Church
Friday: Contending for Spiritual Awakening

One of this century's most significant awakenings began in Wales in 1904, the result of a call to united prayer. According to historian Dr. J. Edwin Orr, Seth Joshua, a Presbyterian evangelist, visited Newcastle Emlyn College in Wales where a young man named Evan Roberts was preparing for the ministry. Roberts was a 26-year-old Welch miner when he felt the call to preach.

During Seth Joshua's visit to the college, the students were stirred to a deep desire for prayer and asked if they could attend his next series of meetings in a nearby city. The request granted, all classes were canceled and the entire student body attended. It was there the students heard Seth Joshua pray passionately, "O God, bend us." Evan Roberts went forward that evening crying out, "O God, bend me."

When the meetings concluded, Roberts returned to the college with his classmates but found he couldn't concentrate on his studies. Something was happening in his heart. "I keep hearing a voice," Roberts told his principal, "that tells me I must go home to speak to the young people in my home church." Roberts wondered if it was the voice of the devil or the voice of the Spirit. The principal answered, "The devil never gives orders like that. You can have a week off."

Young Roberts returned to Loughor and told his pastor he had come home to preach. The pastor was far from comfortable, however, allowing this inexperienced student to address the entire congregation, so he suggested Evan Roberts testify at the prayer meeting on Monday night. Evan agreed, thankful that at least he would have opportunity to speak to some of the congregation.

Attendance was greater than expected at the meeting. The pastor decided not to call on Evan Roberts until the very end. Just before people were ready to depart, the pastor said, "Our young brother, Evan Roberts, feels he has a message for you, if you care to wait."

Only seventeen people remained. Roberts told those present: "I have a message for you from God. You must confess any known sin to God and put any wrong unto man right. Second, you must put away any doubtful habit. Third, you must obey the Spirit promptly. Finally, you must confess your faith in Christ publicly."

According to eyewitnesses, by 10 P.M. all seventeen had responded. The pastor was so moved he asked Evan Roberts if he would be willing to speak at the missions service the following night. Then he asked him to share at the regular Wednesday night meeting. A fourth service was scheduled the following night, and still another. It was decided to continue a second week when the heavens seemed to open.

Soon the main road on which the church was located was packed solid with hungry seekers coming to the service. Shopkeepers even closed early so they, too, could get a seat in the large but packed church.

A Tidal Wave

So powerful was the revival that newspaper reporters were sent to describe the happenings. Like a tidal wave the awakening spread over Wales. In five months 100,000 people met Christ in the immediate region. Judges had no cases to try. There were no robberies, no burglaries, no rapes, no murders. Civic leaders met to discuss what to do with the police now that crime had disappeared. In one community, the sergeant of the police was asked by a reporter, "What do you do with your time?"

"Before the revival," he replied, "we had two main jobs, to prevent crime and to control crowds attending soccer games. Since the revival there is practically no crime. So we just go with the crowds."

When asked what he meant, the sergeant replied, "You know where the crowds are. They are filling the churches."

"But how does that affect the police?" asked the reporter.

"We have seventeen police in our station," replied the sergeant. "Five do nothing but control crowds on their way to prayer meetings."

"What about the other twelve?"

"Oh, we've organized three quartets with those officers," the sergeant responded. "They sing at the churches.

If any church wants a quartet, they just call the police station."

Over the months drunkenness dropped fifty percent; illegitimate births, forty percent in some places. There was even a slowdown in the mines due to the conversion of so many coal miners. Those miners didn't strike; they merely cleaned up the profanity in their language. Horses pulling the carts in the mines didn't understand their "pure" language and had to be retrained.

The Welsh awakening spread throughout the world giving birth to a surge of missionary activity that continues to have impact on the world today.

What an example of revival! The world will be reached for Jesus only by awakened churches that "thrust forth" laborers. That's why Paul told Thessalonian believers that he prayed for them day and night "exceedingly," that he and his co-workers might see them face-to-face and perfect that which was lacking in their faith (1 Thessalonians 3:10). He added: "The Lord make you increase and abound in love one toward another, and toward all men . . . to the end he may stablish your hearts, unblameable in holiness before God . . ." (1 Thessalonians 3:12–13, KJV). These words of Paul provide a unique fourfold prayer pattern specifically touching on interceding for the Church.

The Restoration Focus

First, we must intercede in prayer for the *completion* of the Church. Paul prayed that God would enable him to help "perfect that which is lacking" in the faith of Thessalonian believers. Paul longed to see the Church restored so she might accomplish her supreme task—evangelizing the lost.

When Paul spoke of perfecting the Church, he used a Greek word, *kartartizo,* that elsewhere in the New Testament pictures fishermen mending their nets. Only as their nets were restored or brought to their original condition could they be used again to catch fish.

The same Greek word is found when Paul tells Epaphros, a Colossian believer, that he has labored fervently for him in prayer that he might "stand perfect and complete in all the will of God" (Colossians 4:12). The word is also used in Hebrews 6:1 where we read: "Let us go on to perfection [completion]." In Revelation we discover the Lord's challenge to the seven churches. Speaking to the church of Ephesus regarding restoration, He said, "I have this against you . . . you have left your first love" (Revelation 2:4).

For the Church to fulfill her mission of evangelizing the lost, we must pray for restoration to take place.

The Unity Focus

Second, we must intercede for the *cooperation* of the Church. Paul prayed for a spirit of unity and compassion, that the Thessalonian church would "abound in love one toward another" (1 Thessalonians 3:12).

The early Church *was* united. It was born out of a group of people who were in "one accord" (Acts 2:1). The theme is repeated in Acts when, following an explosive prayer gathering, "the multitude of them that believed were of one heart and one soul" (Acts 4:32).

Paul addressed this theme when later discussing divisions in the churches. To the Corinthians he wrote: "Now I plead with you, brethren, by the name of our Lord Jesus Christ, that you all speak the same thing, and that there would be no divisions among you, but that you be perfectly joined together in the same mind and in the same judgment" (1 Corinthians 1:10).

The word for *abound* in our text (1 Thessalonians 3:12) comes from the Latin *undare,* meaning to rise in waves. Paul was challenging the Thessalonians to allow their love toward each other to rise in great swells, as the waves of the sea rise in response to the tides. Our response to God's love ought to produce waves of love toward our Christian brothers and sisters. If we cannot love those in the Church, we will never love those beyond the Church.

Praise God for thrilling reports of this very spirit of unity presently spreading throughout the Church today! Schools of Prayer, Concerts of Prayer, and interchurch house-to-house evangelism campaigns are uniting thousands of believers in the supreme task of the Church, world evangelization. Intercessors must guard this priceless gift of unity. It is, after all, an answer to Christ's repeated prayer that His disciples would be one (John 17:11, 21).

The Vision Focus

Third, we must intercede for the *commission* of the Church. When Paul prayed that Thessalonian believers abound in love "to all," he was praying that their love for each other would overflow until it had impact on everyone. "All" is not most, or some, or even many. As a preacher once declared, "All means all and that's all all means!" The mission of the Church is to evangelize all the world. And every believer is commissioned to engage in this task.

Christ referred specifically to this commission when He commanded: "Lift up your eyes, and look at the fields"

(John 4:35). Eyes are instruments of vision. Christ was encouraging His disciples to expand the horizons of their inner vision. Later he declared: "Peace be unto you: as my Father hath sent me, even so send I you" (John 20:21, KJV).

Needed in the Church today is an internationalizing of our intercession. Not that we neglect praying for the local church, but that we recognize its significance globally.

One prayer pattern to keep us on target regarding the full sweep of intercession is the Acts 1:8 pattern in which there are three targets for prayer. The *Jerusalem focus* reminds me to pray for those needs close to home, like family, friends, and needs of the local community. The *Judea and Samaria focus* reminds me to pray for needs of my state (or province) as well as my nation. The *"uttermost part" focus* reminds me to pray for activities related to taking the Gospel to distant regions of the world.

The Growth Focus

Finally, we must intercede for the *conviction* of the Church. This concerns spiritual growth in Christ's Body. Numerical growth, though desirable, is meaningless unless the Church grows spiritually. Purity and integrity are essential.

Paul concluded his prayer of desire for the Thessalonians by praying for their hearts to be "unblamable in holiness before God." On another occasion Paul wrote: "Come out from among them [the world] and be separate, says the Lord. Do not touch what is unclean, and I will receive you" (2 Corinthians 6:17).

To Colossian Christians the apostle added:

> As you have therefore received Christ Jesus the Lord, so walk in Him, rooted and built up in Him and established in

> the faith, as you have been taught, abounding in it with thanksgiving. Beware lest anyone cheat you through philosophy and empty deceit, according to the tradition of men, according to the basic principles of the world, and not according to Christ.
>
> (Colossians 2:6–8)

When Paul spoke of being "established in the faith," he used the Greek word *sterizo,* meaning to make firm. We are to engage in those activities that help us firm up our faith. As intercessors, moreover, we should pray that believers everywhere desire new levels of growth that will make this firming up in the faith possible.

eleven
Praying for the Sick and Afflicted
Saturday: Biblical Factors for Physical Restoration

Dealing in prayer with sickness and suffering can be difficult. Almost all intercessors have been confronted with circumstances in which their prayers seemed fruitless. Yet much is said in Scripture about prayer for those who suffer, and no book on intercession would be complete without addressing this matter.

Two words are used by the apostle James when he deals with this matter—*sick* and *afflicted*. He said: "Is any among you afflicted? . . . Is any sick among you? Let him call for the elders of the church; and let them pray . . ." (James 5:13–14, KJV).

Two Greek expressions are used in this passage. *Kakopatheia,* the Greek word translated "affliction," is a reference to anything that causes distress, generally referring to intense suffering caused by circumstances other than illness. In this sense, social distress becomes a focus. The homeless and hungry are not to be forgotten.

In referring to the sick, James uses a different Greek word, *asthenes,* an expression referring to the weak, feeble, or sick.

Thus, in speaking of interceding for the sick and afflicted, we include those who are bound by physical infirmities, but also those oppressed mentally or physically, socially, or spiritually.

Once again we look to Jesus as our supreme example of intercession. Christ had a burden for the sick and afflicted. When Jesus came into the synagogue following His baptism and temptation, He was handed the book of Isaiah and began to read. His words described His own healing mission: "The Spirit of the Lord is upon Me, because He has anointed Me to preach the gospel to the poor. He has sent Me to heal the brokenhearted, to preach deliverance to the captives and recovery of sight to the blind, to set at liberty those who are oppressed, to preach the acceptable year of the Lord" (Luke 4:18–19).

In commissioning His disciples, Jesus appointed them to be healers. "And as you go," He said, "preach, saying, 'The kingdom of heaven is at hand.' Heal the sick, cleanse the lepers, raise the dead, cast out demons. Freely you have received, freely give" (Matthew 10:7–8).

Intercession for the sick is first recorded in Abraham's confrontation with Abimelech when Abraham dwelt in Gerar (Genesis 20:1). Because Abraham feared that telling the truth about his wife, Sarah, might cost them their lives, he lied to Abimelech, saying Sarah was his sister. Abimelech took Sarah to his quarters, no doubt intending to marry her later. That night, however, God came to Abimelech in a dream and pronounced a curse on him and his household because he had approached a married woman.

Abimelech complained bitterly because of Abraham's deception. In fact, he had not yet touched Sarah and God told him he had acted with integrity. But an intercessor was still needed, if the curse was to be lifted. God then told Abimelech, "Now therefore, restore the man's wife; for he is a prophet. And he will pray for you, and you shall live" (Genesis 20:7).

Abimelech obeyed the voice of God and appealed to Abraham. We read: "So Abraham prayed to God; and God healed Abimelech, his wife, and his maid-servants. Then they bore children . . ." (Genesis 20:17).

From such biblical accounts we are able to piece together insights that help us develop a strategy of intercession for the sick and afflicted. Seven factors guide the way.

The Wisdom Factor

First, to intercede for the sick or afflicted we must seek the mind of God for wisdom. "Wisdom is the principal thing," says Proverbs. "And with your wisdom get understanding" (see Proverbs 4:7).

Wisdom is essential. What is the will of God in a

particular circumstance? Jesus taught us to pray, "Thy kingdom come; Thy will be done . . ." but sometimes it is difficult to determine His perfect will in matters regarding physical healing. Some who are sick, for example, need prayer for discipline regarding the proper care of their bodies rather than for a healing of an infirmity caused by that neglect. God looks for healings that last rather than "band-aid solutions" that may lead to worse conditions. God could heal high blood pressure caused by excessive weight in an instant, but He might choose to grant that healing only through the person's discipline of losing thirty or forty pounds. As intercessors, we need wisdom to know how to pray in such matters.

Consider the example of Peter when he was told of the death of Dorcas (Acts 9:39–41). Before Peter commanded Dorcas to rise from the dead, he prayed. Though speculative, this initial prayer could well have been for the wisdom he needed concerning the will of God in the matter. We do know that when Peter finally exercised his authority, he did not ask God to do anything for Dorcas, but rather commanded her to rise.

Wisdom regarding God's will is essential. Years ago I heard the testimony of a Christian mother whose three-year-old daughter had been hit by a car. The doctor's prognosis was bleak. The child would probably die. If she did happen to survive, the child surely would be a "vegetable" as long as she lived.

Shortly after the doctor issued his report, a friend of the mother heard her shout an angry prayer of insistence. "God," she demanded, "either let my daughter live or I will never serve You again!"

The daughter lived, miraculously, but was never able to

think or function beyond the capacity of an infant. Forty years later the mother was still changing her daughter's diapers. She never had even a day to herself for rest and quiet.

Could it be that in God's wisdom it was best to call her daughter home? Surely our Father knows best in these difficult matters and we must seek His wisdom as we pray.

The Willingness Factor

Second, to intercede for the sick or afflicted we must prayerfully determine the willingness of the person to be restored. Some people who suffer do not genuinely long for healing. A person may enjoy receiving the attention an infirmity brings. Others may secretly reject restoration because such healing might require more responsibility on their part.

The willingness factor in praying for the sick must be established if our intercession is to be effective. Pray that the infirm individual will use his or her healing wisely. Ask God to help that person adjust to the ramifications of being well.

The Weakness Factor

Third, to intercede for the sick or afflicted we must seek cautiously to uncover any spiritual weaknesses that may hinder our prayers from being answered.

According to Scripture, sin hinders the potential for seeing God's best released in His children. Isaiah declared: "Behold, the Lord's hand is not shortened that it cannot save; nor His ear heavy, that it cannot hear. But your iniquities have separated you from your God; and your sins have hidden His face from you, so that He will not hear" (Isaiah 59:1–2).

We must avoid being judgmental, but we also need to ask the Lord to reveal any hindrances that might limit the effectiveness of our prayers. Because James linked the confession of sins with physical healing (James 5:16), we have a biblical basis for encouraging the person for whom we are praying to identify and confess any known sins. Seasoned intercessors know that victory over sin is every bit as significant as victory over sickness. Sometimes dealing with sin is the first step in dealing with sickness. Deliverance from sin can be the key to deliverance from disease.

The Word Factor

Fourth, to intercede for the sick or afflicted we must learn to use the power of God's Word as our supreme weapon of attack.

The psalmist linked physical restoration to the power of God's Word when he said: "They cried out to the Lord in their trouble, and He saved them out of their distresses. He sent His word and healed them, and delivered them from their destructions" (Psalm 107:19–20).

In our School of Prayer seminars we challenge participants to bathe their prayers with Scripture. One way to do this is to listen to Scripture on cassettes while you are praying. Take God's promises and declare them in prayer over specific needs on your list.

One School of Prayer participant accepted this challenge and purchased the entire New Testament on cassettes following the seminar. Several days later, while visiting a friend in the hospital, an idea occurred to her for using this new tool. Her friend had been in a coma for many days. Doctors offered little hope of recovery. Nevertheless, the woman sought permission from the head nurse to play cassettes of the Scriptures to her injured friend.

Permission was granted, and a few minutes before noon she placed a cassette player on the bedstand, started it, and headed for the cafeteria for a quick lunch.

While still standing in the cafeteria line, the woman was paged on the hospital intercom and asked to return to her friend's room. She ran upstairs. Her friend was sitting up and talking with a nurse! A twelve-day coma had ended with just a few minutes of recorded Scriptures. God had sent His Word, using a human messenger who believed His promises, and healed her.

The Worship Factor

Fifth, to intercede for the sick or afflicted we must recognize the importance of saturating our prayers with praise and worship.

A spirit of praise is frequently linked to victorious warfare. When God's people were under threat from Moab and Ammon, King Jehoshaphat cried out to God for His strategy for battle. Following a time of sustained worship, Jehoshaphat declared to the people: "Hear me, O Judah and you inhabitants of Jerusalem: Believe in the Lord your God, and you shall be established; believe His prophets, and you shall prosper" (2 Chronicles 20:20). The king then commissioned the singers to enter the battle first. The results were spectacular! We read: "Now when they began to sing and to praise, the Lord set ambushes against the people of Ammon, Moab, and Mount Seir, who had come against Judah; and they were defeated" (2 Chronicles 20:22).

The psalmist also linked worship with warfare: "Let the saints be joyful in glory; let them sing aloud on their beds. Let the high praises of God be in their mouth, and a two-edged sword in their hand, to execute vengeance on the nations, and punishments on the peoples; to bind their kings with chains, and their nobles with fetters of iron" (Psalm 149:5–8). Victory for Paul and Silas in prison also came as the result of prayer mixed with songs of praise (Acts 16:25–26).

My introduction to the power of praise began with a simple song of worship sung over our younger daughter years ago during a serious bout with the flu. Ginger's temperature was 104° and rising when I went into her room to pray. More than a casual prayer was needed.

Recalling the victory of Judah in 2 Chronicles 20:22, I began to sing a song of praise over Ginger. Instantly the fever broke and sweat actually began to pour down her forehead onto my hands.

Years later I shared this experience on television. A woman in California heard the testimony just days before she was to be operated on for a potentially life-threatening condition. At one point her temperature began to rise sharply. Monitors displayed this and other vital signs. Both nurses and family members could see the peril.

Recalling the televised testimony, the woman asked a nurse if her family could sing a song of victory over her. The nurse consented and the family began to blend their voices in praise.

Suddenly all eyes fastened on the monitors displaying the woman's vital signs. A degree at a time the temperature was dropping. The nurse opened her mouth in awe. She had never witnessed anything like it. As the melody ended the display read 98.6. God had met them in their song.

The Warfare Factor

Sixth, to intercede for the sick and afflicted, we must understand and apply principles of spiritual warfare regarding a person's condition.

Much already has been said about developing a warfare strategy in prayer. This certainly applies when praying for the sick or afflicted. As intercessors functioning from a position of authority seated in the heavenlies (Ephesians 2:4–7), we must directly confront the mountain of infirmity before us in prayer (Mark 11:23). We recall again Peter's adventure in authoritative prayer at the Gate Beautiful (Acts 3:1–6).

Peter did not ask God to grant a miracle. He asked God for nothing. Rather, he commanded the lame man directly to rise and walk. His dealing was directly with the infirmity.

Note how Paul told the Ephesians to "stand" against the wiles (schemes) of the devil (Ephesians 6:10–12). Certainly infirmity is a scheme of our enemy to discourage or defeat us. As intercessors we confront these schemes through spiritual warfare. Our stand is not defensive; it is offensive. The disease is our enemy. The name of Jesus is the cure. We must take the cure into the conflict and apply it through our prayers.

The Witness Factor

Finally, to intercede for the sick or afflicted, we must recognize that God's supreme purpose for granting miracles is to reveal Himself. Healing is a witness to the wonder of His Person.

When Jesus and His disciples passed the man blind since birth, as we have already seen, His disciples questioned, "Rabbi, who sinned, this man or his parents, that he was born blind?" (John 9:2). Our Lord responded, "Neither this man nor his parents sinned, but that the works of God should be revealed in him" (John 9:3).

The man's condition was an opportunity for God to reveal the fullness of His power. Miracles open the understanding of many to the mercy of God. Remember, the lame man's healing at the Gate Beautiful resulted in at least 5,000 conversions (Acts 3:1–8; Acts 4:4).

In the Old Testament we also find that God's purpose in answering prayer was to reveal Himself. When Solomon offered his dedicatory prayer over the Temple, he included a petition regarding foreigners in the land. He prayed: "Moreover, concerning a foreigner, who is not of Your people Israel, but has come from a far country for the sake of Your great name and Your mighty hand and Your outstretched arm, when they come and pray in this temple; then hear from heaven Your dwelling place, and do according to all for which the foreigner calls to You, that all people of the earth may know Your name and fear You . . ." (2 Chronicles 6:32–33).

When Hezekiah received an accusatory letter from King Sennacherib denouncing Hezekiah's faith, the king simply spread the letter before the Lord. He then prayed, "Now therefore, O Lord our God, I pray, save us from his hand, that all the kingdoms of the earth may know that You are the Lord God, You alone" (2 Kings 19:19). Again the focus of God's miraculous intervention was that all kingdoms of the earth would know the Lord.

Knowing God is the greatest miracle resulting from our prayers of intercession. In the early years of our twenty-four-hour prayer ministry, I discovered this important secret in a letter of great personal encouragement.

The letter said:

> On January 29 I called your ministry for prayer concerning my sister Mary Jane. She had just been hurt in a terrible car accident. We prayed together and the person I talked to on your prayer line said to call back when the miracle happened.
>
> Well, Mary Jane died on the way to the hospital. But since then many miracles have happened. Mary Jane and her husband had been praying for the Lord to use them in any way He so desired to help the people of their small community seek the Lord. Praise God—at Mary Jane's memorial service about fifty people answered the invitation and came forward to receive Christ. Several cousins have made a commitment, and a long-standing bad relationship between our mother and her sister-in-law seems to be mending. Praise the Lord! Mary's absence hurts, of course, but her five children all belong to the Lord, and they seem to be doing fine. I'm sure that there are more miracles to come. Thank you for your prayers.

Could it be that Mary's homegoing was the real miracle in the battle for her healing? Fifty people met Christ at her memorial service. These friends and loved ones saw the miracle of Mary Jane's life in Christ and in that tragedy realized they, too, needed what she had discovered. What initially appeared as an intercessor's defeat was a fiftyfold victory. Mary Jane wouldn't have wanted it any other way.

twelve
Praying for the Family

Sunday: Prayer Patterns for Healthy Homes

I awakened slowly to the sharp jabbing motions of my wife's hand. I could hear Dee muttering, "Who could that be at this hour?"

It was before 7 A.M. Saturday. Our older daughter Dena, six years of age at the time, had invited her friend Sara from next door to spend the night.

Wiping sleep from my eyes, I opened the front door to discover Sara's nine-year-old sister Julie, the oldest of five children in their family. Julie had been crying. She asked if her sister was up yet, and I told her Sara was asleep in Dena's bedroom. Wiping away tears, Julie insisted that Sara come home right away; it was very important.

I awakened Sara and in a few moments she was on her

way. No explanation was given for the sudden intrusion, and both Dee and I wondered if a tragedy had occurred.

Two hours later, around nine, there was another knock on the door. Sara had returned to retrieve some of her belongings left in her hasty departure. Dena was now awake and I could hear the two six-year-olds conversing.

"Why did you have to leave so early?" Dena quizzed.

"My daddy had to talk to us this morning," Sara responded. "He told us all to sit down so he could tell us a hard thing." Sara's voice cracked and it sounded as if she was holding back tears.

"Daddy told us he was going to be leaving our house this morning," she continued, "because he didn't love Mommy anymore." Attempting to defend her father as best she could, Sara added quickly, "But Dena, don't worry about us. He promised he would never stop loving us. He just doesn't love Mommy anymore."

With that both girls burst into tears. One could almost read Sara's mind: "If Daddy really loved Mommy before, and now he's quit loving her, how can I be sure he'll keep his promise to me?"

Prayer was the only hope for healing that home. Scripture assures us victory if we pray in God's will (1 John 5:14–15) and I knew God desires families to stay together. As sure as I know my name, I knew God wanted their daughters raised by a mom and dad who loved one another. So I began to pray.

By the following Tuesday a strange boldness saturated my prayers. Suddenly I felt as if I was confronting a spirit of lust that Satan had used to deceive that husband into desiring a woman who was not his wife. A strange prayer flowed from my lips. I commanded the man to become sick to his stomach, at that very moment, as he faced the reality of his sin. I recalled praying boldly, "Be nauseated in Jesus' name for what you have done!"

Frankly, I couldn't believe those words had come from my lips. But still I knew the Holy Spirit was guiding my prayer.

The confirmation came the following Saturday when I spoke with the young housewife over our back fence. Her face was aglow. "Dick, I have good news! Bob called yesterday for the first time since he left. Something strange is happening. I can't say there's been a total change, but he did tell me he's been feeling funny."

"What do you mean, feeling funny?"

"Well, last Wednesday Bob decided to go see a psychologist for counseling," she explained. "He said he started feeling guilty on Tuesday afternoon as he thought about our girls not having a daddy. It affected his stomach so much he actually became nauseated and felt like vomiting."

The complete miracle was to require a few more days. By the following week, Bob was back and the children had their daddy home.

The Praying Family

Prayer changes homes! Most believers would agree with that. Yet when it comes to translating this conviction into reality, the Church is sadly deficient.

When I first began to develop a teaching on intercession *for* (as well as *in*) the family, I took a trip to our well-stocked local Christian bookstore. I wanted to check out titles related to praying as a family or praying for families. I discovered a multitude of books related to the family, but, to my dismay, nothing that emphasized prayer in or for the family.

I noticed, for example, a book titled *How to Raise Good Kids*. Surely this would include a chapter on prayer. After all, how can we raise good kids without prayer? Yet nothing was included regarding this important subject. Another title read *How to Really Love Your Child*. Prayer certainly ought to be included here, I thought; but again it was overlooked. There was a book titled *Training Your Child to Handle Money*. This might touch on prayer, I thought, since stewardship and prayer go hand-in-hand. But again, prayer wasn't mentioned. I even found the title *Developing Spiritually Sensitive Children*, convinced it would include a chapter on prayer. Again, prayer was all but overlooked.

Only later would I pick up *The Christian Family* by Larry Christensen, and joyfully discover a chapter titled "The Priesthood of Parents," in which the importance of prayer was discussed.

I could not escape the significance, however, of so many books related to enriching family life in which, for the most part, prayer was either totally ignored or mentioned only in passing. Did not so essential a theme deserve better treatment?

A Rock of Remembrance

We recall Joshua's commitment regarding the spiritual well-being of his household when he stood before God's people declaring: "Choose for yourselves this day whom you will serve, whether the gods which your fathers served that were on the other side of the River, or the gods of the Amorites, in whose land you dwell. But as for me and my house, we will serve the Lord" (Joshua 24:15).

Joshua confirmed this word by establishing a rock of remembrance, about which he declared to all the people: "Behold this stone shall be a witness to us, for it has heard all the words of the Lord which He spoke to us. It shall therefore be a witness to you, lest you deny your God" (Joshua 24:26–27).

Resting in the front flowerbed of our home in California is a large rock over which I have spoken these same words. Inspired by a message from my pastor, Jack Hayford, I stood before that rock and declared aloud, "As for me and my house, we will serve the Lord."

Contemplating this commitment, I realized how essential prayer is to the one God has appointed to serve as head of a household. An absence of prayer from the head will ultimately diminish that person's capacity to make wise decisions, and the whole family will suffer.

Later I read the psalmist's words often quoted when new church buildings are being erected: "Unless the Lord builds the house, they labor in vain who build it" (Psalm 127:1). The context of this psalm deals with the family. Subsequent verses declare, "Behold, children are a heritage from the Lord, the fruit of the womb is His reward, like arrows in the hand of a warrior, so are the children of one's youth" (Psalm 127:3–4). Quite simply, when the psalmist speaks of building a house, he is describing the establishing of a healthy household.

Other biblical injunctions likewise focus on the spiritual well-being of the family. Concerning lessons Israel learned in their wilderness wanderings, Moses declared: "Only take heed to yourself, and diligently keep yourself, lest you forget the things your eyes have seen, and lest they depart from your heart all the days of your life. And teach them to your children and your grandchildren" (Deuteronomy 4:9). The author of Proverbs advises, "Train up a child in the way he should go, and when he is old he will not depart from it" (Proverbs 22:6). Surely prayer ought to be at the heart of showing a child the right path.

To the Ephesians, Paul would later write: "And now a word to you parents. Don't keep on scolding and nagging your children, making them angry and resentful. Rather, bring them up with the loving discipline the Lord Himself approves, with suggestions and godly advice" (Ephesians 6:4, LB). Interestingly, these words on family health immediately precede Scripture's most in-depth analysis of spiritual warfare (Ephesians 6:10–18)!

Because prayer is so essential to communicating godly advice and loving discipline, let us look more closely at several suggestions for developing a praying family.

Praying in the Family

"Like father, like son" is an adage that speaks volumes when it comes to prayer. Are our children learning the importance of prayer *by our example?*

Consider the example of Abraham (Genesis 18:16–22). Here the patriarch speaks with angels who reveal their mission to destroy Sodom and Gomorrah because of sin in the cities. The passage reads:

> Then the men rose from there and looked toward Sodom, and Abraham went with them to send them on the way. And the Lord said, "Shall I hide from Abraham what I am doing, since Abraham shall surely become a great and mighty nation, and all the nations of the earth shall be blessed in him? For I have known him, in order that he may command his children and his household after him,

that they keep the way of the Lord, and do righteousness and justice, that the Lord may bring to Abraham what He has spoken to him."

(Genesis 18:16–19)

The Lord's confidence in Abraham's ability to administrate his household is revealed in the words "For I have known him. . . ." Abraham set an example of one who sought God. Time and again we see Abraham erecting altars to the Lord as focal points for worship.

Do our children see this quality in us? If not, the following suggestions may be helpful.

First, *create a climate of prayer at home.* This begins by communicating with your family the importance of prayer. During our daughters' early years, they would always see Dee reading her Bible when they arrived at the breakfast table. A small thing, perhaps, but vital. It demonstrated the importance of spiritual nourishment.

We should also bring prayer into family activities, such as when going on trips or planning family activities. Prayer is appropriate during times of discipline. When disciplining either of our daughters in their early years, I always assured her that the punishment was not because I didn't love her. Then I would hold the child tightly as we prayed a short prayer of tender dependence on the Holy Spirit to help us live better.

Second, *create a place of prayer in the home.* I call such a place at our family home the "Gap," based on God's message in Ezekiel's day: "I sought for a man among them that should make up the hedge, and stand in the gap before me for the land, that I should not destroy it; but I found none" (Ezekiel 22:30, KJV).

A "Gap" is a place for devotions and family prayers. It

might be located in a large closet, unused room, even a shed in the backyard. Our own family Gap began with a small aluminum shed less than ten feet square. The entire cost, with wood paneling, carpet, and electrical heating, was far less than many families spend on recreation and incidentals for a few months in a year.

A family Gap should minister to the entire family. You might want to buy devotional books suitable for family members of different ages. An inexpensive bulletin board can feature prayer requests from missionaries or evangelism ministries like Every Home for Christ. EHC's World Prayer Map would be especially helpful. (See page 188 for information on the availability of such helpful prayer tools.) A map of the world attached to a wall can give an increased global atmosphere. A trip to a travel agent might yield colorful posters of exotic places.

Be creative in your planning and the result will be a special place of prayer.

Third, *create a program of prayer in the home.* Ask the Holy Spirit to show you a simple plan for developing a daily prayer strategy that you might apply for use with your family. For example, you might want to adopt the seven prayer focuses (one for each day of the week), as outlined in the immediately preceding chapters of this book. With a little creativity, all seven of these focuses, including the family focus, can be adapted to any age group.

Praying for Your Family

Two Scripture passages provide patterns for daily prayer in families. One is from the Old Testament account of King David, while the other is from the New Testament account of our King of kings, Jesus Christ.

In David's prayer for forgiveness we find our first pattern: "Create in me a clean heart, O God, and renew a steadfast spirit within me. Do not cast me away from Your presence, and do not take Your Holy Spirit from me" (Psalm 51:10–11).

Our second pattern emerges from Luke's New Testament description of the early growth years of our Lord. Luke wrote: "And Jesus increased in wisdom and stature, and in favor with God and men" (Luke 2:52).

As our children were growing up I often employed these two passages in daily prayer as a reminder of our family's spiritual and material needs. I would start by asking for a clean heart, following David's plea. Then I would pray for a spirit of purity to permeate my entire family. Next, I would ask the Lord to renew a "steadfast spirit" within me, transferring that quality, too, to the entire household. I would claim a special measure of God's presence for each member of our family as we moved into the day's activities. (Of course, I was praying more for a *recognition* of His presence than for Him to do something He was reluctant to do. God is with us whether we realize it or not, but acknowledging our dependence on Him often leads to blessings we might not otherwise experience.) And finally, I would pray with David, "Take not Your Holy Spirit from me," claiming a special portion of the Holy Spirit in each of us so that we might live a life pleasing to Jesus.

In thinking of Luke's description of Christ's early years, a meaningful fourfold pattern of prayer for our children emerged.

First, I prayed for our children's *spiritual growth.* Luke spoke of Jesus increasing "in favor with God," a reference to our Lord's spiritual growth patterns. Although born without sin, Jesus still had to spend time in prayer and study of Scriptures. Years later, He would confront Satan in the wilderness quoting just the right Scripture for each temptation. This was not because Jesus was programmed from eternity to know the Scriptures, but because He studied the Scriptures as a youth. Remember, when Christ lived on earth, He was a man subjected to all the struggles each of us must face and He had to be mature spiritually to face these temptations without sin.

Second, I prayed for our children's *physical growth.* Jesus not only grew in favor with God but "in stature." This focus allowed me to concentrate a moment's prayer on the physical development of my family, including healthy eating habits and a wise maintenance of our physical "temples." My regular trips to the tennis courts with our daughters in their pre-teen years was but one outflow of this prayer. It led to both girls excelling in four years of high school tennis. During this physical growth focus I would also claim physical health for each of our girls in turn.

Third, I prayed for their *mental growth.* Luke tells us that Jesus increased in wisdom. I petitioned God to help our daughters develop wise stewardship of their mental abilities. I prayed for their grades in school and that God would guide them in their choice of subjects best suited to the field of service to which He would ultimately lead them.

Finally, I prayed for the girls' *social growth.* When the Bible tells us Jesus increased in favor with men, it meant He had gained the respect of those about Him. He was not a social outcast. He was the essence of spirituality but was never religiously obnoxious. Based on Christ's example, I prayed that God would give our children good balance in their social relationships. I also prayed for the friends our daughters would select, and for the girls' ability to discern unhealthy friendships.

As I developed these simple prayer patterns, I was repeatedly reminded that there is no greater gift a parent (or a grandparent or grandchild) can give a child than the covering of prayer. As the noted Norwegian Bible teacher Professor Halesby said: "My friend, if you are not able to leave your children a legacy in the form of goods, do not worry. And do not worry yourself to death either physically or spiritually in order to accumulate a great deal of property for your children. But see to it, night and day, that you pray for them. Then you will leave them a great legacy of answers to prayer, which will follow them all the days of their lives."

Praying as a Family

Christ spoke of the significance of small group prayer: "I say to you that if two of you agree on earth concerning anything that they ask, it will be done for them by My Father in heaven. For where two or three are gathered together in My name, I am there in the midst of them" (Matthew 18:19–20).

Perhaps the most natural of all small prayer groups is the family. Where else do we have an equal opportunity for an ongoing small corporate prayer gathering that can meet on a daily basis?

But to do this in a meaningful way we need a basic plan. Here is a family prayer pattern you may find helpful:

First begin with *a worship focus*. Worship is at the heart of a healthy prayer experience. Worship includes all aspects of prayer that focus on God's nature and character. Praise, thanksgiving, and even singing might be included here. (Please see the author's book *A Celebration of Praise,* Baker Book House, 1984, for suggestions to help you get off to a good start in your time of praise and worship.)

Secondly, include a *Word focus.* Paul told Timothy, ". . . From childhood you have known the Holy Scriptures, which are able to make you wise for salvation through faith which is in Christ Jesus" (2 Timothy 3:15). Someone took time to plant God's Word in Timothy's heart while he was still very young. Consider Paul's words to young Timothy: "I thank God . . . when I call to remembrance the genuine faith that is in you, which dwelt first in your grandmother Lois and your mother Eunice . . ." (2 Timothy 1:3, 5). It appears that it was young Timothy's mother and grandmother who taught this future warrior God's Word.

One never knows when planting Scripture in the heart of a child the extent to which God might someday use those seeds to change nations.

You may wish to use a classic devotional guide such as *Streams in the Desert* or *My Utmost for His Highest.* For younger children you can use such books as *Hurlbut's Story of the Bible* or *Egermeier's Bible Story Book.* Another possible plan is the author's systematic study of God's Word as presented in the book *The University of the Word* (Regal Books, 1983). Because twelve different biblical principles are emphasized in this study, the concepts can become a twelve-month family devotional focus. Each month a different spiritual growth principle would be the focus.

Third, following your important worship and Word focuses, conclude with a *world focus,* interceding for a lost and needy world. You might wish to follow an Acts 1:8

pattern, which speaks of believers receiving power after they have been touched by God's Spirit. As a result, they become witnesses for Jesus in "Jerusalem . . . Judaea, and in Samaria, and unto the uttermost part of the earth"(Acts 1:8, KJV).

Here we find an excellent threefold plan of prayer for family altar. First, *we pray for our Jerusalem*. This concerns local needs, such as our community. Second, *we pray for our Judaea and Samaria*. This involves our state (or, in some countries, our province) and our nation. Third, *we pray for the uttermost parts of the earth* that include unevangelized nations never reached completely with the Gospel.

thirteen
Soul Conflict
Taking Authority Against Spiritual Darkness

In the last chapter I spoke about a family's intercessory headquarters which I call the Gap—in our case the little shed in our backyard dedicated to prayer. The idea of the Gap as a place for personal and family intercession came into being in the latter part of the 1960s during the hippie movement.

There was a very real danger that the youth of our own church would be swept into such lifestyles, and I was concerned. They were seriously at risk unless they were taught the importance of prayer.

So I began planning weekend prayer retreats into the nearby Sierra Nevada Mountains, specifically for the teenagers of our church. The first retreat included 22 participants. We were all inexperienced in prolonged prayer sessions. Not one of us, for instance, knew how to pray an entire night, and frankly we were all about to give up after less than an hour.

Then the youngest participant, a thirteen-year-old, asked us to start praying in a different way—as warriors. He saw himself and his friends as warring against the darkness of the booze-sex-drugs lifestyle of the hippie communes, and he asked us to stand with him all night to "fight the devil." This youth had tears in his eyes as he spoke, and all agreed to go to war along with him.

By three in the morning a spirit of brokenness had settled over our retreat house. The room was warmly lit by a glow from logs burning in a large fireplace, but also from a fire burning within the young people themselves. We all began to weep and cry out. One seventeen-year-old student lay on her face in the middle of the room weeping for the youth of California who were in trouble with drugs.

I was witnessing what our forebears used to call a "spirit of travail," a wonderful word related to the word *work* or *labor*, as in giving birth.

And indeed, the intercessory retreats from our church flourished, until 175 young people were participating. Within a year the Jesus Movement began in many parts of California. At least 800,000 young people would find Christ in those same exciting days.

And amid all this, something profound was happening in my own life. God was placing in my heart a yearning for more of Himself, a hunger that was to explode on a life-changing Wednesday night in 1971.

On that evening I arrived at church an hour-and-a-half before our regular midweek youth intercessory prayer meeting. I made my way to a secluded storage area behind the platform of our church where I often went to find a quiet place to pray. Hidden away amid the boxes of costumes and props for Christmas and Easter pageants, I began to seek the Lord for an outpouring of His Spirit upon the youth of our church.

At first nothing out of the ordinary happened. Then, without much forethought, I asked God a simple, direct question. Hearing His voice in my heart was an entirely new experience, but that night I found I was expecting an answer.

"What do you want me to do with my life?" I asked the Lord.

Suddenly I heard the most startling answer. The words were surprisingly clear: *Because you have asked me this night, I will tell you this night.*

I had never heard the Lord speak so clearly. Tears began to flow as I waited for what was to follow.

The answer came not as a voice but a picture, alive with movement. I saw an army of God's people marching. It was a remarkable sight. The army, six to eight abreast, stretched as far as the eye could see. It formed a vast column that seemed to continue forever.

"Who are these people, Lord," I cried, "and where are they going?"

A quiet answer followed: *This is an army of intercessors who will change the world. I'm calling you to help mobilize this army.*

Before I could respond the picture changed. I was looking at a large white-frame mansion. Coming and going from the building were clean-cut young people carrying Bibles, unusual in a day when communes were everywhere and long-haired youths living together was common.

These are residents at a house of prayer, the Lord told me.

Each young person had made a commitment to give a

significant "time gift" for intercessory prayer. Some were there for a summer, most for an entire year.

Then the Lord took me inside the building. A large sign was attached to the door on my right at the entrance. The sign was hand-painted, as if by one of the young people, and it quoted a portion of Ezekiel: "I sought for a man among them, that should make up the hedge and stand in the gap before me for the land . . ." (Ezekiel 22:30, KJV). Just above the Scripture were the words *The Gap.*

The door opened slowly. Looking inside this room designated the Gap I saw a young lady, perhaps nineteen years of age. She had long brown hair and silver-rimmed glasses and she was kneeling at a small, round table upon which rested a globe. As I watched, she lifted the globe a few inches off the table and began to weep.

Then a young man came into the Gap and the girl transferred her burden to him. After a while he, too, passed the globe to another. This continued as I watched in silence.

"Lord, this is beautiful," I said softly.

He responded with the challenge, *I want you to bring into being exactly what you have seen here.*

The vision was over. There, in the storage room behind the platform of our church, I heard our own young people beginning to arrive for the evening.

That night I shared the vision with our youth. There was unusual excitement and the young people assured me they were ready to help bring my vision to life. I knew that night that God wanted me to find the white-frame building and transform it into a prayer center.

Within six months God did give us our first "house of prayer" in Sacramento, California. Within five years God gave me one hundred young people, each committed to a year of intercession. They supported themselves by "praying in" the finances to help us continue our ministry. Out of those 50,000 continuous hours of prayer, day and night, including holidays, God gave birth to prayer training that ultimately touched over a million believers in more than 120 countries of the world.

It all began when a hundred young people made themselves available for a year of prayer. Later, when asked how my prayer ministry began, I could say, "It started with a century's worth of prayer." One hundred youths sanctifying a year of their lives equalled a century's worth of prayer commitment.

Changing Our World

A second life-changing vision occurred nine years later. By that time the first vision had become a reality. God had given us our prayer center and thousands of additional Gap Ministries had sprung up in houses and churches throughout the world, often in unusual circumstances. A Lutheran day school teacher built a Gap shaped like Noah's ark. There her pre-school children went for as long as thirty minutes a day of prayer. It was often difficult to get the children to stop praying. They had discovered prayer can be fun.

Years later I visited a church in Malaysia that had grown to nearly 5,000 members in less than eight years. This church, thriving in a land where the law prohibits witnessing to a Muslim, had a center where intercessors came for days of concentrated prayer. When entering the center I noticed each door leading to a private prayer room had a Gap sign similar to the one I had first seen in my vision.

Later I learned that a brother from New Zealand was sharing our vision everywhere. He had passed through the region several years earlier.

As the years passed and the army began to increase, God opened the doors for me to take this prayer vision to many nations through the ministry of World Literature Crusade, now Every Home for Christ. The founder, Dr. Jack McAlister, having heard of our prayer ministry and believing prayer to be essential to the ultimate evangelization of the world, asked me to join his staff to develop prayer training for believers of all denominations.

Not realizing I would someday serve Every Home for Christ as their international president, I joined the ministry and developed the Change the World School of Prayer. The School of Prayer was (and continues to be) a training course designed to strengthen believers in their daily devotional habits and to equip them to pray effectively for world evangelization. One important aspect of the training is the challenge for believers to consider giving God a gift of one hour daily for personal prayer. Based on Christ's challenge to His disciples, "Could you not watch one hour?" more than 200,000 Christians have made the commitment. Thousands more have agreed to invest fifteen or thirty minutes a day.

But as the army began to grow, I became increasingly concerned about focusing all this prayer energy on what would bring Christ the most glory. Prayer, after all, is not given as a means to gain increased material or spiritual pleasure, though personal blessings do result from a healthy prayer experience. Rather, prayer is God's supreme gift to assist the Church in establishing His Kingdom throughout the earth.

As I continued my search of the Scriptures concerning

the importance of prayer, I became convinced that believers are engaged in spiritual war that must be waged on biblical principles. Just as Satan has an established order in the invisible realm, so believers must develop a strategy to stand effectively against these forces. The more I traveled, the more convinced I became that every region of the world has a controlling spirit ruling over it. It became evident that something must be developed to restrain these forces.

Which is the background to the second major vision experience of my life. It occurred following several days of fasting and prayer during a trip to Michigan. My devotional time in my motel room beside Lake Michigan began much like that of any other day. I had come to the final chapters of the book of Revelation in my daily Bible reading, and pausing to meditate on the literal nature of the Lamb's Book of Life, I suddenly found myself longing to pray about names *yet to be added* to this most unusual of celestial records. And I blurted out a most unusual prayer.

"Lord," I prayed, "please let me participate in a movement that adds more names to the Book of Life than have been added in all of history."

It was a bold prayer, indeed, but somehow I felt the Holy Spirit had led me to say the words. Tears began to flow as I stood up and walked to the window of my motel room. Before me was the vast expanse of Lake Michigan lying placidly like a giant sheet of glass. As the sun's rays sparkled off the lake, I saw millions of tiny diamond-like bursts of light dancing in the distance. It reminded me of the description in Revelation of the multitude of redeemed humanity who will someday stand upon a sea of glass (Revelation 15:2). Then I recalled the promise of how "blood-washed" souls would come out of every kindred, tongue, people, and nation (Revelation 5:9). I was convinced God had appointed the moment to reveal to me the role of intercessors in global evangelism.

Lifting my face in anticipation, I experienced the second vision that would impact my ministry so strongly.

Before me, in a large arena, stood a multitude representing every age group. I sensed that all these people in the arena were committed intercessors. Each held a page containing names.

I wondered what these names represented, and why everyone in the massive gathering of believers had a personal list.

Suddenly my attention was drawn in the opposite direction. There I saw a throne and an angel who held a huge book. As I watched, each intercessor came to the throne and presented his list of names.

One individual caught my particular attention. She was well beyond seventy years of age. But although her face was wrinkled and her hair gray, she beamed with the joy of Jesus.

Soon she, too, was standing before the angel presenting her list of names. As the angel began recording the names in the great Book, I asked the Lord what all this meant.

"These are the names of souls these warriors helped bring to a knowledge of My salvation."

"Where did the intercessors get these names?" I prayed.

"Come, and I will show you," came the answer.

With that I saw this elderly saint, on her knees, flying swiftly through the heavenlies. It was a strange sight. In my spirit I knew she was entering a level of warfare I had never seen, and that she was flying thousands of miles. In an instant, she descended to hover over a village that seemed to me to be in India, although I had never been there. My attention was drawn to a hut that appeared to be the focus of the saint's intercession.

The hut was modest, even by the standards of the village. Within were a small table, a chair, and a bed. Its lone occupant was a middle-aged man who appeared to be of Indian descent, most likely a Hindu.

As the intercessor continued in prayer above the hut, I noticed that even with the sun shining brightly, the hut was dark.

Then I noticed movement in the village. A man was distributing Gospel literature. He paused at the hut and knocked gently. When the occupant opened the door the worker handed him a Gospel booklet.

Through all this the elderly saint remained stationary in the heavenlies as if waiting for something.

Closing the door, the Hindu read a few sentences that told him about a loving heavenly Father who came to earth in the form of a man, God's only Son, a concept beyond the Hindu's comprehension. He believed there were many gods, perhaps millions. A monkey could be a god, or a cow or snake. Even a tree might be an object of worship. "One God, one Son," he thought. "Nonsense." He tossed the book on the table. It seemed the darkness of the room prevented his comprehension of the truth.

The man's rejection of the message seemed to be the cue the intercessor was waiting for. Into the darkness she plunged, through the roof of the hut, landing on her knees. The Hindu had no idea she was there.

Reaching her hands forward along the floor, with her palms up, the elderly woman appeared to be lifting something. Then I realized what she was doing. She was lifting the darkness in the room! The more she prayed, the more the darkness moved. When she had raised it high enough, she slowly moved from her knees and began pushing the darkness toward the ceiling from a crouched position, a few inches at a time, as she continued her intercession. Before long she had pushed the darkness above the man and was standing stretched to her capacity, warring all the while against the satanic darkness.

The instant the darkness rose above the man's head, he turned again toward the table, gazing intently upon the message he had earlier rejected. Now there was a different look on his face, a look of longing.

He walked to the table and took the booklet into his hand. I could hear his thoughts as he slowly read the opening sentences a second time. "Perhaps I was hasty in rejecting this message," he reasoned. As he read again the claims of Christ, an amazing thing happened. He lifted his face toward heaven, his unseen praying guest contending against the darkness beside him, and he cried out to the Lord, "I believe You are the Son of God!"

Joy flooded the faces of both the new convert and the elderly intercessor. A miracle was happening before my eyes. In that instant a brilliant beam of light penetrated the hut and flowed into the heart of the new believer. He had seen the Light—literally. All darkness in the room vanished. The intercessor's work, at least for the moment, had ended.

Still unseen by the rejoicing Indian, the intercessor stepped from the hut and pulled a piece of paper from her pocket. I recognized it immediately. It was the list she had presented to the angel with the Book. The happy warrior added the man's name to her long list. Then, with a shout of praise, she tucked the list back into her pocket and headed for a hut across the way.

For the next several minutes I sat wondering quietly

about the strange picture I had just witnessed. Had my imagination run wild or had I truly observed an intercessor in action? God's Word would hold my answer. Any vision must find confirmation in God's Word.

Almost immediately I began to recall confirming passages regarding the power of God's light to penetrate the darkness:

> Arise, shine, for your light has come, and the glory of the Lord rises upon you. See . . . thick darkness is over the peoples, but the Lord rises upon you and his glory appears over you. Nations will come to your light, and kings to the brightness of your dawn. Lift up your eyes and look about you: All assemble and come to you; your sons come from afar, and your daughters are carried on the arm. Then you will look and be radiant, your heart will throb and swell with joy; the wealth on the seas will be brought to you, to you the riches of the nations will come.
>
> (Isaiah 60:1–5, NIV)

Other confirming passages followed. As I evaluated these biblical insights, four facts regarding the intercessor's conflict with the darkness on behalf of lost souls emerged.

The Desire of the Lord

Fact one: *It is the Lord's desire to see every person on earth provided access to the Gospel of Jesus Christ.*

This reality is stated throughout the New Testament. Peter wrote, "The Lord is not slack concerning His promise, as some count slackness, but is longsuffering toward us, not willing that any should perish but that all should come to repentance" (2 Peter 3:9). *The Living Bible* renders it: "The Lord isn't really being slow about his promised return, even though it sometimes seems that way. But he is waiting, for the good reason that he is not willing that any should perish, and he is giving more time for sinners to repent."

Of particular interest is the paraphrase of verse 15: "And remember why He is waiting. He is giving us time to get His message of salvation out to others."

Other passages likewise share the importance of "all the world" and "every creature" (Mark 16:15) having access to the Gospel. When Christ discussed end-time events with His disciples, He clearly expressed that total fulfillment of the Great Commission was essential to the wrap-up of this present age. Mark records these words of Christ: "And the gospel must first be preached to all the nations" (Mark 13:10). Matthew includes the promise, "And this gospel of the kingdom will be preached in all the world as a witness to all the nations, and then the end will come" (Matthew 24:14).

Paul later spoke of the harvest, in a context of prayer. To young Timothy he wrote, "Therefore I exhort first of all that supplications, prayers, intercessions, and giving of thanks be made for all men, for kings and all who are in authority, that we may lead a quiet and peaceable life in all godliness and reverence" (1 Timothy 2:1–2). Paul then adds the important ultimate result of these prayers: "For this is good and acceptable in the sight of God our Savior, who desires all men to be saved and to come to the knowledge of the truth" (verses 3–4).

The message is clear. God desires all to have access to

the Gospel, and prayer is at the heart of making that possible. But a second fact is necessary to understand if we're to pursue prayer to its greatest potential.

The Plan of the Enemy

Fact two: *It is Satan's plan to prevent every unbeliever from receiving access to the Gospel of Jesus Christ.* On the surface, this is common sense. Yet we often fail to understand that lost souls, whether family members or unevangelized people groups overseas, are covered with a spiritual darkness they have not, in fact, chosen. True, they are responsible for their sins and cannot be redeemed if they reject salvation, but they did not choose to be born in sin.

Paul instructs Timothy to preach the Gospel so that unbelievers will "come to their senses and escape from the devil's snare, in which they have been caught and held at [Satan's] will" (2 Timothy 2:25–26, NEB).

Satan holds unbelievers in his total control. They are "held at his will" and, according to Ephesians 2:1–2, *Amplified Bible*, "under his control." The unbeliever's darkened spiritual condition is such that until that darkness is removed he cannot see the light. Thus, darkness must be dealt with at a supernatural level if the person is to break through into the brightness of Christ's eternal light.

The more I contemplated this concept, following my vision of the elderly intercessor and the Hindu, the more I wondered if any specific Scripture expressly said such. To my amazement, in my next day's systematic Bible reading I discovered a passage I had read many times before, but had never seen its significance in the context of warring against the darkness on behalf of lost souls.

It was found in Paul's second letter to the Corinthians:

> But even if our gospel is veiled [hidden], it is veiled to those who are perishing, whose minds the god of this age has blinded, who do not believe, lest the light of the gospel of the glory of Christ, who is the image of God, should shine on them.
>
> (2 Corinthians 4:3–4)

Note the paraphrase of this passage: "If the Good News we preach is hidden to anyone, it is hidden from the one who is on the road to eternal death. Satan, who is the god of this evil world, has made him blind, unable to see the glorious light of the Gospel that is shining upon him, or to understand the amazing message we preach about the glory of Christ, who is God" (TLB).

The implication in this passage is clear. Remove the darkness and the light will shine. Yet the one covered with darkness is incapable of removing this darkness on his own.

Further, when a person first receives the Gospel, our enemy immediately attempts to snatch the seed away (see Mark 4:14–15). Do seeds finally take root because an intercessor stands against the enemy, preventing the seed from being snatched away?

This question is vital because the harvest depends on the seed's taking root. Which brings us to fact number three:

The Duty of the Church

Fact Three: *It is the Church's duty to take the Gospel of Jesus Christ to every person on earth.*

Here again is a biblical concept readily accepted by most mature believers. And yet most Christians lack any systematic involvement in communicating the Gospel, whether here or overseas. This, I believe, will soon change radically.

Note again Matthew's familiar record of Christ's words:

> "All authority has been given to Me in heaven and on earth. Go therefore and make disciples of all the nations, baptizing them in the name of the Father and of the Son and of the Holy Spirit, teaching them to observe all things that I have commanded you. . . ."
>
> (Matthew 28:18–20)

Mark's rendering reads:

> "Go into all the world and preach the gospel to every creature."
>
> (Mark 16:15)

Even Old Testament passages prophesied the fulfillment of the Great Commission. Of the Messiah, the psalmist wrote: "Yes, all kings shall fall down before Him; all nations shall serve Him. His name shall endure forever; His name shall continue as long as the sun; and men shall be blessed in Him; all nations shall call Him blessed" (Psalm 72:11, 17). Isaiah said simply, "For the earth shall be full of the knowledge of the Lord as the waters cover the sea" (Isaiah 11:9).

The Church has a duty to take Christ's love to every dark heart on planet earth. And it is here that the intercessor's work becomes absolutely essential.

The Role of the Intercessor

Fact Four: *It is the intercessor's responsibility to hold back the unseen forces of satanic darkness wherever the Gospel of Jesus Christ is shared.*

We know by Scripture that although human beings occupy a physical plane, their actions and activities are controlled from the invisible realm. All warfare for a soul takes place in that same unseen arena. Recall Paul's warfare words to the Ephesian believers that we wrestle "against . . . [the master spirits who are] the world rulers of this present darkness, against the spirit forces of wickedness in the heavenly, (supernatural) sphere" (Ephesians 6:10, 12, AMPLIFIED).

It is because of Paul's awareness of spiritual warfare that he pleaded with the churches repeatedly to remember him in prayer, as he did the Thessalonians: "Finally, brothers, pray for us that the message of the Lord may spread rapidly and be honored, just as it was with you. And pray that we may be delivered from wicked and evil men, for not everyone has faith" (2 Thessalonians 3:1–2, NIV).

In equally strong terms Paul wrote the Romans: "Now I beg you, brethren, through the Lord Jesus Christ, and through the love of the Spirit, that you strive together with me in your prayers to God for me" (Romans 15:30). Paul was convinced that his ministry could go no further than the prayers of his fellow warriors would allow.

The intercessor has a vital role to play in helping unbelievers "come to their senses and escape the snare of the devil." (2 Timothy 2:25–26). And the more I thought about these Bible-based facts, the more convinced I became that intercessors who contend for lost souls do indeed help add names to the Lamb's Book of Life. They may not be aware that they are sweeping through the heavenlies on their knees, or that they are contending against the darkness for a soul who has just been confronted with the claims of Christ, but their prayers make the harvest possible.

The Vision Confirmed

Six years following my unusual vision of the elderly intercessor and her global prayer mission, God confirmed the validity of the vision in an unusual way.

It happened when I made my first trip to India. There I visited all the major regions of that vast and complex land. As I traveled through the countryside I was overwhelmed by the many huts that looked exactly like the hut I first observed in my prayer time six years earlier.

Departing India with a most unusual burden for these masses, I headed home. Somewhere over the vast expanse of the Pacific I picked up a challenging book I'd been given in Calcutta, Paul Pillai's book *India's Search for the Unknown Christ*. Unexpectedly, when I came to page 212, I couldn't keep back the tears. The author told of a Hindu leader in the Arya Samag sect who lived many years ago in the region of Rajasthan. He was an angry man consumed with a passion to fight all Christian work. More than once he had stopped young Christians who were witnessing and removed their Bibles and publicly burned them.

On one such occasion Paul Pillai himself had been part of a team who encountered this hostility. They had been going house-to-house and standing on street corners distributing small Gospels of John.

Suddenly the angry man appeared and demanded their Gospel booklets. Keeping only one, perhaps as evidence, he set the remainder on fire. Then he threatened to kill anyone on the team who continued witnessing for Jesus. The man left the scene angrily with his evidence in hand, a lone copy of John's Gospel.

Three weeks later Paul Pillai received a letter from that same man. He wrote that he had taken the Gospel of John home with him and after reading a few pages tossed it on the table in his hut, convinced it was filled with lies. But that night, in the blackness of the evening, he felt a strange presence enter the room. The man couldn't get his mind off the booklet on the table. Finally he stood and made his way in darkness toward the table.

As he picked up the booklet that second time, a supernatural light illumined the room. He looked down at the booklet and read: "He that believeth on him is not condemned: but he that believeth not is condemned already, because he hath not believed in the name of the only begotten Son of God. And this is the condemnation, that light is come into the world, and men loved darkness rather than light, because their deeds were evil. For every one that doeth evil hateth the light, neither cometh to the light . . ." (John 3:18–20, KJV).

In that instant he knelt down and received Christ as Savior. He declared later that in his search for truth, his eyes had been blinded by his own preconceived images.

Although my vision of six years earlier had several differences with the story I read, I was overwhelmed by the similarities. Had the unusual presence in the Hindu man's room been the working of the Holy Spirit in response to an intercessor's prayers? Or had the intercessor actually been there, in spirit, as the result of the operation of the Holy Spirit released through that intercessor's prayers?

I had no answers. But I became convinced that prayer plays a vital role in the conflict for a soul. It had happened with me. True, by an act of my own will, I had chosen to believe. But somewhere, somehow, an intercessor confronted the darkness on my behalf. In my case I know the identity of the intercessor. It was my mother. She loved me on her knees. Her intercession drove away the darkness so that the light of Christ might penetrate my heart during days of youthful rebellion.

Beloved intercessor, the world is waiting for your love. I invite you to be a praying participant today in seeing names added to that glorious celestial record John describes in Revelation. Our final chapter will tell you how you can be involved in the greatest harvest in the history of the church—if we will pray.

fourteen
Prayer Travelers
Mobilizing a Movement of World Prayer Missionaries

The gifted writer S. D. Gordon said, "The real victory in all service is won beforehand in prayer. Service is merely gathering up the results." Expanding on this thought as related to the Great Commission, W. Stanley Mooneyham adds, "Let us stop complaining that we don't have enough people, enough money, enough tools. That simply is not true. There is no shortage of anything we need—except of vision and prayer and will. Prayer is the one resource immediately available to us all. If more Christians were on their knees praying, more Christians would be on their feet evangelizing."

The missionary leader continues, "Robert Speer, a great Presbyterian missions pioneer and leader, wrote: 'The evangelization of the world depends first upon a revival of prayer. Deeper than the need for workers; deeper, far, than the need for money; deep down at the bottom of our spiritual lives, is the need for the forgotten secret of prevailing, worldwide prayer. Missions have progressed slowly abroad because piety and prayer have been shallow at home.' "

A Call for World Prayer Missionaries

The vision that came to me in 1971, of the elderly saint warring against darkness, was the stimulus for a highly focused work that we call World Prayer Missionaries.

Simply stated, a World Prayer Missionary is any follower of Jesus who will go daily in prayer to a specific region of the world to engage in a carefully planned strategy of spiritual warfare.

The World Prayer Missionary selects a specific country, a region or province of that country, and even a base city when possible. Just as a conventional missionary must determine what country God wants him to evangelize, and what city in that country to live in, the World Prayer Missionary must define his or her specific focuses carefully for prayer. And just as a conventional missionary must seek God for an evangelism strategy regarding his or her area of responsibility, the World Prayer Missionary must seek the Holy Spirit for a specific prayer strategy regarding his area of prayer focus.

A Bible Basis for the World Prayer Missionary

From a biblical standpoint the World Prayer Missionary has a fourfold function:

First, *the World Prayer Missionary is a forerunner.* Isaiah wrote: "For Zion's sake I will not hold My peace, and for Jerusalem's sake I will not rest, until her righteousness goes forth as brightness, and her salvation as a lamp that burns. The Gentiles shall see your righteousness, and all kings your glory . . ." (Isaiah 62:1–2).

The prophet continues, "Go through, go through the gates! Prepare the way for the people; build up, build up the highway! Take out the stones, lift up a banner for the peoples!" (Isaiah 62:10).

Isaiah speaks here of a forerunner, an individual who helps prepare the way for others to follow. The World Prayer Missionary serves this function. He or she goes into spiritual warfare long before conventional workers enter the conflict. Because the obstacles that hinder evangelism originate in the unseen realm, we must deal with them in this same realm. Thus, the World Prayer Missionary enters the conflict in advance of the missionary or Christian worker. He or she goes to places that even missionaries cannot go.

Second, *the World Prayer Missionary is himself or herself an actual, spiritual war club.* A World Prayer Missionary actually becomes a weapon in God's hands. The prophet Isaiah referred to God's watchmen as "a crown of glory in the hand of the Lord, and a royal diadem in the hand of your God" (Isaiah 62:3). Note God's description of King Cyrus: "You are My battle-ax and weapon of war: for with you I will break the nation in pieces; with you I will destroy kingdoms; with you I will break in pieces the horse and its rider" (Jeremiah 51:20–21). *The New International Version* says of Cyrus, "You are my war club."

True, this passage is speaking of an earthly king, Cyrus, and not specifically of intercessors. Still, it reminds us that in every generation God will raise up His people to carry out His purposes.

Third, *the World Prayer Missionary is a threshing sledge.*

Here we find a most unique description of one who is called to the ministry of destroying Satan's works through prayer. Isaiah wrote, "Behold, I will make you into a new threshing sledge with sharp teeth; you shall thresh the mountains and beat them small, and make the hills like chaff" (Isaiah 41:15).

When Isaiah spoke of a "threshing sledge" he employed the Hebrew word *mowrag,* meaning to pulverize completely, or to crush and grind at the same time. The teeth of the sledge are both new and sharp. They are capable of pulverizing all that Satan would raise up to block God's plan.

This is the work of the World Prayer Missionary. He or she selects a region of the world, identifies opposing spiritual forces in that region, and through prayer pulverizes them completely.

Fourth, *the World Prayer Missionary is a ruling authority.* Through Jeremiah God declared, "See, I have this day set you over the nations and over the kingdoms, to root out and to pull down, to destroy and to throw down, to build and to plant" (Jeremiah 1:10).

The World Prayer Missionary is a ruler. In prayer, under the full authority and supervision of Jesus Christ, the Head of the Church, he or she rules over geographic regions of the earth.

Qualifications

Note these words of Christ to His disciples: "Have faith in God. For assuredly, I say to you, whoever says to this mountain, 'Be removed and be cast into the sea,' and does not doubt in his heart, but believes that those things he says will come to pass, he will have whatever he says" (Mark 11:22–23).

An evaluation of this passage reveals three qualifications regarding candidates for the office of a World Prayer Missionary.

First is the *eligibility factor.* Note the words *Whoever says to this mountain.* Any believer in right standing with the Lord is eligible to be a mountain-mover. No matter what a person's gifts or abilities, the willing warrior is qualified to be a World Prayer Missionary. Availability is the key. It is as if the Lord is saying, "Give Me a believer who is available, and I can work out all the details necessary to give that person the strength to fulfill any task to which I might call him."

Second is the *authority factor.* In Mark 11:22–23 Jesus pictures a confident disciple taking direct authority against an inanimate object. A confident intercessor is convinced of his position in Christ and puts his conviction into words. Power is released not so much by his faith as by the declaration of his lips expressing that faith.

Finally is the *certainty factor.* Here we see Christ's emphasis on our need for absolute assurance that He will carry out what we command with our lips, providing our commands measure up to His will. He says, "Whosoever says . . . and does not doubt . . ." (Mark 11:23). Note the words *and does not doubt.* A spirit of certainty is absolutely essential for a successful World Prayer Missionary. The degree to which we are certain God is going to respond to our prayers will be the degree to which we will see that response become a reality.

Defining Our Focus

How do you determine your country, region, and base city as a World Prayer Missionary? The steps are simple:

First, *establish a systematic prayer strategy*. Set aside time over the next several days to pray about which region God wants you to target in your prayers. You may wish to use a book such as *Operation World*, Patrick Johnstone, STL Books, William Carey Library, or the *World Prayer Map*, Every Home for Christ, P.O. Box 7139, Canoga Park, CA 91304–7139.

Second, *pray systematically for several nations to help you select your country*. If you use the World Prayer Map, you will note the map is divided into 31 groups of seven countries. This allows you to pray for the entire world each month. You may wish to devote an entire month to the process of selecting a country. As you pray daily, note any countries to which you feel drawn for more concentrated prayer. Be especially sensitive to countries under Communist or Muslem dominance.

Third, *prayerfully narrow your focus to cover a region rather than the whole country*.

China provides a good example. This vast land is populated with more than a billion people. Focusing on all of China might be too general. Thus, the World Prayer Missionary might pray daily for one of China's almost thirty provinces and autonomous regions. The same would apply for the Soviet Union with fifteen republics, or India with twenty-two states. As the army of World Prayer Missionaries increases, all provinces and regions of the world will be covered.

Fourth, *search out specific information you can use as prayer fuel for your region of focus*. *Operation World* is an excellent source to help get you started. If, for example, you were to select the closed Communist country of Albania, you might list on 3 x 5 cards these facts for later use in your daily prayer strategy: Albania has a population of 3,000,000. The capital city is Tirana, with a population of 175,000 souls. Albania's specific peoples: Albanians (95%), Greeks (2.5%), and gypsies (2.4%). Albania is Europe's poorest and least-developed country. Its government is considered one of Europe's most ruthless Communist regimes. Albania's government leaders boast that their nation is the first officially atheistic state in the world. Atheism is the official state religion of Albania.

Number each of your facts because it is from this list that you will later compile a seven-day prayer strategy.

Fifth, *take a strategy development trip to your public library.* A visit to the library will greatly assist you in planning your strategy. Upon arrival ask the librarian where the encyclopedias and world atlases are found. If permitted, make a photocopy of the best map you can find of your country. Read the main article about your country in an encyclopedia such as *World Book.* As you work, begin translating simple facts about a nation and its peoples into potential prayer requests.

Take, for example, the Kwangtung province in southern China with a population exceeding 50 million. There are at least twenty large cities in the province, with Canton serving as its capital. All of these cities should be on your list. Later, when you implement them into your seven-day prayer strategy, you might list several of these cities for each day, thus allowing you to pray for all the main cities of that province each week. Remember, a missionary planning to go to a region would need to study cities targeted for ministry. As committed World Prayer Missionaries we need to take our calling just as seriously.

You'll also want to determine your base city as a World

Prayer Missionary. Generally, this will be the capital city of the nation or province.

When reading the primary article about your country, be sure to note the listing of other articles in that encyclopedia related to that same theme.

Sixth, *develop a spiritual warfare strategy for your region of focus.* After you have gleaned some basic information concerning your country, use it as the basis for developing a seven-day prayer strategy.

To accomplish this, you'll need to prepare "Prayer Warfare Strategy Cards" for each day of the week. Eventually you may have as many as two or even three cards for each day.

Next, divide all your facts into seven groups. From these lists you will develop a seven-day prayer strategy for your nation.

On one side of each card, note the day of the week and list that day's prayer facts. Certain facts you will want to include each day are your base city and other general prayer targets, like the overall population of the country. Then for each day in the week write the names of several cities that will be your intercessory targets. If you're praying for a larger country like China or India, and you do not feel directed to focus on just one province, divide the provinces up, praying for several each day so that once a week you have included all by name. The goal is to include enough in prayer each day to cover all your regions every seven days.

To give a hypothetical example, if your master list of general facts about your country includes twenty-eight focuses, and if, in addition, there are twenty-one main cities, you would pray for four different fact-focuses and three different cities (in addition to your base city) each day. In total you would have eight separate prayer opportunities per day.

On the opposite side of each 3 x 5 card you might wish to print several key verses of Scripture that you can use to keep the power of God's Word in your praying. List your favorite verses, plus some of the many positive verses recorded in this book.

Some sample verses might include Jeremiah 51:20, Isaiah 41:15, Jeremiah 1:10, 1 John 4:4, Matthew 28:18, Matthew 19:26, Luke 9:1–2, Luke 10:19, Micah 3:8, Mark 11:23, and Matthew 16:19.

Elsewhere on these cards you might want to include some of the suggestions for prayer as shared in our weekly guide to intercession presented earlier in this book.

Seventh, *develop your prayer mission both within and without your prayer closet*. Jesus said, "Men ought always to pray and not to faint" (Luke 18:1, KJV); and Paul wrote, "Pray without ceasing" (1 Thessalonians 5:17). This is the spirit of the World Prayer Missionary. We should take our prayer burden with us wherever we can. When a missionary goes to a land, he or she is consumed with that culture. No matter what that worker does, or where he goes in that land, he is still a missionary.

The World Prayer Missionary must cultivate this same quality. Our country of focus ought to go with us wherever we go. It's easy to tuck the cards with a day's strategy into pocket or purse to be prayed over whenever there's a pause in the day. And always remember, as a World Prayer Missionary you may be a housewife, schoolteacher, car salesman, or carpenter—but your real calling is a mission of prayer. You may go physically to a place of employment, but your heart is going to Europe, Asia, or Africa.

Ultimate Victory

Several weeks after the World Prayer Missionary concept was first introduced through our ministry, we began to receive scores of commitment cards from intercessors indicating they wished to enlist. On each card the intercessor noted the country he or she had selected for daily prayer.

As the cards began to arrive I decided it would be good to have special prayer over these firstfruits of a program I believed would greatly honor the Lord in the future.

It happened to be our usual monthly day of prayer and several of our regular intercessors had gathered, along with a new, older brother I had not met before. He introduced himself as Armando, and I recognized an accent that originated somewhere in Europe. Later I learned Armando was born near the Albanian border.

God had sent Armando that day to deliver an important message.

We gathered in our small prayer chapel and after a season of worship began to pray over the numerous World Prayer Missionary commitment cards. The lights were turned out in the prayer room except for a lighted globe of the earth near the center of the small room. It served as a special focus for what was about to happen.

As each warrior took a handful of cards we began to pray, one at a time. We held the cards before the Lord, thanking Him for these pioneer prayer missionaries. They were the first of what I believed would become a vast army of committed intercessors. They would be, I believed, an army that would ultimately bind or restrain satanic power over every geographic region on earth. At one point in our prayer I expressed these feelings with the remark, "Wouldn't it be beautiful if an army of intercessors would someday rise up and restrain all demonic activity, confronting *every* demon at the same time throughout the world?"

I thought little of the theological implications of that remark until it was Armando's time to pray. Even the flavor of the brother's accent added something of significance to what God was about to say.

Armando began to pray a simple prayer of God's blessing on all these who were enlisting in the new army. Then he paused, and the look on his face was one of wonder. He began to nod his head, as tears ran down his face. He clutched his handful of commitment cards more tightly and lifted them toward the globe, pointing with the cards.

"God . . . He just talk to my heart," Armando said. "He tell me I must tell you that as soon as you raise up an army that binds every demon on earth, His Kingdom shall come."

The authority with which my brother spoke was remarkable. His statement was so absolute that it took my breath away. I wondered if there was any clear biblical basis for making such a statement. After all, God's Word alone is the standard upon which we must base all perceived divine guidance.

A few days later I read John's description of a war to end all wars in the heavenlies (Revelation 12:7–11). There I found a unique confirmation of Armando's insight.

As described in Revelation, Michael, one of God's chief angelic officers, leads his angelic army against Satan's demonic forces and overcomes them. Satan's defeat is so final, he and his demonic hordes are forced forever from the heavenlies. Most noteworthy is the fact that although angelic forces defeat Satan, they do so because saints on earth are applying their weaponry—"the blood of the Lamb and the word of their testimony" (Revelation 12:11).

While meditating on these thoughts I read a footnote in the margin of my Bible. The commentary explained that something would happen in the future, a mysterious miracle in the heavenlies, that would render Satan incapable of functioning any longer with his demonic powers in that vast, invisible arena. The commentary suggested that no one could know for certain what the mystery would be, but somehow the application of the blood of the Lamb and the word of the saints' testimony would make it impossible for Satan to operate any longer in that unseen sphere.

Could it be that a great army of intercessors, highly trained and deeply committed, might be a part of the cleansing of the heavenlies in this final spiritual battle? Was this what Armando was sensing in his spirit?

The answer, of course, will be known only when the full record of history is written and we stand before God on the threshold of eternity.

We *can* know this. Our prayers not only make a difference; in God's eyes they *are* the difference. If one person's prayers can restrain a demonic spirit, a thousand intercessors focusing their prayers on specific regions of the world can restrain the demonic spirits that reign there.

Imagine what could happen if our prayer army increased until every demonic spirit over every geographic region of the world was restrained at the very same moment! As soon as every spirit is bound in prayer, which will permit the Gospel to be preached fully in all nations, His Kingdom will be established.

Perhaps this is what Jesus had in mind when He said, ". . . This gospel of the kingdom will be preached in all the world as a witness to all the nations, and then the end will come" (Matthew 24:14).

For more information on the ministry of Every Home for Christ, write one of the following:

Every Home for Christ
P.O. Box 35930
Colorado Springs, CO 80935-3593
USA

Every Home for Christ
P.O. Box 3636
Guelph, Ontario, N1H 7S2
Canada

Every Home for Christ
P.O. Box 168
Penshurst, N.S.W. 2222
Australia

Every Home for Christ
P.O. Box 7256
Hennopsmeer, 0046
South Africa

Dick Eastman is international president of Every Home for Christ (formerly World Literature Crusade), president of the National Prayer Committee, and the originator of the Change-the-World School of Prayer. He has taught and ministered in scores of nations.

Eastman studied at Carthage College, Moody Bible Institute, North Central Bible College, and the University of Wisconsin at Madison, all in the USA. He holds a B.A. degree in Bible and theology and an M.S. in journalism.

He is the author of ten books, three of which are included in this omnibus edition and three of which are listed on page 2.